THE

NOISY

GOD WHISPERS

PERSONAL REFLECTIONS FROM THE JOURNAL OF:

Julia Monnin

VOLUME I: MY WANDERINGS

ISBN: 0692930671
ISBN-13: 978-0692930670

Cover design by Kecia Flaute

For more information visit:
www.juliamonnin.com

FIRST EDITION

DEDICATION

This book is dedicated to all of my brothers and sisters in Christ, those in this life and in the next, whose constant intercession and prayer have kept me moving forward. Especially to my Spiritual Sister, St. Teresa of Avila, whose guidance and inspiration have made me feel like I'm not alone. They are her words, written at the beginning of her work *The Way of Perfection*, that I now echo as my own:

"In all that I say in this book I submit to what our Mother the Holy Roman Church holds. If there should be anything contrary to that, it will be due to my not understanding the matter. And so I beg the learned men who will see this work to look it over carefully and to correct any mistake there may be as to what the Church holds, as well as any other mistakes in other matters. If there should be anything good in this work, may it be for the honor and glory of God and the service of His most Blessed Mother, our Lady and Patroness, whose habit I wear despite my being very unworthy to do so."

(From *The Way of Perfection* by St. Teresa of Avila as translated by Kieran Kavanaugh, O.C.D. and Otilio Rodriguez O.C.D., published by ICS Publications, Washington, D.C., 1980)

When I came to you, brothers, proclaiming the mystery of God, I did not come with sublimity of words or of wisdom. For I resolved to know nothing while I was with you except Jesus Christ, and him crucified. I came to you in weakness and fear and much trembling, and my message and my proclamation were not with persuasive [words of] wisdom, but with a demonstration of spirit and power, so that your faith might rest not on human wisdom but on the power of God.

(1 Corinthians 2:1-5)

TABLE OF CONTENTS

INTRODUCTION

Over a year ago I felt an inner desire to write; to start a journal. The words I wrote in this journal were just my thoughts on paper, nothing more. I wasn't writing them for anyone else. They were meant for just me and God. A few months ago, however, I felt an inner desire to not only write but to share. Sharing my writing, though, has never been part of my plan. No, I have never thought my words would mean anything to anyone else, but it's becoming more and more clear that God's plans are different than my own. Yes, the doors seem to be opening all around me to share my writing, and, I must say, it's scary to even consider! I mean, what will people think? Who am I to do this? What can I say that hasn't already been said a million times before by millions of other people? Still, though the fears about sharing are real, the desire to share is real, too, and, try as I may, I simply cannot ignore it any longer. I can't help but think that if even one person is helped by reading my journal, then it will be worth sharing. I also can't help but think that this inner desire to share is, in fact, coming from God. I mean, where else would it be coming from? It certainly isn't coming from me! No, I have been quite happy with my little life and career. I have been quite happy hanging out in my nice little comfort zone. To be honest, this whole "mission" thing has turned my life upside down!

Yes, I'll admit it. I have been content sitting in the background. I have been content having "my thing" and letting others have "their thing." In fact, "You do your thing, I'll do my thing, and we'll all be happy," was kind of becoming my motto, but something inside tells me this isn't the life I'm called to live. Yeah, something inside tells me this "writing thing" is a huge part of why I'm here, and I can't just keep ignoring the feeling. I can't just keep pretending like I'm not seeing all the people around me struggling. I can't just keep looking past those people searching for more who are lost on their way when I know God has given me the knowledge and the ability to help. Still, I've come a long way from the girl who would do anything to be the center of attention, so the thought of making my private journal public goes against everything in me. Even so, faith tells me the reason this desire to share won't go away is because doing so is part of why I'm here. I guess time will tell if I'm right...

* The above is taken from Reflection #120, *The Inner Desire*

HOW TO USE THIS BOOK

To read this book put the letters together from left to right to form words, the words together to form sentences, the sentences to form paragraphs, and the paragraphs to form the reflection. And, now that I'm done being sarcastic, no, I'm not about to tell you there is a "correct" way to read this book. You can read it however you wish! What I do want to offer you, though, is a recommendation for proceeding. This recommendation is simple: *Don't rush through reading this book.* Instead, chew it. Read it slowly over the course of several months, or maybe even years, (after all, it took me years to write it) and let it help you "tune-in" to the voice of God guiding you and directing you in your own life; that very voice that has been doing so from the very first moment of your existence. Why? Because once you know what His voice "sounds" like, I'm certain you'll "hear" it just like I do. Yes, and that's when you'll start getting your answers. So, to be very clear, this is *not* a "do what I did, and you'll get what I got" kind of a book. The spiritual life doesn't work like that. There is no "one-size-fits-all" approach to this, so, please, don't expect to find your answers in this book because they aren't in here. They aren't in any book for that matter. Well, no book other than God's, that is. And that's where the *Read, Think, Pray* section comes in.

As you will see, this book is comprised of 191 short reflections from my journal dated March 20, 2013 to February 18, 2015. Each short reflection is followed by an even shorter prayer and then concludes with a *Read, Think, Pray* section. (Or with an inspirational quote or short story that has helped me on my journey which ties in to my reflection.) The *Read, Think, Pray* section is meant to help guide you through the process of *Lectio Divina,* (Latin for "Divine Reading"). To go through this process simply _Read_ the Scripture text, _Think_ about what that text is saying to you personally, (meditate, ponder, contemplate) and _Pray_ about what you have discovered. Look, I'm no expert on Sacred Scripture or on Lectio Divina, but I have found this process to be quite helpful in my own life, and I do, therefore, want to offer it as a suggestion to you. Whether or not you actually decide to utilize this section of the book is, of course, your choice. (As I'm sure you know, though, God's Word is much better than my own.)

Oh, and one more thing: the answer is "No." No, I did *not* exclude any of my journal entries from this book. They are all in here, - the good, the bad and the ugly - and not because I love them all. (Or because I think I have everything figured out...Remember, it's a journal...I'm learning more and more as I go.) I have included all of them because I don't want you to lose sight of the fact that the journey to God is a process. I don't want you to forget that sinners don't become saints overnight. I would be doing no one any good if my little story made you assume otherwise.

With that, I leave you to begin. May God inspire you as you continue your journey.

Happy Reflecting!

Julia

PROLOGUE

I had no idea at the time, but in 2013 my entire life changed. Yes, unbeknownst to me, God was making something new in my life. God was sending me on a journey. I had no idea it was happening. I had no idea where the road was leading. To be honest, I had no idea I was even on the road to begin with. No, I had no idea. I had no idea.

It all began so simply, so ordinarily. How could I have known? How could I have guessed? How could I have even imagined? No, it wasn't possible. I couldn't have known. I couldn't have guessed. I couldn't have imagined.

It wasn't time for me to know. No, I wasn't supposed to know. All I was supposed to do was keep working, keep striving, keep looking. The destination, and the journey there, wasn't up to me. It was all up to God. It was all in His hands. It was all in His time. All I could do was keep moving forward. All I could do was keep searching...

THE FOUNDATION

NEW BEGINNINGS

3/20/2013

And so it begins...My husband and I bought our first home. Since moving into this home I have spent my mornings (my best mornings anyway) sitting in our living room looking out at the beauty of God that surrounds me outside my window. I spend this time in prayer and silence, preparing for my day to come. It is during this time in the silence that the Lord speaks to me; not in an audible voice, but in the stillness of my heart. This is what has prompted me to write. Yes, this is what has inspired me to pick up this pen. I don't want to forget these moments; these times when I am filled with such peace and when the meaning of life seems so clear.

Not surprisingly, much had to happen before I could get to this point. Yes, not surprisingly, much had to change. Things had to get real dirty, real messy before getting here. To be honest, my life had to be turned upside down, but I seem to be on the other side of it now. Yes, now everything in life seems new. Life is more beautiful, happiness is more joyful, love is more real. And that is another reason I have decided to start a journal. My journey, you see, has shown me that a life with Christ is better (way better) than a life without him, and, though I can't be

2

certain what the future holds, I'm pretty sure he's not done proving that to me. I want to start taking notes!

Prayer

Thank you, Lord, for the gift of life, and thank you for making something new in mine. I love you, my God, and I praise you! Keep me in your loving presence now and forever. AMEN. I love you! I thank you! I praise you!

Read, Think, Pray: Isaiah 43:18-19

REFLECTION #2

A LOOK BACK

3/20/2013

I wish I didn't have to go here. I wish what I'm about to say didn't need to be said. I wish I could just skip over it and get to the good part, but I can't. No, I can't go around it. I can't take it away. I can't pretend it didn't happen because it happened. Yes, it is a part of my journey; a very important part that I can't just gloss over. Before I go any further, though, I want to warn you. Hold on tight! It's about to get a little bumpy.

Let me start by answering a simple question: "No." No, my life wasn't always filled with peace. No, things didn't always make this much sense to me. No, I wasn't always this in love with life or with God. As is probably often the case, my journey back to God wasn't easy. It was quite the opposite actually. Yes, in all actuality it was filled with suffering. It was filled with pain. It was filled with hurt. It was filled with fear. It was filled with doubt. It was filled with worry. It was filled with trials and tests and tribulations. Why, you ask? Because that's just the way it is...No, wait; that's not the right answer....There's more; there's always more...I have come to learn that the real reason there was so

3

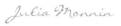

much pain and suffering on my journey back to God was because of love. Yes, I have come to learn it was all because of Love.

God, you see, loved me too much to let me die in my sin. He loved me too much to let me walk away. He loved me too much to let me turn my back on Him forever. I'll admit, it didn't feel like love when it was all happening, - when I first came face-to-face with my sin - but that's what it was. Yeah, it's easy to see now that I'm out of it; now that the pain is behind me. It *was* about love. It was always about love. It *is* always about love. This love is just sometimes wearing a painful, burdensome disguise.

For me, the most painful part of my journey happened a few years in. Yeah, you heard me right. It took me years to find my way back to God and many more years (many, many more years) to find my way out of the habitual sin that had taken root in my life. None of it happened overnight. None of it was easy. None of it was a "quick fix." It was slow. It was burdensome. It was painful. But it was all because of love. Yes, it was all because of Love.

Though it was difficult, I continued to put one foot in front of the other year after year. I continued to move forward, and with each tiny step came a little more light; a little more joy; a little more freedom. Things got so good at one point, in fact, that I thought for sure I was getting close to the end. I thought for sure the worst was behind me. I thought for sure I was out of the woods. - I was wrong. - Oh, yes, I was so very, very wrong. You see, just when I had seen enough of the light to know I never wanted to go back into the darkness, the real test came. This is when God opened the door for what was to become my biggest trial; my biggest obstacle; my biggest hurdle. This is when God asked me to do the unthinkable. This is when He asked me to forgive. He asked me to admit my mistakes, to bring them to the light, to apologize and seek forgiveness. He asked me to let go, forgive, and move on.

Yes, the time eventually came for me to not only beg for mercy but to accept it; to admit what was done, to let the cards fall where they may, to forgive myself, (and others) and to move on. Doing this was, without a doubt, the hardest thing I have ever done in my life. It was so hard, in fact, that I ignored God's request for years. I just couldn't overcome my fear. There was a part of my life that I wanted to keep hidden and seeking forgiveness meant exposing it. It meant bringing it to the light, and I was afraid of what that would mean. Yeah, I was afraid of what others would think. I was afraid I would never truly be forgiven. To be honest, I was afraid my life would be ruined. - I had believed a lie. - I had forgotten that the truth is what would set me free. I, instead, was convinced it would only lead to more hurt and pain.

Like the good Father that He is, God never gave up on me, though. Yes, through it all, He continued to fill me with the desire to come into the light and to seek forgiveness. Although I ignored Him for years, I learned that God is very persistent. I learned, in fact, that when it comes to saving His children, He is even more stubborn than I am! After realizing this, I also realized that the gentle nudging I was feeling from Him was never going to stop. Yes, I realized that I was never going to be happy if I didn't do what He was asking. I realized that in order to be set free from my past, I was going to have to bring it to the light...All of it...And so, after years of trying to ignore God's voice of reason, the time came when I could no longer be disobedient; when I could no longer run and hide. At this point my prayer quickly became, *"Lord, Give me courage. Give me strength. Give me mercy."* Then finally, after what seemed like an eternity, I did it: I came into the light. I sought the forgiveness I so desperately needed. I said out loud the things I thought for sure I never would; the things I thought for sure I would take to my grave.

I wish I could tell you this was the end of the pain. I wish I could tell you it all immediately got better from that point on, but it didn't. In fact, at first, it got much worse. It made my life more messy. It made things more ugly. It made things more confusing and hurtful. Yes, stepping out of the darkness had ripped open the scab that was holding my heart together, and I was bleeding all over the place. It was a rough time in my

"Stepping out of the darkness had ripped open the scab that was holding my heart together, and I was bleeding all over the place."

5

life, but (I knew it then, and I know it now) it had to be done. I had to swallow my pride, admit my many mistakes, let go of the guilt, and attempt to start over if I ever wanted to be happy again. Yes, even if it meant I would lose everything in the process. There was no other way. Trust me, I would have taken it had there been. I would have stayed in hiding forever if there had been another way out of the mess. But there wasn't. It had to be done. Things had to get ripped apart before they could get put back together.

Though this was a grueling time in my life, it didn't take long for me to realize that God had not abandoned me. Yes, though things got really ugly, it didn't take long for me to realize that He had been with me every step of the way. He was with me in the lows. He was with me in the pain. He was with me in the tears. He was with me when I needed a friend and all my friends had "fallen asleep" and "scattered" (Luke 22:45, Matthew 26:56). He was with me when the fear was consuming me and I was "sweating blood" (Luke 22:44). Yes, He was with me through it all. This, as I later realized, was my agony. This was my condemnation, my scourging, my carrying of the cross, my crucifixion. It was torturous, painful, and ugly. The big difference, though, between mine and Christ's was that I was not blameless. Yes, I, unlike Jesus, deserved to die. I deserved to suffer. I deserved to lose everything. Oh, but you know I didn't, right? Yes, you know this wasn't the end, don't you? You know my story doesn't stop here in the midst of all of this pain and suffering, correct? This was the crucifixion, sure, but the crucifixion is not the end. Oh, please tell me you know the crucifixion is not the end!...There's more; there's always more!...The resurrection was just around the corner. And that "corner" is where I am today.

Prayer

Thank you, my God, for bringing me out of the darkness. Thank you for healing me. Thank you for saving me. Thank you for setting me free. May I never again refuse to accept your mercy. May I never again refuse to live in the light. May I never again refuse to receive your love. I love you! I thank you! I praise you!

Read, Think, Pray: 1 Timothy 1:13-17

PERPETUAL DOING

3/25/2013

I need to constantly remind myself that the to-do list never ends. I need to constantly remind myself that there will always be things to do; that there will always be people demanding my time and attention; that there will always be fires to put out and problems to solve. Why? Because there are always reasons, lots and lots of reasons, *not* to do something I know I should. Yes, although there are duties in my life that I must fulfill, I must remember that I am a human *being* not a human *doing*. If I ever lose sight of this, I have no doubt that I will, once again, become one of those people who are always super busy doing absolutely nothing.

Oh, it's easy to fall into the trap of perpetual doing...Soooo easy...I have learned, though, that the answers come in the silence. I have learned that I can't hear the whispering voice of God in a room full of noise. I have learned that I have to turn the noise down; I have to shut it off; I have to embrace the silence because "the silence" is where I find God. Yes, I have learned there is nothing - absolutely nothing - more important than spending time with my Father, and that is why I picked up my pen today. I, you see, am in need of a reality check, so here goes...

Dear Julia: Stop making excuses for why you are not spending quality time with God every day. You are not fooling anyone; not even yourself. You say that you don't have enough time, but come on. Who do you think you're kidding? You know who God is. You know that He is a limitless God who always gives in abundance, so do you honestly think you're going to convince yourself that this limitless, abundant God that you know and love is somehow limiting your time? Seriously, come on. God is not just another "someone" demanding your attention. He is not just another "something" to squeeze in to your already busy day. He is not just another part of your life; He is the reason for it! Don't you see? Without Him, nothing else matters. I repeat, without Him nothing else matters! Quit acting like you don't know this. Please, quit! You were created by God and for God. You were made by Love and for Love. You are here to serve God, but you spend most of your time serving your to-do list...Stop!...Slow down. Run to the silence. Spend some time with your Father. He's waiting.

We are here to serve God, but most of us spend our time serving our to-do lists.

Prayer

Be with me as I pray, Lord. Be with me as I sit. Be with me as I breathe. Help me to always be mindful of you and of the gifts you've given me. Help me to open my heart up to you and to your guidance. Give me courage, Lord. Show me how to overcome my fear of the silence. Remind me that your love casts out all fear (1 John 4:18). May I never again allow myself to be overcome by the many distractions of this world. May I never again put my to-do list ahead of you. Teach me how to embrace the silence, Lord. Teach me how to ask you better questions. Teach me how to slow down and listen to you. Teach me how to be.
I love you! I thank you! I praise you!

Read, Think, Pray: Hosea 6:1-3

REFLECTION #4

CHILDLIKE TRUST

3/26/2013

I have to think it saddens our Creator, our God, our Father when we don't trust in Him; when we doubt in His presence, in His power, in His goodness; when we doubt that He can, will, and is taking care. I mean, in one breath we say, "Jesus rose from the dead." "God parted the Red Sea." "Christ walked on water." But in the next we say, "How will I ever do all of this?" "I'll never have enough." "Why did this happen?" Yes, I have to think that if we *truly* believed, we wouldn't doubt. I have to think that if we *truly* believed, we wouldn't worry. I have to think that if we *truly* believed, we wouldn't fear.

Perhaps we just need a reminder: A loving father would *never* leave his child. A loving father would *never* abandon his kin. A loving father would *never* walk away...Never!

Earthly relationships are not perfect. Earthly relationships disappoint, fall apart, and even dissolve, but our relationship with God is *not* an earthly one. We are made in His image, yes, but our sin messes up our God-like image. We are human and imperfect; He is not. We shouldn't compare God to those who have hurt us. We shouldn't compare Him to those who have let us down. We shouldn't compare Him to those who have left because He will *never* leave. He is our Father; our loving, merciful, omnipotent Father. He has *not* abandoned us. He has *not* stopped caring. He has *not* stopped paying attention. Trust in Him. Have the faith of a child; a child who doesn't know emotional hurt, pain, or fear; a child who only knows love. God is with us, and He always will be. He will show us the Way (John 14:6). We just have to let Him do it.

Prayer

Be with me, Lord. Break down my walls.
Increase my faith and trust in you.
I love you! I thank you! I praise you!

Read, Think, Pray: Matthew 18:1-4

REFLECTION #5

THE SHORTCUT

3/28/2013

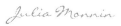

I can clearly remember the time when going to "extra" Mass during the week was just another thing my parents made me do. Christmas, Lent, and Easter were the worst. "Extra" Masses during these times seemed endless. And now, by the grace of God, I see the beauty of Mass and joyfully await the coming of these celebrations. Oh, how much the Lord has changed me! He has made the impossible (i.e., my conversion) possible, and all I had to do was turn to Him and ask for help!

I'll admit, though, I did have a secret weapon when it came to my conversion. Yes, God did, in fact, give me a shortcut; an "easy" way; a fast track. What was it? It was Mary, his Mother. Yes, I have no doubt that the miracle of my transformation (and I assure you, it *was* a miracle) came from Mary's intercession, for I am convinced that it was *not* a coincidence that my transformation began the moment my own mother (my earthly mother) began hers. You see, the moment she began falling in love with Christ (through a special devotion to Mary) was the moment I began falling in love with him, too. This was the time that Christ, through his Mother, started working on me. This was the time that he, through her, began opening my heart. This was the time that he, through her, began opening my eyes. Yes, this was the time. This was the time that I began to see the error of my ways. This was the time that I began to realize how far I had fallen. This was the time that God began calling me back to Him. And I'm certain it wasn't because of anything I was doing. Yeah, I'm certain that if it would have been left up to me, I would have continued digging my own grave. Yes, I'm certain. I'm certain it wasn't me. I'm certain it was my mom. I'm certain it was my Mother.

You can say what you want about Mary. Over the years there has been a lot of confusion about her and about her role, but to me this role has always been easy to understand: Mary's mission on earth was to bear Christ; to bring him into this world and to raise him. Mary's mission in eternity is to raise us; to bring us into God's world, Heaven. Some will doubt this simplicity. Some will argue that "no one comes to the Father except through [the Son]" (John 14:6). And I would like to second that by saying, of course no one does! But why do so many of us assume that there is only one way to the Son?

In my life, Mary was the way to the Son. You can try to go around her if you want, but, in my life, she was the shortcut. She didn't make the impossible things possible. No, that was God. She just made them easier. And I needed (and still need) things as easy as they can get!

Prayer

Pray for us, O Holy Mother of God,
that we may be made worthy of the promises of Christ.
Open our eyes. Open our minds. Open our hearts.
Show us the Way. Show us your Son.
I love you! I thank you! I praise you!

Read, Think, Pray: Revelation 12

"When the Holy Spirit finds that a soul has drawn close to Mary, his dear and inseparable spouse, he quickens his activity of forming Jesus Christ in it." - St. Louis de Montfort

Mom: *Thank you for praying for me and for my conversion before I ever knew I needed one. Thank you for leading by example; for opening your heart up to Jesus and his Mother. Thank you for letting God transform you because without your transformation mine would not have been possible. Yes, I'm certain mine would not have been possible! God used you to bring me into this world, and He used you again to show me the next. Not only would I have never been born without you, without you I would have never lived; without you I would have died...forever. Thank you for being such a wonderful instrument in His hands. I love you!*

-Julia

THE QUESTION

4/1/2013

Here it is, my God. Here it is. Here is *the* question you have been waiting for me to ask you: What do *you* want from me, Lord?...What do *you* want me to do?...How do *you* want me to serve you?

At times I feel like I'm doing exactly what you're asking me to do, and at other times, I wonder if I'm even getting close...Is this what you want? Is this what I'm here to do? Am I doing enough?...I've been trying, Lord, that's for sure. Yes, I've been trying. I'm just not sure I've been trying my best. This, however, seems like a turning point for me. Yes, this seems like a big moment. And not just because I'm asking better questions. No, I've been asking you questions like this for awhile now. It's just that now I actually *want* to hear the answer. Yes, now I actually *want* to know what it is that you want me to know.

Sure, I've been trying to go where it is you're leading me, but let's be honest, I have not been trying whole-heartedly. No, I have not been giving you my best effort. I guess there was a part of me that was afraid. I guess there was a part of me that was doubting you. I guess there was a part of me that was more focused on me than it was on you. - Yeah, I guess. - Up until this point I have been dipping my toe into your waters slowly wading in, slowly getting deeper and deeper, but I'm done with that. This is it. I trust you. I'm jumping in.

And so I'm in. - Yes, I am in. - I am in. I am yours. I am ready. Show me, Lord, what I'm missing. Show me what you want me to do. Open doors around me. Open my eyes to see your face, my ears to hear your voice, and my mouth to proclaim your praise. Give me courage, Lord. Give me the courage to do whatever it is you are asking me to do. Put me to work; grant that my work may somehow lead people to you. We are a tired, distracted, worn-out people, Lord, so consumed with ourselves that we're failing to see the big picture; so consumed with ourselves that we're failing to see you. Have mercy on those of us who are blinded by the distractions. Have mercy on those of us who are blinded by the busyness. Have mercy on those of us who are blinded by the noise. Use me as your instrument, Lord, for I am your handiwork. I am your creation. And this is why I am here. Perfect my character. Train me in virtue. Increase my love. May my life do one thing: point others to you.

Prayer

Thank you for all you have given me, Lord. Thank you for guiding me to this moment. Yes, the time is here. The time is here when I finally realize that all I have is actually yours; that all I do is actually for you; that all I am is actually you yourself. And, so, I pray: Show me, Lord, how to best share the gifts you have given me. Bless those people my life is meant to touch. Fill them, and me, with the power of your Spirit. Fill them, and me, with your goodness and kindness. Fill them, and me, with your mercy and love.
I love you! I thank you! I praise you!

Read, Think, Pray: Isaiah 50:4-5

REFLECTION #7

DETERMINED

4/3/2013

It seems to me that most women (at least most of the women I know) are born with the skill of being domestic. They can cook and clean, wipe noses and change diapers all at, seemingly, the same time. They are able to love and care for those around them without the least bit of concern for themselves. I, however, did not seem to inherit this gene. Most of the time this doesn't bother me much, I just laugh it off and accept the fact that I have other gifts. Yesterday, however, was a different story, and in the battle between myself and the kitchen, the kitchen came out on top: Kitchen – 1, Julia – 0

Yes, in an attempt to be a better wife to my husband, Tony, I decided to spend my day as a domesticated housewife. I cleaned and ironed and tried to cook him a nice meal. I got one of his mom's recipes after she assured me it was "so easy" to cook. I did *exactly* as I was instructed, but when he came home from work all I could do was look at him and ask, "What's plan B?...Is frozen pizza OK?" At this point, I threw in the towel. The game was over. I had lost and felt so defeated. I went into another

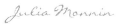

room and wept. This, you see, was more than a meal to me. It was a sign of my womanhood. To me, failing at this meant that I would never live up to the standards of my mother, grandmothers, or in-laws. It meant that I would never be the wife I wanted to be. Oh, I am not intimidated by much. I am not defeated by much. But one thing is for sure: the kitchen is *not* my friend!

As with most things, though, this is not the end of the story. Yes, there were many life lessons all tucked into this one, epic failure. First off, I was, once again, reminded of how loving and supportive my husband is, who, instead of complaining, insisted this loss wasn't my fault but the equipment I was using. (He's very wise.) Secondly, I realized that hidden beneath the subpar cooking was a lesson on the importance of perseverance. As you can tell I was quick to give up; quick to leave the kitchen and never want to return. This incident, however, reminded me that some things just don't come easily at first, and that that's OK. It reminded me that failing a few times is not a reason to stop trying. It reminded me that I shouldn't be so quick to give up, and that I should instead pick myself up and try again remembering that the things in life that are most worthwhile usually take persistent, diligent effort. Last, but certainly not least, this experience gave me some new-found respect for the women in my life, especially my own mother. I realized that she can, not only, run a household and take care of children without blinking an eye, she is also super resilient in other areas of her life where things don't come so easily. Every day, for example, she "goes to war" with the computer. Often she loses, but she always returns the next day and tries again. She is determined to master it. I, however, was quick to give up and walk away when things got a little hard. Perhaps next time I'll not only look to her for guidance in the kitchen, I'll look to her for guidance in life, as well.

So, I began this day with the intention of being a better wife to my husband, and I guess that, even though the meal failed, I did do just that. Yes, I learned that the number one rule of being a good wife (and of being good at anything for that matter) is being

The number one rule of being good at anything is being determined to be.

determined to be. Now I just pray this determination pays off.

Prayer

Help me, Lord, to accept my weaknesses for what they are but to always work to improve in all areas of my life. Inspire me to do more and to get better. Pick me up when I fall and give me the courage to try again. Help me to overcome the temptation of feeling sorry for myself because "I can't do what every other woman seems to be able to do with such ease." Help me, my God, to carry this cross, and fill me with the determination to keep trying remembering that "I have the strength for everything through [you] who empowers me" (Philippians 4:13). Yes, even the strength to (maybe someday) learn how to cook! I love you! I thank you! I praise you!

Read, Think, Pray: 1 Corinthians 9:24-27

REFLECTION #8

IMPOSSIBLE POSSIBILITIES

4/9/2013

People can change. Period. Although I'll admit I didn't always believe this, time has proven to me that I was wrong. Yes, time has proven to me that I was very, very wrong. I will say this, though, it is true that people can't change on their own. Yeah, I'll give you that one. We are, simply put, too lost in our sin to ever find our way out. We are too enslaved by our passions to ever set ourselves free. We are too wounded to ever put ourselves back together. None of this, though, means that change is impossible. Yes, none of this means that our limitations are somehow God's. Sure, change may be impossible for us, but it is *not* impossible for God...Nothing is.

I, of course, can't say that change is easy, though. No, it never is. All I can really say is that early on in my spiritual journey I, too, thought that change was impossible. Yeah, I, too, had let evil win for so many years

15

that it had an overwhelmingly tight grip on me; a grip so tight it seemed impossible that it would ever be loosened. In spite of how impossible things seemed, though, I always knew I had choices, and I chose to keep moving forward. I chose to refuse to give in to the temptation to stay where I was, or (even worse) to fall back into my old habits. Yes, I chose to go to war.

After years of fighting, desperately trying to free myself from the many sins that had ahold of me, I was tired, worn out, and beat up. Apparently this was all part of God's plan, though, because this was the very thing that finally dropped me to my knees. Yes, after years of fighting in vain I finally came to my senses. I finally realized that it wasn't enough for me to admit I wanted out, I also had to admit I needed help getting there. I had to admit I couldn't do it on my own. I had to admit I needed a Savior.

"After years of fighting in vain I finally came to my senses. I finally realized that it wasn't enough for me to admit I wanted out, I also had to admit I needed help getting there... I had to admit I needed a Savior."

As soon as I came to this realization, the real change started to take place. This is when the good in me began to prevail over the evil; the despair began to turn into hope; the death began to turn into new life. Yes, I finally let God in. I finally let Him do what He came here to do. I finally let Him save me, and the change that began happening in me was proof that He was doing just that.

For years I believed the lie that I had made my bed and that I was going to have to lie in it, but I was wrong. So very, very wrong. In time, God showed me that He is not only willing to help us get out of our messy, dark, sinful beds, He is also willing (in fact, more than willing) to help us remake them. I, you see, am proof that change is possible because God changed me, and that is why I'm convinced He can change others, too. After all, why would I be the only one?

Prayer

You know me, Lord. You know my strengths, and you know my weaknesses. You know my wins, and you know my losses. You know my good deeds, and you know my not-so-good ones. Set me free from the sin that enslaves me. Set me free from the pain of my past. Set me free from the fear. Help me to become all I was created to become. Work a miracle in my life, Lord. Change me. Make me new.
I love you! I thank you! I praise you!

Read, Think, Pray: 1 Corinthians 15:51-52

REFLECTION #9

AWESTRUCK

4/11/2013

After years of failing, years of not caring, years of searching, and years of fighting, I'm happy to say, "I am a child of the Light!" Look, I know this is not mind-blowing news to some. In fact, it isn't really mind-blowing news to me either. Yes, I have always known I'm a child of the Light. There were just so many years I didn't understand what it meant, followed by so many years I didn't care what it meant, followed by so many years I thought I had screwed up too bad to ever be allowed to embrace what it meant that this simple statement of truth has now taken on whole new meaning in my life. Oh, and this whole new meaning is why I'm excited. Yes, it's not about where I came from, it's about who I am: I am a child of the Light!

This newfound zeal for life often leaves me feeling inspired. It often drives me to do more. It often fills me with awe. Yes, the Spirit is alive and at work in my life. It is taking me to places I never thought I would

17

go; places I never thought I would *want* to go. It is guiding my hands, guiding my tongue, and guiding my heart. How, though, could I ever put into words all that is going on inside? How could I ever say all that needs to be said or do all that needs to be done? I guess the truth is I can't, and won't, because that's not why the Lord has opened my mouth in the first place. No, I'm not here to say it all or do it all, I'm only here to say some of it; to do some of it. I can promise you this, though, I will never let what I can't do or say stop me from doing or saying what I can, and this is something I can say: I'm in love!...I'm awestruck!

Dear God, Creator of the Universe, Maker of all that is, all that was, and all that ever will be: I am, once again, amazed by your glory, by your majesty, and by your mystery. I sit now on a plane flying above the clouds looking down at your creation. How do you do it? Everything so intricately woven together; the past, present, and future all tied together and completely dependent on one another. Your creation is, and always will be, a mystery; a beautiful mystery.

As I begin these next few days at a conference with colleagues, I pray that your Spirit is alive in me. I pray that this Spirit speaks to me and shows me what I need to learn in order to grow and change and become more of the person you created me to be. I pray that this Spirit speaks through me. I pray that I am an instrument in your hands; that I am a living example of your goodness and truth, your love and compassion.

Keep me focused this weekend, Lord. Help me to be energized, helpful, loving, and patient. Help me to show my love and appreciation of you by being a gift to those around me. Someday, my God, I hope to join you, and all the angels and saints, in heaven. In the meantime, I will serve you! Be with me, Lord. My eyes, my ears, and my heart are wide open. Come, continue to reveal to me your plan for my life.

Prayer

Fill me with new life, Lord. Fill me with new hope. Fill me with new zeal. Give me the courage to expect more from you; the courage to ask more of you. I want, more than anything, Lord, to do whatever it is you are asking of me. I want, more than anything, to become the person you created me to be. I do not fear the road ahead, my God, for you are my

Father, and I know you are with me always. Yes, I know you will always take care. I don't need to know the how, or the why, or the when, Lord, just let me get to know you, for you are all that I need. Yes, you, my God, are more than enough...You, my God, are way more than enough. I love you! I thank you! I praise you!

Read, Think, Pray: Luke 5:26

"There are only two ways to live your life. One is as though nothing is a miracle. The other is as though everything is a miracle." - Albert Einstein

REFLECTION #10

WORDS THAT SPEAK

4/15/2013

Have you ever heard something that immediately "spoke" to you? Something that immediately stopped you in your tracks? Something that immediately made you shut up and listen? Well, my answer is, "Yes!" Moments like these are what I like to call "aha moments," and since "tuning-in" to God I have them all the time. I haven't always been "tuned-in," though. Yeah, there was definitely a time when, although I'm sure God was speaking, I never heard a word.

Simply put, my life used to be very noisy. I rarely let the silence in. I was always moving, always doing, always talking. I was never listening. I think that's why I still remember some of my first "aha moments." These moments, you see, left me speechless, and, at that time in my life, I was *never* speechless. No, never. I was never at a loss for words. I always had an answer, always had a reason, always had an excuse. In fact, I could talk my way out of just about anything. But there came a time when all this changed; a time when I could no longer fool anyone, not even myself. This is when God started "waking me up" spiritually speaking. He did this by sending people into my life to knock some sense into me. He did this by sending people into my life to help me get back on the straight and narrow. Though their words always made me

mad at first because they "afflicted me so much in my comfort," they are what got me to start taking action. Yes, they are what got me to start paying attention. Here are a few examples of them...

One time someone asked me if I was really happy. It was an honest question with well-meaning intentions, but it ticked me off. Why? Because, though I knew deep down my answer was "no," I thought no one else could tell. Yeah, I thought I was hiding it well. The question, though, proved that I wasn't fooling anyone, so I shut up and listened. The wheels began to turn...One time someone pointed out that if I could schedule my workouts in and make sure I had time for them, then I should be able to schedule my prayer in and make sure I had time for it, too. Oh, this someone saw right through my excuses for avoiding prayer. I wanted to argue with her but quickly realized I couldn't, so I shut up and listened. The wheels continued to turn...One time (that same) someone asked me what I thought about when I first woke up in the morning. I didn't have an answer. To be honest, I had no idea. The concept of "thinking about what you're thinking about" was foreign to me. Thoughts came in and went out, and I never stopped to wonder why. After a few moments of silence, though, she went on to say that God should be the first thing on my mind when I wake up. Well, I may not have been able to tell you what I *was* thinking about when I first woke up, but I could tell you for sure what I *wasn't*; I was *not* thinking about God! So, yeah, I got her point. I shut up and listened. The wheels kept on turning.

These moments (and all the "aha moments" I've had since) had one thing in common: they all made me shut up and listen. They made me start asking myself better questions. They made me start taking action. They were the initial seeds God planted in my life; the initial wake-up calls. They were so simple, so small, so ordinary, but they are what started me on my journey back to Him. They are what began my process of change. They are what made me realize that words, even if they are just said in passing, speak. (I'm just glad I finally shut up long enough to hear them!)

Prayer

Thank you, my God, for the ability to learn and for the grace to want to. Thank you for waking me up and for enlightening me. I know you have a plan for my life; please continue to unveil this plan to me. I know you have all the answers; please continue to fill me with your wisdom and knowledge. I know you are all-powerful; please continue to give me your strength. I open myself up to you, Lord. Come, teach me how to live. I love you! I thank you! I praise you!

Read, Think, Pray: Hebrews 4:12-13

REFLECTION #11

YOUNG WISDOM

4/22/2013

My wheels started turning recently when someone told me that the children of today will be the ones who bring their parents back to church. I wonder, could this be? Is there any truth to this? It does seem like we, the adults of today, are the ones who are the most lost at times. It does seem like we strive for things like power, possessions, and pleasure, and, therefore, have no time to strive for things like virtue, sacrifice, and love. It does seem like we are the ones who have no time to pray once a week let alone "without ceasing" (1 Thessalonians 5:17). Yes, it does seem like our secular life of "working" and "spending" has no room for God. Don't get me wrong, I don't think most of us believe that religion is "wrong," I just think we are too busy to give it much thought. There are just always places to go and people to see. With that being said, maybe it *will* be the children of today who wake us up. Maybe it *will* be the children of today who teach us. Maybe it *will* be the children of today who bring us back to church; who bring us back to God. Yes, maybe it *will* be the children of today who bring us home...Maybe, just maybe.

By the time we reach adulthood most of us are beat up, damaged, and tired. We are worn out rats in the rat race of life. Young people, however, are none of these things. They are not overly educated like most of us are. They don't have a lifetime of pain, hurt, and lies to overcome. They don't have hardened hearts keeping them from understanding the truth like we sometimes do. They are open. They are inspired. They are full of life. Maybe they *are* the solution to the Godlessness of our time. If this is true, could they be who the Lord is calling me to serve? Have I been overlooking these young people who are coming after me; these people who are the leaders of tomorrow? Have I been "eating my young" instead of nurturing them, listening to them, and learning from them? Yes, perhaps the time has come for me to start giving them more attention. Perhaps they really *will* be the ones God uses to bring us back to Him...Yes, perhaps.

I don't know where the road is taking me, but I do know this: I know that I am here for a reason. I know that Truth exists. I know that God exists. I can see Him at work, and I can see the beauty and genius of religion. Yes, I am comforted by the fact that there is a place in this world where I can go to find truth; a place that always stands up for what is true even if it's not easy, widely accepted, or popular. In a world full of lies, I needed a place to go for truth, and I found this place. Now I wonder if I should start to take this role of passing this truth on to the young people of today more seriously. Maybe I *should* stop questioning their young wisdom and start embracing it. Yes, maybe, just maybe, there's more...Oh, the road is leading me somewhere...I'm just not sure where.

"In a world full of lies, I needed a place to go for truth...I found this place."

Prayer

Show me how to stop putting boundaries on the people and places you are leading me to, Lord. Inspire me to live the authentic, abundant life you call each of us to live, and show me how you want me to serve you. Inspire the young people of today, Lord, and fill them, and all of us, with courage and zeal.
I love you! I thank you! I praise you!

Read, Think, Pray: 1 Timothy 4:12

"My Lord God, I have no idea where I am going. I do not see the road ahead of me. I cannot know for certain where it will end. Nor do I really know myself, and the fact that I think that I am following your will does not mean that I am actually doing so. But I believe that the desire to please you does in fact please you. And I hope I have that desire in all that I am doing. I hope that I will never do anything apart from that desire. And I know that if I do this you will lead me by the right road though I may know nothing about it. Therefore will I trust you always though I may seem to be lost and in the shadow of death. I will not fear, for you are ever with me, and you will never leave me to face my perils alone." - Thomas Merton, *Thoughts in Solitude*

REFLECTION #12

SWEET SMELLING ROSES

4/27/2013

My husband and I recently invited two Christ-like people into our home. Opening our house up to a few people who could breathe a little life into it helped it feel more like a home; our home. That's really all it took. Now I feel settled. Now I feel at peace. Now I feel like we weren't the only ones who moved. Now I feel like God moved with us. (Oh, and in case you're wondering, this visit did require a home-cooked meal. Yes, I gave the kitchen another try, and guess what? It actually tasted pretty good! With God everything really *is* possible! It's tied up: Kitchen - 1, Julia - 1)

The spiritual fruits of this simple act of hospitality got me thinking. If all it took to help turn this ordinary house into a home was for me to invite a few good and holy people inside, I wonder what would happen if we invited a few good and holy people inside our hearts?...The possibilities, to me, seem endless.

Someone once told me "if you run with skunk sooner or later you'll start to smell like one." I have never forgotten these words. As I recall this sound advice, I can't help but be led in another direction. I can't help but think if this is true, (which I think it is) then the opposite must be true, too. I mean, maybe all it takes to smell like a rose is to start running around with a few of them. I suppose if sin is contagious, then holiness is, too, right? Yes, perhaps I will never be any good to anyone if there is always a part of me that smells. Perhaps the best way I can help others is by first helping myself. Perhaps it's time I start taking up residence in a field of blooming flowers instead of running around with a group of smelly skunk.

The truth is, the goal of the Christian life is to become like Christ, and there are just some people out there who are farther along on their journeys than others. There are just some people out there who are so united with Christ that his presence radiates through them. These people have a way of drawing others to them. They are a reminder to us of Christ's love, Christ's mercy, and Christ's goodness. It's easy for me to spot these people now, and, at this stage of my journey, I'm finding it really important to surround myself with them. After all, the world is really noisy, and as one freshly removed from its influence I have to be leery of those forces trying to pull me away. I must not fear or worry or doubt, but I must not be stupid either. I must know what my triggers are. I must know how and when and where my temptations lie, and I must surround myself with people who can guide, challenge, and encourage me so that I am able to stay on this path of truth and righteousness that I worked so hard to get back on.

Yes, from now on I will pay more attention to who I'm letting into my life. From now on I will be a little more selective. From now on I will choose to open myself up to those people who help me be a better me. Hopefully I, too, am soon smelling like a rose!

Prayer

Thank you, Lord, for the gift of good and holy people. People who are much farther along on their spiritual journey than I. People who encourage, guide, and challenge me to grow. People who help me keep my fire lit. Thank you for giving us the opportunity to sit down with a few of these people and enjoy their ordinary, but holy, company. Bless those people in the world, Lord, who hear your voice and are following you. Encourage them. Strengthen them. Inspire them. May I one day become one of these people, and may we all one day join you in heaven. I love you! I thank you! I praise you!

Read, Think, Pray: 1 Corinthians 15:33, Sirach 37:11-15

"The virtuous soul that is alone and without a master is like a lone burning coal; it will grow colder rather than hotter." - St. John of the Cross

REFLECTION #13

A NEW NORMAL

5/8/2013

For years I have been changing on the inside. To the outside world, I'm sure I don't look much different; to the outside world, I'm sure I'm *not* much different. Up until this point most of the change that has been happening is change within; change that I'm sure is only noticeable to God (and to those closest to me). I suppose this change is starting to trickle outside me and into my life, but I'm still a work in progress. I still have much in my outer life I need to work on...Ok, who am I kidding? I still have much in my inner life I need to work on, too!...Yes, the change has started and the pruning is underway, but there is still much to do before any of this produces any lasting fruit. I know this, and I'm ready and willing to do the work. I'm ready and willing to be led wherever it is the Lord leads. That is why when I felt the gentle nudging from God about a year ago to start thinking about working from home, I took it seriously. I continued to pray and discern and respond. Was I "hearing" correctly? Was this really what He was asking of me? Was this really what was coming next? Was this really even possible?

Time proved that this *was* the next step in my journey, so I began making the transition. I didn't rush it. I didn't push it. I didn't turn into a crazy person. I just kept praying, looking, and responding. I just kept taking steps - tiny, little steps - towards the goal. It was a slow process, but I eventually got there. I eventually got to the point where I was working from home; the point where, though the work I was doing did not change, the location of where I was doing it did..."Now what?" I found myself asking God..."Now what?"

As I sat in prayer reflecting on this transition and asking God the "Now what?" question, (and more questions like it) I found myself thinking about the week I just had. It was obvious that I was feeling somewhat guilty about my lack of presence at the office. Sure, I had been talking about and preparing for this moment for months, but I couldn't help but feel bad about it now that it was here. I couldn't help but feel like I was "abandoning" my team. (A team which includes my husband since it is *his* office that I work in.) Yes, though it was as clear as is humanly possible that this is what God asked me to do, it was also clear that I was struggling with the transition. I guess there was just a part of me that felt uncomfortable with the change.

As I worked through the emotions I wondered where they were coming from and why they were so intense. After all, this change wasn't *my* idea. God put it on my heart, and I had been processing it mentally, emotionally, and physically for months. I knew He was the one asking me to make the transition, and so, out of obedience, I did it. I took the steps necessary to make it happen. It was *His* idea, not mine, so why couldn't I just be on board with it? Why couldn't I just trust that this was the right move? Why couldn't I just trust that this was for the best? Now that the time had come, I was filled with doubt. I seemed to be having a hard time adjusting to all the changes. I seemed to be having a hard time finding a new routine. I seemed to be having a hard time finding peace. Yes, I was struggling. I was uncomfortable, overwhelmed, and doubtful..."Now what?" I found myself asking God again..."Now what?"

"Get used to this," I finally "heard" God tell me one day in prayer. "This is your new normal."

And, so, I say, "OK, my Lord. I hear you. And, though I still have more questions than I have answers, the doubt is now gone. Yes, I am now, once again, excited about the road ahead. (But I must admit, I have no idea where it's going!)"

Prayer

Pour out your blessings upon me as I continue my journey, Lord.
May your will be done in my life...Always!
I love you! I thank you! I praise you!

Read, Think, Pray: Proverbs 16:1-3

REFLECTION #14

THE TEMPLE OF GOD

5/16/2014

I, for one, have not done much thinking about my body being "the temple of God." (Remember, I'm new to all this spiritual stuff, and to the one who only sees the physical world, little thought is ever really given to what is happening spiritually.) Anyway, this is probably why it surprised me when I recently read in Dr. John Wood's book, *Ordinary Lives, Extraordinary Mission*, that choosing habits that create a destructive lifestyle (like drinking, smoking, not exercising, etc.) is like slowly killing ourselves...Say what now, Dr. Wood?...I guess I had never thought about the fact that choosing *not* to take care of yourself day after day is one way of destroying the gift of the body God has given you. Now that this has been brought to my attention, though, I will tell you this: I will never look at exercise in the same way again!

Oh, and this couldn't have come at a better time. Yes, I needed some fresh insight into this idea of "working out." You see, the issue in this area for me has never been *not* working out. No, I have been doing so regularly for most of my adult life. The issue instead has been *why* I work out. Yeah, for years my reason for doing so was pretty limited. Diet and exercise were really only about one thing: having the perfect figure. I worked out because I wanted to look like the people on TV and in the magazines. I dieted for the same reasons. Both were strictly done in vain. Because of this attitude, I quickly lost balance and became obsessed, spending hours every day working out and countless more

27

"counting calories." At one point during the heart of this obsession, my mom reached out to me to try to knock some sense into me. (Yes, it was another one of life's "aha moments.") Oh, and I remember exactly what she said to me like it was yesterday..."We can lose balance with everything in life," she wisely pointed out trying to get me to see how obsessed I had become. "We can even lose balance with those things that are 'good' for us; things like working out."...Well, like most motherly advice given to a teenage daughter, it took some time for this to actually sink in. (Lots of time!)

After years of being tormented by the number on the scale, I eventually came to my senses. Yes, I eventually realized the truth: I was addicted to dieting and working out. I later realized why. I, you see, was starving for love. I was so uncomfortable with who I was that I was certain no one would love me if I didn't love myself, and I was also certain that I would never love myself if I didn't look "the right" way. I was obsessed with having "the perfect" figure because I thought for sure it would result in me receiving "the perfect" love. This all seems ridiculous to me now, but it was anything *but* ridiculous to me at that time in my life. Yes, at that time, my life revolved around what I thought others thought about me, and since I related this to how I looked, my life revolved around maintaining a certain appearance. Perhaps others can't relate, but in my situation it was pretty simple: since I didn't feel loved, (and I didn't feel loved because I didn't know *God's* love) I did stupid - and I mean stupid - things to try to fill the void... It's a good thing God showed up when He did, isn't it?

> *"Since I didn't feel loved, (and I didn't feel loved because I didn't know God's love) I did stupid - and I mean stupid - things to try to fill the void."*

Prayer

Thank you, Lord, for all the gifts you have given me including

the gift of my physical body. Help me to love every part of my being. (Yes, even the parts that I don't really like.) I love you, my Lord, and I want to become the person you created me to be. I want to be set free from the slavery of having "the perfect" figure. So, show me how to better embrace what my body really is: your holy temple.
I love you! I thank you! I praise you!

Read, Think, Pray: 1 Corinthians 3:16-17, 1 Corinthians 6:12-14

REFLECTION #15

THIRTY YEARS IN THE MAKING

5/19/2013

It's here! The time I've been waiting for these past few years is finally here! Look, I know many people don't look forward to this day. I know for many people this is a day of "what if's," and "now what's," and "sad goodbye's to the best days of our lives," but this is *not* what this day is for me. No, I've been waiting for this day to get here like a young child waiting for Christmas morning; filled with excited anticipation. I guess I've always known that something special was going to happen in my life once I got to this point. Yeah, I guess I've always known that my life was going to change drastically at this stage of the game. I guess I've always known that something more was in store for me and that this would be the time of fulfillment. Yes, I have been waiting, - patiently waiting - and the time is here! It's finally here! So, it is with great joy that I say, "Goodbye 20s! So long! What's done is done, and what's there is staying there. I'm not bringing any of that with me into this next phase of my journey. Your reign has come to an end! Goodbye 20-something- year-old Julia. Hello 30-something-year-old me! I've been waiting to meet you. I can't wait to see what you have in store!"

Yes, Lord, thirty short years ago you brought me into this world. Thirty short years ago, you breathed new life in me as I left the comfort of my mother's womb and entered the world of the unknown. It's obvious, my

God, that you have been with me at every moment of my journey. It's obvious that you have been pouring your blessings out into my life from that very day. It is also obvious that, though your gifts have been many, my bad decisions have been, too. As I take some time to reflect and look back on the first thirty years of my life, I am finding it somewhat hard to believe who I was then and who I am now. I am finding it somewhat hard to believe how much you have worked in my life. I am finding it somewhat hard to believe how miraculous my transformation really is. If this wasn't my life, if I hadn't experienced it for myself, if it hadn't happened directly to me, then I might not believe it. I might be skeptical. I might be a critic. But this _is_ my life. I _did_ go through all of it. It _did_ all happen to me. And, though it's obvious that those who have not seen and still believe are blessed, (John 20:29) it's also obvious that seeing is believing. Oh, and I see now, Lord! I see it all quite clearly! Yes, it is all strikingly visible!

Prayer

Send your Spirit upon me as I begin this next phase of my
life, Lord. Fill me with your love and goodness. Fill me with your
wisdom and understanding. Fill me with your peace and joy.
May my 30s bring me into a new chapter in my life; a chapter
that is completely and totally devoted to you.
I love you! I thank you! I praise you!

Read, Think, Pray: Psalm 139:1-16

REFLECTION #16

REALITY CHECK

6/4/2013

The celebration has come to an end, and now all I can see is the mess of the party. Don't get me wrong, the celebration was awesome, much needed, and filled with pure joy, but the time has come to get back to work. Yes, the time has come for the vacation to end. The time has come for me to get real; to be honest with myself. The truth is, it's been a while since I've picked this journal up; since I've taken the time to put on paper all that's been going on in my life. I guess that pretty much sums up where my mind has been these past few weeks. Yeah, I got a little lost in the celebration. I overdid it a bit. I became a little too concerned with worldly things and lost sight of what is really important. Oh, how quickly the noise drowns out the silence!

Now I have more questions. Now there is more I want to know, so I'll start where I always start; I'll start with the why. *Why, Lord, why? Why is it so easy to get lost in the busyness of our earthly lives? Why is it so easy to get lost in the noise? I know better! I know true peace and happiness only come from you, so why was it so easy for me to let the noise in and to choose to lose sight of what really matters in the process? Why was it so easy for me to embrace the noise instead of the silence when I know what is really best; when I know what is really true; when I know the noise is just trying to distract me? I must try again, Lord. I must try again. Have mercy on me, and help me to make a more diligent effort to overcome my tendency to become of this world. Help me to remember that, although I am here to live in this world, I am not of it, and never will be. Help me, Lord! Help me to turn down the noise that I willingly turned back up.*

"Although I am here to live in this world, I am not of it, and never will be."

These past few weeks were a blur. The month is already over, but what can I do about any of that now? It is behind me, and I must simply try again. I must learn from these mistakes. I must do a better job at embracing the silence - of taking the time to think and respond to God's voice - instead of just running around and reacting to the noises of the world. Yes, I must.

Now that I have taken this time to refocus and re-center myself, I can already feel my mind making the change I know is necessary. Yes, I once again feel the peace, joy, and happiness that come when I'm focused on what is really important. This is going to be a better month, I just know it. Yes, this is going to be a more fruitful month, I can already tell.

Prayer

Thank you, Lord, for calling me back to you. Thank you for sending your Spirit upon me and for redirecting me. Keep me focused, energized, encouraged, humble, and filled with childlike faith as I move forward. Teach me to trust more in you! I love you! I thank you! I praise you!

Read, Think, Pray: 1 John 1:8-9

REFLECTION #17

A MOMENT OF THANKS

6/8/2013

How easy it is to tell someone, "Thank You!" How simple these words and how deserving so many people are of hearing them. From the moment we begin to speak our parents do their best to teach us manners; to ingrain in us the importance of saying "please" and "thank you." Why, then, do so many of us fail to acknowledge our gratitude once we reach adulthood? Are we just not grateful for anything anymore? Are we just so miserable we can't find anyone to thank or anything to be thankful for? Although I think this might be true for some people, I have a hard time believing this is the case for most. I think most of us *are* grateful, I just think we assume others don't want to hear about how grateful we are, or we assume others already know how grateful we are. Yeah, I think we often make the assumption that others already know that their hard work was noticed and appreciated, but - and this is a big but - unless we get really good at reading people's minds, I think it's wise that we don't assume.

With that being said, I'm learning that there is one, more than any other, who gets thanked the least. I'm learning that there is one, more than any other, who is taken for granted the most. That one is *the* One; that One is God. Recognizing that I am often one of these people taking God for granted, I now turn to Him with a grateful heart and say...

Thank You, my God! Thank you for all of the gifts you have given me! Thank you for my husband, Tony. Thank you for our marriage. Thank you for our daughter, Faith, in heaven with you. Thank you for the failures that have taught us how to live and for the successes that have come along the way. Thank you for your continuous help and guidance in all areas of our lives. Thank you for our home and for our family and for our friends, and for bringing so many of them together to share in our joy and to celebrate with us these past few weeks. Life is a gift, my Lord, and I thank you for it! I thank you for all of it! May I never stop singing your praises!

Prayer

Fill me with a grateful and humble heart, Lord. Show me how to generously share all the gifts you have given me. Make me a better example of your love and goodness. Make me more like you. May others see you in me. May others know you and your love because of my life. May I be a source of your hope, peace, and love to everyone I meet, and may I never stop thanking you along the way! I love you! I thank you! I praise you!

Read, Think, Pray: Psalm 103

LOVING MORE

6/19/2013

I have become so much removed from the girl of my past that, although I will never forget where I came from, I often forget how miserable the darkness is. Today, however, I was reminded of this misery because the past few nights I have had dreams in which this girl from my past showed herself again; dreams in which I fell into old habits; dreams in which I was not acting in ways that are consistent with a life of one living in the light. In these dreams I found myself being tempted in the same ways I used to be, and (in these dreams) I gave in to these temptations. Look, I know that dreams are dreams, but in the midst of them they seem real, and that is why I woke up this morning in a panic. I, you see, was having flashbacks of my past self, this self that I have worked so hard to let go of. In an instant, I found myself tempted to let the guilt and shame back in. In an instant, I could feel the evil around me trying to get me to go back into hiding; trying to get me to go back into the darkness. The questions I had been tormented with for years began to replay themselves in my head...

"How could you?" that nagging voice inside kept saying trying to belittle me. "Who do you think you are? Look at all you've done! Look at how disgusting and sinful you are! You will *never* be free from these things. Never! You will *never* be able to undo what you have done! You might as well give up," it continued. "You're as good as finished anyway."

It didn't take long for me to realize these thoughts were not coming from God. Yeah, it didn't take long for me to realize I was being attacked by the evil one. This evil was desperately trying to scare me into turning around. It was desperately trying to scare me into running back into the darkness. The problem for it, though, is I'm onto it! Yes, though its tactics worked on me for years, I'm not so quick to be fooled now. No, now I know the truth. I know God cares more about where I'm going than about where I've been. I know my sins died with Christ. And that is why I refused to take the bait.

God cares more about where you're going than about where you've been.

In the midst of the tormenting, I remained calm, took a deep breath, and centered my mind and heart back on my Savior. I stopped dialoguing with the devil and started conversing with Christ, and eventually the evil fled. As it did, I once again "heard" Christ's whisper calling me back...

"Yes," he gently called out comforting me in my affliction. "Yes, you have made some mistakes, but I died to erase those mistakes. They no longer exist. I repeat, they no longer exist! Don't be fooled by the lies of the enemy. Remember, your past does *not* define you. Besides, look at the good our Father is bringing out of this. Look at how He's straightening your crooked lines. As crazy as it sounds this was all worked into His plan. Yes, even your sin. Your massive conversion would *not* have been possible without your massive fall, for, as you know, 'the one whose larger debt is forgiven loves more' (Luke 7:40-43). You see, my beloved, your many sins have been forgiven, and that is why you are filled with such great love. Yes, that is why you know what love really is. So, don't be fooled! Instead, go in peace. Your faith has saved you."

And, so, go in peace, I shall.

Prayer

Thank you, Lord, for all of the blessings you have given me.
Thank you, Lord for loving me, for forgiving me, and for saving me.
I love you, my dear Savior; my brother; my friend. I love you!
(And, though you tell me it's impossible, I will always love you more!)
I love you! I thank you! I praise you!

Read, Think, Pray: Isaiah 42:16, Luke 7:36-50

REFLECTION #19

THE PATH TO SAINTHOOD

7/17/2013

"The only thing keeping me from being the saint I was created to be is me." - I heard this from someone earlier today, and it has been replaying in my mind ever since. There must be a reason for it. Yeah, there must be a reason I'm still thinking about it. Let's dive in...

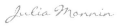

I know God wants nothing more than for me to one day join Him in heaven, so I know His goal is for me to become a saint. (After all, a saint is someone who is living in heaven with Him.) That's not the issue for me; that's not the area of confusion; that's not what's holding me back. No, the question for me has never been *what* the goal is, the question for me has always been, *"How?"* How do I go about reaching this goal? How do I go about fulfilling my mission?...Oh, and *what*, by the way, is my mission to begin with?...Yeah, the time has come for me to ask more questions. I must return to prayer and contemplation. I must return to the search.

It's true: this *has* been a year of searching for me, and I'm just now realizing how inconsistent I've been during this search. This year has been filled with so many highs and so many lows. There have been times I've felt so close to God that it seems as if I'm in heaven already, but there have been other times I've gotten so busy and distracted that I don't even know which way I'm going. I know there is more to all of this, though. Yeah, I know there is still much I am missing. I know I still have much more to learn...much, much more.

I think the great challenge of life is to learn how to live *in* the world without becoming *of* it; to learn to keep our eyes, minds, and hearts focused on God and eternity instead of on the millions of distractions that are constantly pulling us out of focus. I'm not there yet. I'm not where I want to be. And I don't think I'm where God wants me to be either. Yeah, I think He wants more for me. In fact, I know He does.

I must not get discouraged, though. I must remember that if the Lord is allowing me to be challenged right now, then it can only mean I'm ready for it. Though I find it hard to believe I'm ready, it's obvious He thinks differently, so I return, once again, to my prayer...

Yes, Lord, it's true. I know it's true. The only thing keeping me from being the saint you created me to be is me. So, how about I just get out of your way, and let you go to work? How about I just spend more time praying and less time preaching? How about I just wait more patiently for you to unveil all of this to me instead of pushing you for answers? Yeah, how about I just trust? How about I just ask, think, pray, respond, and trust? After all, if you say I'm ready to be pruned, Lord, then I'm ready. If you say I'm ready for the challenge, then I'm ready. Yes, Lord, I'm ready. Let us continue on this path to sainthood.

Prayer

Thank you, Lord, for gently calling me back to you. Give me the grace and strength I need to continue. Give me the courage to take the next step. Give me a faith so strong and a confidence so steadfast that I'm like the Peter who walked on water, not the Peter who fell in. I love you! I thank you! I praise you!

Read, Think, Pray: Matthew 14:27-31

REFLECTION #20

NOTE TO SELF

8/7/2013

It wasn't until I began my journey back to God that I started paying closer attention to my thoughts. The advice I was given early on was to "start thinking about what you're thinking about," and doing so has proven to be fruitful in my life. Thoughts, after all, have to be coming from somewhere, and once I started "tuning in" to them it started to become clear which of them were coming from God and which of them weren't. It also started to become clear which of them were productive, helpful, and healthy and which of them were anything but.

Through the years I've learned that some thoughts come and go. Some, however, seem to reappear over and over again. I've gotten into the habit of paying attention to these reoccurring thoughts because I've learned that if the message keeps coming up in my life, (and, of course, it's a healthy message) then there must be a reason for it. It is, in fact, often in these reoccurring thoughts that I "hear" the voice of God, and that is why I've finally decided not to ignore this particular one that has been coming up in my life these past several months. So, just in case

I ever forget what seems to be an obvious truth to me now, here is a quick note to self...

Dear Julia:

Remember, the most important things in your life are your relationships. First on this list is your relationship with God. Take note of what you heard the other day, and make sure you never forget it because the message in this advice states what is of the utmost importance. Yes, "everyone really should spend at least thirty minutes a day with God, except, of course, those people who are really busy; those people need to spend at least an hour."*...Oh, and don't forget that this advice comes with the key words "at least." These really are the minimum requirements...Life, you see, will get busy. The world will try to distract you and get you to lose focus, but there is <u>nothing</u> more important than spending time with your Creator. There is really no acceptable reason not to spend time with God, for no matter what is going on, no one can keep you from praying. No matter what duties you have in life, no one can stop you from inviting God in to help you with them, and that, of course, is a form of prayer and a way to grow in your relationship with Him. So, I guess what I'm telling you is, don't make excuses when it comes to your prayer life! When it comes to your relationship with God there is no excuse <u>not</u> to spend time with Him.

After your divine relationship, the most important relationship you have is with your husband. Your marriage is a vocation, a divine calling. Do not take it for granted. Do not overlook your husband. He comes right after God, and not just sometimes, all of the time. Make your marriage a priority in your life, and it will not fail. Build it on a solid foundation, and it will weather any storm. Be a good wife, honor your husband, and thank God for him daily. He is a gift to you and is as much a part of this journey as you are.

These two relationships should be your primary focus, but they are, of course, not the only ones that are of importance to you. Though you have left the home and should cling to your husband, don't forget why you are here in the first place and where you come from. Yes, your extended family and friends and neighbors, even those who are complete strangers, are of great importance, too. Christ lives in all these people, so when you spend time with them you are spending time with the Lord. Soak in their love and give it back to them in return. Good friends are scarce, and you have hit the jackpot. Be thankful for your many loving, supportive relationships. They, too, are a gift from God.

I know you are a worker, Julia. I know there is work to be done, and you are one of the people the Lord is asking to do it, but one thing is for sure: you will not be on your deathbed wishing you had spent more time working. You will not be on your deathbed wishing you had accumulated more stuff. All that will matter at that point is what you are leaving behind in the lives of those people whom you have touched. Don't live so that people will remember what you did or what you had along the way. Live so that people will remember who you are.

You, my friend, are nothing without God and without the people around you that love, support, and challenge you to be the person you were created to be. It will seem crazy to many in the world that you spend so much time and energy nurturing, growing, and working on your relationships, but don't let that stop you from doing it because there is no better way to spend your life. In fact, that's really the only reason you are here to begin with. Yes, it's true. It's all about relationships.

And with that I say, "Note to self, complete."

Prayer

Help me, my God, to be loving and generous to everyone in my life. Help me to prioritize my life and to spend quality time with everyone you have surrounded me with, especially you. Remind me often that life is not about what I do, it's about who I am. Remind me often that life is not about living in solitude, it's about living in communion. Remind me often that life is not about what I have, it's about who I have with me. Oh, and remind me often that, above all else, the most important being I have with me is you.
I love you! I thank you! I praise you!

Read, Think, Pray: Mark 12:30-31

* "Half an hour's meditation each day is essential, except when you are busy. Then a full hour is needed." - St. Francis de Sales

SELF-CONDEMNATION

9/10/2013

Due to a recent experience in my own life, I just realized how hard it is to watch someone you love beat themselves up over a silly (or even not so silly) mistake. Yes, it's emotionally painful to watch a loved one stew in their own self-hatred. Now, I have to ask: If a situation like this is so painful for me, a mere human incapable of loving perfectly, what must it feel like for God?

It must be excruciating for God to watch us, His beloved children, torture ourselves. It must be excruciating for Him to watch us agonize over every little mistake we've ever made. It must be excruciating for Him to watch us rake our own selves over the coals. Yes, it must.

I think the world tries to make us believe that self-condemnation is a requirement of humility because it somehow seems noble to beat ourselves up when we know we've messed up. As it's been said, though, "true humility does not require that we think less of ourselves, just that we think of ourselves less." With that being said, I think we would be more pleasing to God if we learned how to accept His love and mercy instead of repeatedly telling Him how stupid we are.

> *Self-condemnation is not a requirement of humility.*

Prayer

Show me what you see when you look at me, Lord.
Show me how to learn from the past, not live in it. Show me how
to forgive, especially when it comes to forgiving myself.
I love you! I thank you! I praise you!

Read, Think, Pray: 1 John 2:1-2

GOD'S PLAN

10/7/2013

I was recently asked the question, *"With all the messed up things happening in our world today, do you really think God cares whether or not I use contraception?"*...Hmmm...Well, in short, yes. But before I go any further I will admit, I'm probably not the best person to answer this question. To be honest, I know very little about the Church's teaching on the "Theology of the Body." I am, however, always happy to share what I'm learning about God and about life, and I think that's why this particular person asked me this question and not someone else who is more of an "expert" in this area. Regardless, I answered her question the only way I knew how: by looking at it from the perspective of a loving Father. So, yes, my answer was (and still is) "Yes," but I think I should explain why.

Yes, I *do* think God cares (and cares very deeply for that matter) whether or not we use contraception, but not for the reasons one might expect. In fact, I think His take on this has little to do with the "rules," for He, Himself tells us that He wants love, not sacrifice (Hosea 6:6). Yes, He is a God of love. He *is* love. He is *not* a "follow the rules or else!" kind of God. No, as I see it, the "rules" exist out of love. They exist because He knows the things that will hurt us, and, as any loving father would, He wants to keep us away from those things. To me, the "rules" are more of a head thing, and this, as I see it, is a heart thing. It's much deeper than a "rule."

So what is the heart thing? Well, to me, it's trust. Yes, to me it's trust. I mean, if we *really* believed that God had our best interests at heart; that He only wants what's best for us; that He would never allow anything to happen to us that He couldn't bring good from; that He is our kind, compassionate, merciful, loving, all-knowing Father, then contraception wouldn't even be a topic of conversation, would it? Wouldn't we just *trust* in God's will? As I see it, the fact that we think we somehow know what's best and think that He couldn't possibly understand our needs, wants, and desires is just an example of us

41

putting our will before His. This is why I think He "cares" whether or not we use contraception. To me, using it is a statement of distrust. It's proof that we think we know better. It's proof that we think our way (and our plans) are best.

What do I know, though? I mean, seriously. This particular "rule" is an easy one for me to follow. After all, I don't have a house full of kids tugging at me at every waking moment. In fact, I would love nothing more than for God to give me a few of them. But, like all things, whether or not this actually happens is completely up to Him. His plans are what I want, not mine.

Prayer

Increase my trust in you, my God. Show me how to trust more in you and less in myself. You know what is best for me, Lord. You know what I desire and what I need and what will most fulfill me. Show me, therefore, how to surrender my life to you. Show me how to trust in you more completely. Show me how to let go of the control. Show me how to let go of my plans and embrace yours.
I love you! I thank you! I praise you!

Read, Think, Pray: Romans 12:1-2

REFLECTION #23

BACKSEAT DRIVER

10/20/2013

Ok, ok let's get real. I know this "trust" thing isn't easy to master. Yeah, I know it's our life's work to learn how to let go and surrender to God. The truth is, there are some areas in my life that I have let go of and surrendered to God easily, but there are other areas that I'm still working on. Even so, I'm certain the freedom is in the surrender. Yes, I'm certain the only way to receive "the peace the world cannot give"

(John 14:27) is to surrender our lives to Christ, so I'm back to asking why. Yes, I'm back to asking God why.

Why is it so hard to trust in you, God? Why do I want so badly to work out every detail of every situation? Why do I try so hard to have complete control over everything? Life is soooo much easier when I give up control; when I just do my best and accept every outcome with joy and trust in your Divine Plan. Why, then, is it so difficult for me to do this? Why, God? Why? I feel like it should be easier to "turn it over" and "to offer it up," but these are obviously not easy things to do. Why is that? Why is it so hard, Lord? Why is it so hard?

I think most of us find it difficult to totally surrender ourselves to God. I think, though, that as long as we are *trying* to surrender, as long as we are *trying* to let go, as long as we are *trying* to give it our best effort then what we are doing *is* pleasing to God. Yeah, I think God is more concerned with the journey we are on than with our immediate results. I think all He really wants from us is a little forward motion.

"I think God is more concerned with the journey we are on than with our immediate results. I think all He really wants from us is a little forward motion."

I have been moving forward, little by little, these past several years, and I've learned in the process that the only times I've found true peace in my life are those times when I've surrendered. Yes, I've learned that in order to accept the gift of Christ's peace, I have to - very willingly - become a passenger on the journey. I mean, let's be honest. He really *is* the One driving anyway. Yeah, we are kidding ourselves to think we have control over any of this, so we might as well make it easy on ourselves and enjoy the ride, right? We would be stupid not to, wouldn't we?...Why, then, is there still a part of me that wants to do the stupid thing and try to take control?...Why, then, is there still a part of me that wants to make things harder than they need to be?

I want to know how to trust. I want to know how to willingly let God drive while I joyfully enjoy the journey. I want to be a carefree passenger, but let's be honest, I'm a backseat driver! I'm hoping this, too, will one day change.

Prayer

I want to trust you, my Lord. I want to surrender myself to you. I want to do your will, be a perfect instrument in your hands, and trust you to work out all the details. But I need help. Please, help me! Help me to trust. Help me to let go. Help me to surrender. I love you! I thank you! I praise you!

Read, Think, Pray: Philippians 2:5-8

REFLECTION #24

A GOOD EYE

10/22/2013

The darkness of the world can feel overpowering at times. We turn on the news and read the paper only to find more pain, more anger, more death. Sometimes the world seems so messed up that we wonder if God has forgotten about us. Yeah, sometimes things make so little sense that, although we want to believe in God and trust that He is in control, it's hard to imagine that an all-powerful, all-knowing, all-loving Father would allow such terrible things to happen. Even so, though it would be easy to let the worry and fear set in and lead me into despair, I find comfort in the truth. And the truth is, God has not gone anywhere; God has not abandoned or forgotten about us; God knows *exactly* what is going on.

Yes, as I see it, the issue here is *not* with God's apparent lack of grace or lack of blessings or lack of presence, care, and/or concern. The issue here is with what we are choosing to see. You see, I believe that if we make a conscious effort to see God's grace at work in what is good, beautiful, and right in our lives, (and in the world) then we will easily see it, but I also believe that if we allow what is bad, ugly, and wrong to consume us, then all we'll see is the darkness. I mean, sure, life has its ups and downs and comes with its fair share of sorrows, challenges, and even tragedies, but if we look for the good in life, we will always find it. Why? Because it is always there! Yes, I firmly believe that God's goodness far outweighs any evil in this world. I just think it takes a good eye to see it.

Prayer

Open my eyes to see the good that is around me, Lord.
Keep me focused on you and on your goodness and truth. I trust
in you, and I know you haven't left me. Yes, I know there is no reason for
me to live in fear and lose hope. Give me, therefore, good eyes, Lord.
Give me eyes that see you, and your goodness, in all.
I love you! I thank you! I praise you!

Read, Think, Pray: Proverbs 16:4, Matthew 6:22-23

"Each creature in the world will lift our hearts to God if we look at it with a good eye." - St. Felix of Cantalice

REFLECTION #25

TRACES OF EVIL

10/24/2013

I've got some more questions for you, my God. I've got some more questions...If Christ is the answer and prayer is what leads to him, then why do even prayerful people live chaotic, stressful, worrisome lives?...If, then, why?

I found myself thinking about this question as I noticed that many of us (myself included) are prayerful people, "doing" all the right things, but are still stressed out, super busy, and living less than virtuous lives. It just got me wondering why. I mean, the point of prayer is to bring us closer to God not turn us into crazy people, right? Yes, I know the answers come in the silence. I know the only way to "bear fruit that will remain" (John 15:16) is to become people of prayer, so I have to wonder what is going on. I have to wonder, could there be traces of evil even in our times of prayer?

It didn't take long for me to realize that the answer to this question is, "Yes!" (I mean, of course the answer is yes!) After all, if your primary goal was to keep someone from growing in their relationship with God, then wouldn't you focus your attention on the people in prayer? Wouldn't you focus your attention on the people trying to make changes in their lives? Wouldn't you focus your attention on the people going to church? Yes, of course you would! You would do everything in your power to complicate their lives. You would do everything in your power to drown out the simplicity. You would do everything in your power to turn up the noise.

Look, I've learned over the years that we shouldn't pay too much attention to the evil lurking around us because God is much greater than all of it, but I've also learned that it isn't wise to ignore it either. Yes, I've learned that if we want to set ourselves up to win, then we need to be on guard and have a general understanding of what we're up against. With that being said, I'm going to take this time to remind myself of the truth.

The truth is, prayer is simple. The truth is, prayer should be heartfelt and childlike. The truth is, prayer should help me grow in my relationship with Christ. The truth is, prayer should make me want to be a better me... (If it doesn't, then maybe something is trying to stand in my way.)

"Prayer should make me want to be a better me."

46

Prayer

Show me where and how evil is working in my life, Lord. Teach me how to embrace your Spirit, especially in times of prayer. May my focus always be on one thing: growing in my relationship with you. I love you! I thank you! I praise you!

Read, Think, Pray: Luke 18:9-14

REFLECTION #26

THE WHY

11/4/2013

My journey back to God has taught me much over the years, but there is one lesson, before all others, that laid the foundation. That one lesson is this: having a basic understanding of the *whats* and the *hows* of the spiritual life is not enough. We must also understand the *why*.

You see, we can know the *what* (for example, the Sacrament of Reconciliation) and know the *how*, (how to proceed through the process from examination to penance) but if we don't understand the *why*, then many of us will miss the point. Yeah, if we don't understand the *why* then many of us will lack any motivation to go, and, if we do go, it will probably only be because "we have to." The problem with this, of course, is that in order to truly experience all the

"In order to truly experience all the Church offers us, we have to move past the point of doing things because we have to, and start doing them because we want to."

47

Church offers us, we have to move past the point of doing things because "we have to," and start doing them because we want to. This, at least in my opinion, will only happen if we come to understand the *why*.

In my own life, knowing that "I'm not supposed to do this," was never enough to keep me from doing it. It wasn't until I understood *why* I wasn't supposed to do it that I actually started overcoming the many temptations of this world. Now, I'm not saying that understanding the *why* meant that I never made another bad decision, I'm just saying it empowered me to make better ones. Yeah, I'm just saying that all ignorance of the *why* ever did was set me up to fail.

So, yes, to me ignorance is *not* bliss. In fact, if my journey is proof of anything, it's proof that "the why" is the foundation of it all.

Prayer

Help me to come to know and understand the whys, Lord, especially the whys of your Church. Change me on the inside and help me go from doing things out of obligation, to doing them out of love. I love you! I thank you! I praise you!

Read, Think, Pray: Proverbs 9:10

REFLECTION #27

WORRIED WORRYING

11/9/2013

After being on the receiving end of a few worry-filled conversations one evening, I returned home distressed. I just couldn't make sense of what I had been hearing. I guess I had no idea how many people (good, church-going people) live lives of worry. I am, after all, a glass-half-full kind of a person, so I guess I was just surprised by how many glass-half-empty kind of people there really are.

Regardless, as I returned home I just couldn't get out of my head all that I had heard. The more I thought about what these people said, the more I realized how alone I was in my thinking. Since no one shared my optimistic, faith-filled attitude, I began wondering if maybe I was the one looking at things wrong. (After all, I have been wrong once or twice before!) In all seriousness, I really began to think that I was missing something, so I went to my husband for help...

"Do I not worry enough?" I asked him after I arrived home. "Everyone seems to be so worried about everything. I mean, I care about how things turn out. In fact, I care very much! But they've got me wondering. Do you think my lack of worry is a sign that I don't care enough?"

Answering my question with a question he said, "So, are you saying that you're worried about your lack of worry?"

He didn't have to say anything else. As soon as he said it out loud I realized how silly my doubt was. Yes, his wise response reminded me that worry is not from God and that I have nothing to worry about regarding my apparent lack of it. It's a good thing I brought it up, huh? I mean, seriously. Can you imagine where that train of thought could have taken me had he not shed some light on it?

Oh, this has been a good reminder for me. Yes, this has reminded me that it's good to say out loud the fear and worry-filled thoughts running through our minds because some of them are just plain ridiculous!

Prayer

*Come into my life, Lord, and fill me with your love and truth.
Help me to trust in you more completely, so that I can live in
peaceful confidence instead of in fear-filled doubt. Show
me how to worry less and trust in you more.
I love you! I thank you! I praise you!*

Read, Think, Pray: Matthew 6:27

A RESTFUL HEART

12/11/2013

My Lord and My God,

This all seems so simple, yet I'm finding that the problem for many of us is that we are addicted to doing. I'm finding that even when we take the time to pray, we are praying in a spirit of "*doing*" with our minds and our hearts far from being centered on you. Why is "*being*" so difficult? The answers come in the silence. The peace we all seek comes from spending time with you, - from centering ourselves on you - but we are hamsters on a wheel running and running and running but getting nowhere. Teach us, my Lord, how to *do* all you ask, but in a spirit of *be*ing.

Last year, Lord, I felt you calling me to start working from home. As you may recall, this was difficult for me. Out of obedience to you, though, I slowly began making the transition. The months that followed were torture, but I made myself sit back and watch as everyone "learned to fly." I must admit, when I felt you calling me to work from home, I assumed children would be soon to follow, but this, as you also know, has yet to happen. Even so, I am beginning to understand why you asked me to do this. Yes, I am beginning to see the fruits of this transition. My entire day is now spent in silence. I read, write, pray, and work all in silence. After a year of doing this, I have grown closer and closer to you. I mean, how could I not have? Now you are as real to me as the birds outside my window. Yes, I know you are here. I feel your presence stirring within me. I hear your voice calling out to my heart.

There are times, Lord, that I become too concerned with worldly things, but every time this happens you always make me aware of it and call me back. Yes, you always call me back into the silence and fill me with the peace I know can only come from you. Thank you! It's so easy to get swallowed up by the world, and I am in constant need of your redirection.

50

As I continue to grow closer and closer to you, Lord, I can feel you calling me to give up more and more of myself. I can feel you working to release me from my fears and free me from my sins. Please continue your work in me! I know, Lord, that I am not perfect, but I believe that, with you, I am perfectible. Help me, therefore, to become the saint I was created to be. Not, of course, for my gain, but for your glory.

Help me also, Lord, to do all you call me to do in a spirit of humility, for it seems to me that you are starting to reveal to me some of the longings and wearinesses of the souls around me. If this is truly what is happening, then I want to use it for good. Yes, use me as your instrument; as your humble instrument. May my life point others directly to you.

The words you spoke to us through your servant Augustine are ringing true in my life, Lord. Yes, *our hearts truly are restless until they rest in you.* I have found this rest, and now that I have it, I realize it wasn't really that hard to find to begin with. And, with that being said, I now rest in your presence and pray: *Show me how to simplify my life, Lord. Show me what is truly important. Show me how to live in your peace, forever.*

Prayer

All that I am, all that I have, and all that I do, Lord,
is from you, with you, and for you. I love you with every part
of my being. May I go forth proving this love to you.
I love you! I thank you! I praise you!

Read, Think, Pray: Psalm 131

"You have made us for yourself, O Lord, and our heart is restless until it rests in you." - St. Augustine

THE PRUNING

WAITING

12/16/2013

"What God does in us while we are waiting is often more important than what we are waiting for." - Ben Patterson

I heard this quote today while listening to a homily by Fr. Mike Schmitz, and it has opened my mind to a whole new level of understanding. Waiting, you see, has always been the hardest part for me because I am a textbook overachiever. I often find myself wanting things done yesterday, racing to get to wherever it is I am going, pushing to finish whatever it is I have started. I'm always ready to move on to the next thing, always ready for what is coming next, but these simple words shed new light on this area of my life. Now I am seeing life from a whole new perspective.

Oh, Lord, I now see why "the wait" is so important. I now have a better understanding of your why behind the wait. Yes, I can see how much growth this wait has produced in my life, and growth is the goal, isn't it?

You know, my Lord, that the waiting can be torturous at times, but I'm certain your plan is much better than mine, and, though I know it doesn't always seem like it, I really do trust you. I know you haven't left

53

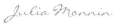

my side. I know you have heard our prayers and only want what's best for us, so all I really want to say is, thank you. Thank you for giving us this opportunity to grow closer to you. Thank you for making us wait.

Give me eyes of faith, Lord. Allow me to see things as you see them, always trusting in your Divine Providence, for I know that you are my loving Father, and I know there is a reason for this. Yes, I know there is a reason we do not have children in this life, and I no longer feel the need to ask you "why?" or "why not?" I know you are taking perfect care, and I want you to know, Lord, that the only thing I want is to one day join you in heaven. So, if waiting is a part of me getting there, - a part of us getting there - then bring it on! I trust in you and in your plan for our marriage. I am not a victim of the past. I do not fear the future. I follow you blindly wherever you go.

Prayer

Help me to wait well by living a life that's pleasing to you, Lord. Teach me. Show me. Guide me. Remind me often that you are the One who is all-knowing, not me. Jesus, I trust in you! I love you! I thank you! I praise you!

Read, Think, Pray: James 5:7-8

REFLECTION #30

MATTHEW, CHAPTER 6

12/17/2013

You never cease to amaze me, my God; my loving omnipotent Father. I pray, you answer. The answers rarely come how and when I expect, but they always comes. Yes, Lord, I have been asking you to guide me, and you have been answering me by showing me the areas of my life I still need to work on. The change you have made in me so far is really quite unbelievable, and yet the more I humble myself, the more you reveal. The more I open myself up to you, the more you show me. The more I accept your graces, the more graces you give...It really is that simple, isn't it?

Today in prayer I began to meditate on humility. The question I was reflecting on was, *"What does humility mean to you?"* After some thought, my search for answers led me to the Gospel of Matthew, Chapter 6. How can it be that this *one* chapter contains *everything* I have been working on these past few months?...*Everything!*

I long to be a humble person. This chapter opens with what it means to be humble; to do all for your glory and for no other reason (Verses 1-4). I struggle with prayer becoming repetitive and lacking heart. You show me what it means to pray in meaningful ways with great love (Verses 5-18). I pray that you show me how to best use the resources you are sending into my life, that you show me how to be a good steward of all the gifts you give me, and you tell me to "store up treasures in heaven" (Verses 19-21). I say, "Give me eyes of faith so I can see things how you see them." And you respond, "If your eye is sound, your whole body will be filled with light" (Verses 22-23). I ask you to free me from the slavery of vanity. I ask you to help me to be less concerned with how I look and what I wear and more concerned with you, and you say, "Do not worry about your body, what you will wear. Is not the body more than clothing?" (Verses 24-32). I pray, "Help me to be present in all that I do. Teach me to live for today and not fear tomorrow." And you tell me, "Do not worry about tomorrow; tomorrow will take care of itself" (Verse 34). "Seek first the kingdom of God and his righteousness, and all these things will be given you besides" (Verse 33)...All I can say is, WOW, you're good! Thank you! I hear you.

Prayer

Thank you, Lord! Thank you for, once again, amazing me by your powerful presence in my life! Help me to become a person who lives by your Truth revealed to us in Matthew, Chapter 6, for it seems to me that a person who can do this will, most certainly, be on the path that leads to you.
I love you! I thank you! I praise you!

Read, Think, Pray: Matthew 6

ANSWERED WITHIN

12/19/2013

The truth about you and about your love is becoming more and more clear to me, Lord. I am now realizing that there is no *one* person that has all the answers we seek in our lives. My mentors don't have all the answers. My parish priest doesn't have all the answers. My parents don't have all the answers. I certainly don't have all the answers. (Though I often think I do!)

I guess there are times in each our lives when we think we are the ones with the answers; when we think we have it figured out and have learned everything there is to learn. And you know what else? I'm also realizing that we not only think we have all the answers for our own life, we also often think we have all the answers for other people's lives, too, don't we? Yes, we think we somehow know what others should do and how they should change. Oh, it's so very easy to pull the splinters out of other people's eyes and ignore the wooden beams in our own (Matthew 7:1-5). It's no wonder you warned us about this!

If we are honest with ourselves, Lord, I think we will discover that there is much we don't know; that there is always more to learn, always ways to grow, and always much that needs to change. I guess on the surface this might seem discouraging, but the truth is, *we* don't have to have all of the answers, do we? No, this isn't dependent on *us* having it all figured out, is it? All that matters is that *you* know; that *you* have all of the answers; that *you* have it all figured out, isn't it?

Oh, Lord, if only we come to you with humble hearts and admit that we don't know, that we can't do it by ourselves, and that we need you, then the floodgates open, and we begin to receive the graces you are pouring into our lives. That is when we start to figure things out. That is when life starts to make sense. That is when everything starts to come together. We just have to start looking in for answers instead of out, don't we?

Yes, Lord, in the silence and stillness of our hearts lies you and every answer to every question we could ever have. The abundant life (John 10:10) comes from letting go of our pride and approaching you with a humble heart. Yes, of course! It's so simple and yet so hard to just let go and let you take the reins, but that is the very thing (and only thing) we need to do in order to receive all it is you want to give us, isn't it?

"In the silence and stillness of our hearts lies God and every answer to every question we could ever have."

Oh, Lord, I think I'm starting to understand, and, as always, I thank you for opening my eyes. I thank you for opening my eyes to see what's been alive in my heart all along.

Prayer

Show me how to approach you with a sincere and humble heart, Lord. Unveil to me your will for my life, and guide me to a life of complete and total surrender.
I love you! I thank you! I praise you!

Read, Think, Pray: Sirach 3:17-24

REFLECTION #32

A BIRTHDAY GIFT

12/25/2013

Today we celebrate you, my Lord and Savior. Today we celebrate you coming into this world. In this moment, I am overcome with emotion. I just can't put into words my gratitude and joy. I just can't seem to express the deepness of my love for you, but I suppose that is one of the wonderful things about our relationship. I don't have to. Yes, Lord, you know my heart, and in this moment my heart is overflowing with love: love for you for coming to save us; love for Mary for saying "yes" to your will; love for Joseph for humbly and obediently following you and trusting in your plan. Yes, my salvation, and the salvation of the world, was dependent on this; on you coming here. My human mind just can't fathom the bigness of this event. All I can do is sit in joy, wonder, and amazement at all the gifts we have been given; your gift of self being at the top of this list.

Yes, Lord, today I am speechless. You have left me speechless. So, I will simply breathe in the joy that surrounds me. I will simply breathe in your abundance and give thanks.

I thank you, my Lord, for the gift of life, and I thank you for giving us your very self. (Oh, and by the way, Happy Birthday!)

Prayer

My Lord, I believe! Today, and all days, I celebrate you by celebrating life. What an amazing gift! Though I am unworthy of all of this, - though I am unworthy of you - I long to be made worthy and will rest confidently in your arms knowing that you love me, not in spite of my unworthiness, but because of it. I love you! I thank you! I praise you!

Read, Think, Pray: Luke 2:1-14

REFLECTION #33

A YEAR IN REVIEW

1/1/2014

Another year has come and gone, Lord. Although it seems like time goes by a little faster with each passing year, I'm not complaining. No, even though it flew by, 2013 was a wonderful year; one that I would never have guessed would have turned out like it did, but one that I am grateful for nonetheless. It is in this gratitude that I now take this time to tell you, thank you!

Throughout this year, Lord, I felt you drawing me closer and closer to you. Yes, week after week I felt you showing me how to let go of my old self and how to become more of the person you created me to be. Thank you! Thank you for all of it! Sure, there have been ups and downs, highs and lows, but they have all brought me closer to you. And, for this, I am forever grateful. Yes, it was all worth it. Every last second of it was worth it.

I have learned much this year, my God. First on this list is realizing (not for the first time, but hopefully for the last) that you know best and that I can trust you. Yes, you have proven yourself to me over and over again, and I think I'm finally starting to get the message. On top of that, you continue to show me exactly what I need to do to unite myself more and more with you and less and less with the world. So, again, I say, thank you! Thank you! Thank you! Thank you! Please don't stop your work in me!

Since I know there is still much more that needs to be done in me, Lord, I now recommit myself to you by making a few resolutions.* With your help, I resolve to:

1) Be joyful at all times: May I seek your consolation and always hope in your promises.
2) Treat everyone like a celebrity: Everyone is special in your eyes. May I love them like you do.
3) Spend time doing things that may seem like "wasted" time to everyone else: May I remember that time spent with you and for you is *never* wasted.

Be with me as I continue my journey towards you, Lord. May these resolutions produce great fruit in my life; fruit that will last.

Read, Think, Pray: John 15:8

* These were resolutions I heard during a homily given by a visiting priest at a neighboring parish on 12/31/2013. I liked them so much I chose to make them my own.

REFLECTION #34

GOOD VS. EVIL

1/8/2014

I've been asking you since the first of the year, Lord, to *"remove all the trappings of my life that prevent my openness to you."* Well, we are eight days into the year, and I just want to say, you are wasting no time! I feel like I am being purged of my past desires to put myself first, to worship the almighty dollar, and to value my reputation with others more than my relationship with you. This journey to sainthood is no joke! Seriously, why is it so hard? I know what is right, I know what is good, I know what is just, but the world would love nothing more than to pull me back in to my old ways. I'm fighting the war of good vs. evil, and I'm feeling the pain of the fight!

A quick look into my past reminds me that my old self was not very honest. Yeah, I lied often by twisting the truth. I mean, if I didn't have anything to hide, I was honest, (who wouldn't be) but if I feared getting into trouble or tarnishing my reputation I could, and would, talk myself out of anything. By the end, I would probably even have others feeling sorry for me even if I was the one at fault. Yes, I was manipulative, that's for sure. There are times now, Lord, that I'm tempted to fall back into these old ways; tempted to tell just one more "little white lie." Oh, but it feels so wrong and dirty now. I wouldn't have cared about this years ago. No, it wouldn't have bothered me. I wouldn't have even blinked an eye. My conscience was deafened. My soul was dying. I was numb to these sins and others like them. But my soul is alive now, and my conscience speaks loudly. Yes, now it is impossible to ignore. When I sin, or when I am even tempted to sin, my inner voice shouts out its words of warning begging me not to take a wrong turn.

I want so badly to live in you alone, Lord, but Satan works hard at getting me to look back. It's an internal struggle of good vs. evil, and the battle is intense. Oh, how I wish I could go back to my childhood and early adulthood and stop the bad habits from ever starting. They were so small and innocent in the beginning, but I guess that's how all large, habitual sin starts and takes hold, isn't it? Even so, I have no reason to hold on to these things of my past, so I let them go. I turn to you. Come, free me from these sins that have been enslaving me for years. Give me the strength to resist the many temptations that are now bearing down on me. As tempting as it is to beat myself up about my past mistakes, Lord, I'm not going there. I refuse to look back! I refuse to waste time in self-pity and fear! You know my heart, and you know how sorry I really am, so I will pick myself up, dust myself off, repent, and move forward. I know your mercy is greater than any of my sin, so I graciously accept your mercy. Please give me the strength to try again. "Whatever is true, whatever is honorable, whatever is just, whatever is pure, whatever is lovely, whatever is gracious," (Philippians 4:8) this is what I want. I will think of these things. I choose these things.

A few weeks ago, Lord, I felt like you were starting to reveal to me some of the longings and wearinesses of the souls around me. I now see that what you are actually revealing to me is the danger and consequence of sin. I am moved with pity as you show me how our sin, large and small, damages our relationship with you. It is never worth it! My heart aches for those who, like me for so many years, are choosing sin over you. Forgive them, Father, they know not what they do! No, there is no way they know. No one would choose sin if they really understood what it is I am now understanding. No one would!

Yes, Lord, by your great grace I now know the danger of sin, and I want nothing more to do with it. Help me to overcome any desires and temptations that would lead me to sin. Help me to sin no more. I cannot do this alone, for I, as you know, am so very weak. Yes, this fight proves how weak I really am! In you, though, my Lord, I have strength. In you, I can do whatever it is you ask of me. In you, I can be made new. In you, I can learn how to live a life of perfect love; a love that fears nothing, a love that seeks no personal gain, a love that loves just to love and to love alone. This is what I want, Lord. This is all that I want. Fight for me! I am at war!

Prayer

Thank you for showing me the light, Lord. Thank you for showing me what needs to change in order for me to continue on this path of holiness. Have mercy on me, a poor sinner, for I refuse to give up the fight. I refuse to turn around. I know this fighting will be worth it in the end, and I trust that you are here with me. I, therefore, don't ask that you take it away, I simply ask that you fill me with the strength I need to continue. Strengthen me, my God. Let the good in me prevail. I love you! I thank you! I praise you!

Read, Think, Pray: Exodus 14:14, Romans 7:13-25

REFLECTION #35

FRUITFUL PRUNING

1/9/2014

Are you noticing, Lord, the many ups and downs of my life these past few months? I mean, if I didn't have a basic understanding of the spiritual life and the war within, then I would be convinced that I was losing my mind! Honestly, I just went from being in an intense battle to now rejoicing in your goodness. You are pruning me, aren't you? Yes, I'm convinced that you are, but this pruning feels nothing like getting a haircut. It, instead, feels more like ripping open a scab. Now, though, that the scab has been ripped off and is healing properly, I am once again filled with joy. I can now see the fruit being produced on this stem, so again, I thank you! I thank you! I thank you! I thank you! I thank you, Lord, for pruning me so that I can heal; so that I can be made new; so that I can bear greater, more lasting fruit!

Yes, I am once again on a spiritual high as I reflect on this pruning you have done in me and on the miraculous growth that is coming from it. You know that I spent much of last year in prayer, study, and meditation. You know that I spent much of last year at Mass, Adoration, and in the confessional. Oh, and I can now see the fruit this has been producing. I can now see that these have been the very things strengthening me for the fight. Yes, I'm certain that, without them, I would have lost. So, thank you! Thank you! Thank you! Thank you! Thank you for strengthening me before I knew I was going to need it.

I have heard it said, Lord, that the more one loves you, the more one will want to love you, and I think this best describes what has been going on with me. Yes, I love you so much, but I want to love you so much more. No matter what I do it will never be enough. I simply cannot love you enough! You are so good to me, my God, and I thank you! I thank you! I thank you! I thank you! I thank you for pruning me and for showing me what life is really about.

The more one loves God, the more one will want to love God.

Prayer

I love you, my Lord, and the more I love you, the more I want to love you, and the more I know you, the more I want to know you. You are my God, my loving Father. You are my rock, my refuge, and my shield. Be with me in the days ahead. Prune me if you must, and continue your great work in me. Jesus, I trust in you! I love you! I thank you! I praise you!

Read, Think, Pray: John 15:1-2

REFLECTION #36

SIMPLE MINDS

1/9/2014

I am realizing many things, my Lord; many things that are filling me with deep gratitude and great joy. For starters, I think there was a part of me that falsely believed I would never be good enough to do your work because I would never be smart enough. Oh, but I'm realizing that one doesn't have to be a highly-educated scholar to be your faithful disciple. Yes, I know this is not a requirement because I'm always amazed at how much I don't know. In all honesty, it's actually shocking to me how simple-minded I really am.

I remember, for example, being at my parents' house last year when it finally dawned on me who Peter was. I asked my dad, "Dad, is Peter, - you know, Peter, 'the Rock of the Church,' (Matthew 16:18) Peter, 'the one who holds the keys to the kingdom of heaven' (Matthew 16:19) - the same Peter who denied Jesus three times?" (John 18:17, 25-27)

"Yeeees," he replied in a slow, drawn-out way making it clear that he was trying to be loving and understanding but also clear that he was astonished by the fact that I was unaware of this. Well, needless to say, my mind was blown. (On a side note, I, too, was shocked. I mean, how had I never put that together before?)

In any event, that's just one story of many. Yeah, as if I needed any more proof of my elementary understanding of things, you, my Lord, reminded me again of my simple-mindedness here recently when, after watching a video about how scientists are discovering that the earth and human race are somehow "special" in terms of the universe, I reacted by wondering, "Is this seriously news to some people? I mean, of course the earth and the human race are special! All you need to understand that is a little faith, right? After all, God didn't become a planet, or a star, or a plant, or an animal, or even an angel. No, He became man, and if that's not proof that, out of all of creation, human beings have some special favor in His eyes, then I don't know what is!"

Oh, yes, it's true; very true. You, my God, have given me a simple mind. I guess it's always been relatively easy for me to see the simplicity behind all the complexity. Even so, I know that doesn't mean I'm ignorant. I know that doesn't mean I'm naive. I know that doesn't mean I don't understand. Yes, I know. I know because in you, Lord, I believe. I know because in you, Lord, I find meaning. I know because in you, Lord, I have purpose. And, as long as I remember this, then my life, and the universe I live in, makes perfect sense.

Prayer

Bless those whom you have called to work in the field of science, Lord. May their findings prove what faith already knows; that you are God and that we are created by you and for you. Yes, may science test faith, and may it, in so doing, glorify your Holy Name!
I love you! I thank you! I praise you!

Read, Think, Pray: Genesis 1

"To one who has faith, no explanation is necessary. To one without faith, no explanation is possible." – St. Thomas Aquinas

REFLECTION #37

THE ROOT OF ALL EVIL

1/13/2014

I am feeling very distraught and overwhelmed today, Lord. Since turning my life around and finding my way back to you, I rarely find myself in moods like this. I am usually hopeful and optimistic no matter what the world is throwing at me, but something is different today. Today I am not feeling myself and, quite honestly, it's awful. I feel like the weight of the world is on my shoulders. I feel so much pressure. I know no one is putting this pressure on me. I know I am doing this to myself, but I just can't seem to shut off the voice inside my head that is telling me what a failure I am. I feel like I'm drowning. I have to be missing something.

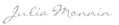

There has to be more to this. This can't be part of the abundant life you promised us. It just can't be! I feel so trapped. What is really going on?

Today you seem to have guided me to another area of my life that needs some work; my financial life. I know, Lord, that until very recently I've had a poor relationship with money. Yes, I know that I've always been a wasteful spender. I know that my attitude of, *"Why wait to buy tomorrow what I <u>want</u> today?"* has always been incredibly irresponsible. And that's why I've been working to change it. Yes, and now that I've been working to change it, I realize, more than ever, the pull money has in my life. I realize, more than ever, the attention money gets day in and day out. And you know what? I hate it! Yeah, I hate the idea that "success" is somehow dependent upon money. Oh, I know money has nothing to do with the person I am, but it often feels like it does, and that is why I'm turning to you now in prayer. I want to know why, Lord. I want to know why money feels so important when I know it really isn't. I want to know what I'm missing. Please, tell me what I'm missing.

I came into this world with nothing, Lord, and I will leave it with nothing, but in the "real world" money has a way of making me think that it is the only important thing in life. It has a way of making me think that it comes before everything else. It has a way of making me think that it is the reason I do anything; that it is what motivates me and keeps me going. Well, I hate it! Yes, I hate the lies associated with money! You, my God, are my only motivation. You, my God, are my only reason for being. You, my God, are the only reason I work, play, rest, and live. Money somehow makes me forget this, though. Money somehow makes me feel like less of a person. Money somehow makes me want to crawl into a hole. Money somehow makes me feel defeated. Money somehow sucks the life out of me.

I know, Lord, that money can't buy happiness. Yes, I know it can't! I know that true happiness and joy come from you and you alone. I know. I know. I know. I just had a day of feeling like I failed you. I just had a day of feeling like the world got the best of me. I just had a day of letting money control me and of letting that tormenting voice inside me win.

Oh, but this battle has stirred a fire in me, for never before have I been so determined to be set free from money's grasp! You, my good God, have let me feel the weight of this disordered attachment, and now I want nothing more than to be detached from it!

Help me, Lord! Set me free! I am a slave to the almighty dollar! Free me! Break the chains! Loosen its grip! Help me to love people and use money, not use people and love money. Help me to manage all that you give me in ways that are pleasing to you. Help me to learn from the past and move forward loving, serving, and giving. Help me get back to the simplicity I had in my life when I didn't have a dime to my name. Oh, how I long for that simplicity. Where did that girl go? She was irresponsible, sure, but she was *not* attached to money, and detachment from this is what I need now more than anything. Yes, Lord, detach me from this, and show me how to be a better steward. Help me to rid myself of the things in my life that create unnecessary noise and chaos; the things that create unnecessary expense. Help me to become a better steward of all your gifts, especially your gift of money, for it's true that though "I" may have earned it with the work I'm doing, *you* are the only reason I have this work to begin with because *you* are the One who has given me the talents, abilities, and opportunities to do it in the first place. Yes, this all comes from you and belongs to you. May it all glorify your great name!

Forgive me, Lord, for being so selfish, greedy, wasteful, and irresponsible for so many years. Forgive me, Lord, for allowing self-doubt to lead me into despair. You are so much bigger than all of this, and I know you can conquer this for me. Besides, I know of no other inanimate object that is so easy to value in such a disordered way. Yes, Lord, I now know. I now know that the love of money really *is* the root of all evil.

Prayer

Money is just money, Lord, and stuff is just stuff. These things, in no way, define me. These things, in no way, dictate who I am or who I was created to be. May I never again forget that. May I never again be fooled into believing the many lies this world has about money and belongings. May I never again put money ahead of others. Most importantly, may I never again put money ahead of you. Yes, you, Lord, are my God, and you, and you alone, are worthy of my

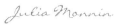

> *love, attention, and worship. So, uproot the love of money in*
> *my life, and fill it with what really matters: love of you.*
> *I love you! I thank you! I praise you!*

Read, Think, Pray: 1 Timothy 6:10

REFLECTION #38

JOYFUL LEADERSHIP

1/15/2014

I'm back at the top of a hill on this spiritual rollercoaster you've had me on these past few weeks, Lord. Yes, today is a new day, a fresh start, and I'm as excited as I've ever been! Oh, how I love mornings like these; mornings when I just get to sit and be with you. Thank you for this great gift, Lord! Thank you for being here with me day in and day out. Thank you for calling me back into the silence.

I'm reflecting now, Lord, on the book study that, with your help and guidance, I began last night. This, as you know, was one of the many small group discussions I've led in the past few years, and, I must admit, I always feel so alive after them! Oh, I know those participating are inspired by them, too, but I would be shocked to find out they were as inspired by them as I am. Yes, Lord, it is in giving that we receive, and I am receiving so much from these little meetings. I'm falling in love with this role, and I thank you for the opportunity and talents to share in this way. Yes, I thank you! I absolutely *love* having a place where I can talk about how awesome you are!

I know I'm not doing or saying anything new. I know your message is so simple it's stupid, but it's easy for us to get lost and consumed by the world. It's easy for us to lose our way and get off the straight and narrow. Yes, it's easy for us to get distracted and pulled away from what's really important. That's why it helps to share like this. Yeah, that's why it helps to share with others in a loving, non-judgmental way.

I think many overlook discussions like these because they seem too simple to be beneficial, but I see how important they are. Yeah, I see how powerful they can be. I see how easily and fruitfully you work through them. And that is why I am, once again, filled with gratitude. Yes, that is why I am, once again, crying out, thank you! Thank you, Lord, for inspiring me to do this! Thank you for including me in this work! Thank you for making it so easy for me to express my great love for you and your great love for us! May this, and all things, give you great glory!

Prayer

You, my God, are what we need. You, my God, are what we desire. You, my God, are what we long for. Use me as your instrument to help others find you. Use me as your instrument to share your great love. Use me as your instrument to spread your Good News. May all I think, say, and do lead others to you. I love you! I thank you! I praise you!

Read, Think, Pray: Romans 12:3-8

REFLECTION #39

THE FATAL FLAW

1/16/2014

Have mercy on me, Lord, for I have, once again, fallen. Yes, my extreme high has, once again, been followed by an extreme low. I have, once again, found myself in a valley. There's more pruning going on, isn't there?

Yes, as you know, Lord, my life has taken a wrong turn, so I'm turning to you now with a simple question, why? Why is this happening? What are you trying to teach me through it? Speak, Lord. Your servant is listening.

Oh, I see! Of course! That's it! That's what I've been missing! Oh, thank you! Thank you! Thank you! Thank you! I just realized what was going on. I just realized what happened. I just realized the fatal flaw.

There was a part of me that felt like I didn't need you anymore, wasn't there? There was a part of me that thought I could somehow do this without you; that thought I could somehow just coast on by from here on out because I had it all figured out, huh? Oh, forgive me, Lord! Forgive me! That was a huge mistake! Yes, I was so very wrong! So very, very wrong! I don't have anything figured out! Nothing!

I didn't do this on purpose. You know I didn't do this on purpose. It just seems like the more things started to make sense to me about you and about life, the more I began taking back the control; the more I began depending on myself instead of on you. Aaahhh! It all happened so slowly I didn't even realize what was going on! It's no wonder fear, worry, and anxiety all began to rear their ugly heads! I mean, if I stop trusting in you, then it will only be a matter of time until I lose all sense of peace, meaning, and purpose in my life. If I stop depending on you, then I will, undoubtedly, fall on my face. Oh, thank you, Lord! Thank you! Thank you for lovingly calling me back into your arms. Thank you for lovingly reminding me that I am completely dependent on you. Thank you for lovingly reminding me *not* to take back hold of the reins. Yes, Lord, I am kidding myself to think I have this figured out and don't need you anymore, and this proves it! I need you now more than ever!

> *"If I stop depending on you, Lord, then I will, undoubtedly, fall on my face."*

Prayer

With your help, Lord, I will simplify my life so that I am not so easily distracted and pulled away from you. With your help, I will simplify my life so that I am not so easily confused and filled with distrust. With your help, I will simplify my life so that I am not so easily misguided and led astray. Help me, Lord, and strengthen me!

> *I give it all back to you and trust that you will take perfect care.*
> *I love you! I thank you! I praise you!*

Read, Think, Pray: 2 Corinthians 1:3-7

REFLECTION #40

SWIMMING UPSTREAM

1/18/2014

Today I'm spending time with you at a retreat, Lord; a retreat focused on our ordinary, but holy, lives. As I sit and look around, I'm finding myself wondering what it is you are doing with me, for it is becoming more and more clear that you must have plans for me that are not "normal" for someone my age. Yes, it is becoming more and more clear that you must be calling me to something "different." If not, then where is everyone else? Where are all the other 30-something year olds?

I don't feel young in terms of the world and in my knowledge of you. In fact, this so called "early" conversion doesn't seem early to me at all. But when I'm serving you and spending time with you at "church things," everyone else seems to be (at least) a decade older than me, so I've got to think that it *is* uncommon for someone my age to be so committed to you. Yes, all signs (so far) seem to be pointing to "Yes." Yes, I am swimming upstream.

I'm starting to notice, Lord. I'm starting to notice that I *am* a little different than most people around me. But it doesn't bother me. No, it doesn't bother me at all. I, you see, am convinced that "different" isn't a bad thing. In fact, I *want* to be different...Different in a good way.

Prayer

Thank you, Lord, for the graces you've given me to get to know you

so "early" in life. Give me the courage to continue my swim upstream.
Make me different, Lord; different in a good way.
I love you! I thank you! I praise you!

Read, Think, Pray: Philippians 3:17-21

REFLECTION #41

UNKNOWINGLY DISCOVERED

1/28/2014

Oh, my wise and loving God, you are so very good; you are so very loving; you are so very powerful. Thank you! Thank you for proving yourself to me again. Thank you for showing me how you are at work in my life.

In case you're wondering, (which I know you're really not) let me be more clear. Last weekend at a seminar you, my good God, sent me a little message. This message came when someone came up to my husband and I during a break to thank us for inspiring him during a talk we gave at a conference nearly three years ago. He said, "I can't really remember what you two talked about, but I remember how much it impacted me, so I just wanted to say thank you." After conversing with him a little, I couldn't help but be intrigued by the fact that he was moved by the presentation but couldn't really remember what it was about. Oh, yes, his words got my wheels turning, (as I'm sure you planned them to) and I began to wonder how something could impact someone enough that they remembered it doing so but had no idea what was actually discussed. I pondered the idea.

As I did, I remembered that, at that particular conference, we were asked to speak about the "success" we had experienced in our business. Yes, we were asked to talk about our "secret." Oh, but we knew there was no "secret" to our so-called "success," so our entire presentation simply gave credit where credit was due: to you. I mean, though we

72

didn't give a sermon or anything, everything we said centered on you and on the importance of trusting in your plan for our lives. In a way, I guess we talked about Truth while talking about truth. (If that even makes any sense.) Anyway, as I continued thinking about our presentation, something "clicked." As it did, I came to this realization:

Our words impacted that man that day because, as we spoke to his ears, you, my Lord, spoke to his heart. Yes, whether he realized it or not, somewhere in the midst of that ordinary presentation given in that ordinary conference room, he found answers to his extraordinary search: his search for you.

He, my Lord, unknowingly discovered you, and that is why he never forgot the impact. For who, Lord, could ever forget that moment when they encounter you?

Who, Lord, could ever forget that moment when they encounter you?"

Oh, my good God, I'm not sure this was the point, but, yes, I'm amazed! You are so very awesome, and I am in awe! Thank you for reminding me that you have been at work - yes, even through me - all along.

Prayer

Bless those people who have, or will, hear me speak, Lord. Pour out your Spirit upon us so that your words, spoken through me, impact lives. As I speak to their ears, Lord, you speak to their hearts. I love you! I thank you! I praise you!

Read, Think, Pray: Acts 17:22-28

A GRACE-FILLED MOMENT

1/29/2014

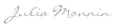

For a while now, Lord, I have been sitting with you in prayer. Though this time spent with you is not abnormal, the fruits of it certainly are. Yes, today my prayer seemed more heartfelt and inspired and less rigid and formal. I truly felt your presence, the presence of the holy angels, and the presence of all the saints and heavenly hosts I asked to pray with me. It was a beautiful experience. One that words will never fully describe. What else can I say, but, thank you?

I'm certain, Lord, that time spent with you is always well spent and is never wasted, but something was different about today. Yes, today it was as if a little piece of heaven came down to earth and hung out in my living room. It is something I will never forget.

You are so good to me, my God, and you are fulfilling every promise you ever made to me. Today you showed me (once again) that "to everyone who has, more will be given" (Matthew 25:29). Oh, Lord, I have been given so much and in your great love and generosity, you keep giving me more. How will I ever repay you?

Prayer

May my heart always be open to receiving whatever it is you want to give me, Lord. Yes, even if it's a gift I've never received before; even if it's a gift I don't exactly know what to do with. I love you! I thank you! I praise you!

Read, Think, Pray: Proverbs 11:24-26

REFLECTION #43

AN OPEN HEART

2/4/2014

For the past few weeks, Lord, I have been reflecting on a quote from your great servant St. Francis deSales. It reads: *"Blessed are those whose hearts are ever open to God's inspiration; they will never lack what they need to live good holy lives, or to perform properly the duties of their state."* Something about these words speaks to my heart. I wonder, what could you be trying to tell me through them? What is it that you want me to know?

I think you brought these words into my life to comfort me, Lord, for I am realizing there is a part of me that's afraid I'm going to somehow mess all of this up for you. I am realizing there is a part of me that's afraid I'm going to somehow do something you didn't ask me to do, or not do something you did ask me to do, or, quite frankly, just do something wrong all together. These words have reminded me, though, that I need *not* be afraid. Yes, these words have reminded me that all that's really required for you to work through me is an open heart. Well, my God, that is something I can give you. Yes, with your help, I will *keep my heart open to your inspiration* and trust that *I will never lack anything I need.*

Prayer

I love you, my Lord, and I thank you. I thank you for giving me more opportunities to learn and grow. I thank you for calling me back into your peace. May my heart always be open to your inspiration, and may I move forward fearlessly, knowing that I will never lack what I need. I love you! I thank you! I praise you!

Read, Think, Pray: Ephesians 1:18-21

REFLECTION #44

ENDLESS OPPORTUNITIES

2/7/2014

Opportunity, my God. That's all I need to do your work. I just need an opportunity. I just need another chance.

I know, Lord, that I sometimes miss opportunities to do good. Yeah, I know that I sometimes don't recognize them for what they really are; I sometimes ignore them because I'm "too busy" with other things; I sometimes just come up short. Yes, I know I have room to improve, but I *want* to live my life in ways that are pleasing to you. I *want* to be a useful instrument in your hands. I *want* to make good use of every opportunity you give me. Oh, and I think that's why it's so easy for me to get mad at myself when I feel like I've done (or not done) something to disappoint you. Even so, I'm learning this is *not* how you see things, is it?

Yes, I'm certain there are times (lots and lots of times) that I handle things less than perfectly, but you never give up on me, do you? You never call me names, do you? You never beat me up or lower your expectations of me, do you? No, this isn't you! I know this isn't you! You, instead, always give me another chance. You, instead, always encourage me to try again. You, instead, always pick me up, dust me off, and give me another opportunity to do your work, to be your voice, to embody your presence. Thank you, my Lord! Thank you for not giving up on me! Your opportunities really are endless, and I thank you for every last one of them!

Prayer

I can't promise you, Lord, that I will never fall, but I can promise you that I will always get back up. Yes, I can promise you that I will always try again. Strengthen me for the journey, and give me the courage to embrace the next opportunity you send my way. I love you! I thank you! I praise you!

Read, Think, Pray: Sirach 2

REFLECTION #45

BE STILL

2/7/2014

76

You tell us, my Lord, "Be still and know" (Psalm 46:11). I thought I had a good understanding of what this really meant, but yesterday I was given instruction (a penance actually) to dive into this passage a little more, so without delay, I headed to the Adoration Chapel and began to ponder.

"Be still and know."...Hmmm...What does this really mean? What are you trying to tell me? What am I still missing?...I spend most of my days in silence, Lord. This can't be what you're telling me. No, it can't be. I spend much time every day in prayer and study getting to know you better. This can't be it either, can it? No, I don't think this is it either. There's got to be something else. There's got to be something more.

As I continued reflecting, I was led to some other areas of Scripture where you say something similar. Eventually, when I was least expecting it, it hit me like a ton of bricks. Oh, yes, your Spirit spoke loud and clear. I "heard" exactly what you were saying, and there was no denying what you were asking me to do. No, there was no denying your call-to-action. The answer was too clear, too obvious, too direct. It was impossible to misunderstand. To be honest, I found the bluntness of your message quite humorous. It was so funny to me, in fact, that I had to hold in my laughter so that I didn't disturb those praying next to me. OK, so, yes, the silence is necessary. Yes, prayer and study are musts, but there's more. There *is* something more. This time, my Lord, your message was different. Yes, this time, my Lord, your message was new.

As you know, I've been having a hard time living in the present these past few weeks. Yes, as you know, I've been having a hard time "actively listening" to those around me. (You know, listening more than I talk.) I had come to realize what you were asking me to do before this little penance, and you kept giving me opportunities to do it, - to listen and not fix - but I just kept opening my mouth. Oh, it's easy to know *what* I'm supposed to do, but it's a lot harder to do it, and this is where my struggle has been. Yes, I've been struggling listening and not coming up with solutions in my head, holding my tongue and not telling people what I think they should do. I've been struggling keeping my mouth shut even when I know this is exactly what you are asking of me.

Apparently you knew my disobedience would need more than a gentle nudge to right itself. Yeah, apparently you knew I would need to hear things in a more "matter-of-fact" way before I would start taking action.

Apparently you knew I would need you to just tell me like it is. How do I know? Well, my prayerful searching led to the discovery that "Be Still" can also be translated as "Shut Up." HaHaHa! How funny! I mean, seriously. After hearing it put so directly, how could I deny what it was you were telling me? How could I ignore such an obvious statement of truth? No, I can't ignore it anymore. I can't pretend I don't know what you're asking of me. You, my God, want me to shut up! Yes, you, my God, want me to "be still" and listen. Oh, I knew I was talking too much! Yeah, I knew I needed to zip my lips! I guess I just needed you to "give it to me straight" before this knowing could become doing, huh?

HaHaHa! You actually told me to shut up! Seriously, HAHAHA! I'm still laughing! You, my God, always know exactly what to say to get my attention. (And you always know when I need a good laugh, too!)

Prayer

Oh, Lord, I talk too much. Show me how to quiet my mind and my tongue. Show me how to live in the present and let you do the fixing. Show me how to get out of your way and let you do the work. Give me faith to trust in your process. Give me ears that listen and a mouth that speaks only when you open it!
I love you! I thank you! I praise you!

Read, Think, Pray: Psalm 141:3

REFLECTION #46

A LOVE LETTER

2/8/2014

My heart is overflowing with love for you, my God. How could I ever show you how much I love you? How, Lord? How?

I find myself thinking about all the times you've answered my prayers. I find myself thinking about all the times you've worked a miracle in my life. I find myself thinking about all the wonderful people you put in my life, - like those in the amazing family I was born into and those in the amazing family I married into - the people who have shown me what love really is. You have been filling my life with gifts from the very first moment of my existence. How, then, could I *not* love you with everything that I am? How, Lord? How? It would be impossible for me *not* to love you. It would be impossible for me to walk away. It would be impossible for me to turn around.

I am finding, Lord, that the more I give to you and for you, the more you give to me. I will never be able to out give you or out love you, will I? No, I will never be able to out give you, for you *are* the Great Giver. I will never be able to out love you, for you *are* Love. Oh, Lord, my cup is overflowing, my heart is aflame, and I want to share this abundance with everyone I meet!

"I will never be able to out give you, Lord, for you are the Great Giver. I will never be able to out love you, for you are Love."

I trust in you, my Lord, and I know that you will never steer me wrong. I know that, as long as my heart is open to you, you will give me everything I need to do your work. How, then, could I doubt?

Oh, I say that, but there is a lesser part of me that still wants to doubt. Yes, there is a lesser part of me that wants to doubt my skills and abilities, my knowledge and talents, my resources and connections. There is a lesser part of me that wants to doubt ME, and this scares me into thinking things like, "What if I don't hear you correctly? What if I don't hear you at all because I'm too busy and distracted with worldly things? What if I hear you but lack the courage to do what you're asking?" Your response in times like these, though, is always the same. "Impossible," you tell me, "for I am with you. I am working through you. I have it all figured out. Yes, it is impossible for you to 'mess' anything up, my dear child, so do not doubt. Do not worry. Do not fear. I am with you and always will be. I will take perfect care."

And, so, Lord, I know you are here. Yes, I know that, even when I fail, you will still be here. This, Lord, is enough. Yes, you, Lord, are enough. I love you and trust you. I praise you and thank you. I worship you and adore you. Let it be done to me according to your will.

> ## Prayer
> *I know you are always with me, Lord, and that is enough.*
> *Yes, Lord, I know your love, and your love is, and*
> *always will be, enough...more than enough!*
> *I love you! I thank you! I praise you!*

Read, Think, Pray: 1 John 4:7-19

REFLECTION #47

LET GOD BE GOD

2/10/2014

I've been given the advice *"let God be God"* often, and, after reflecting on it some more this morning, I now find myself wondering how well I'm actually living it out. Yeah, I wonder, do I, my God, do a good job letting you be you? I'm such a control freak, such an organizer, such a planner. Do I let go enough so that you can work freely through me? Do I, Lord? Do I?

There are times when I think I do this quite well. After all, skills of leadership, organization, and planning are gifts and talents that come from you, so I know they're not "bad." As with all things, though, there are times when I lose balance; times when these good qualities and traits become disordered passions; times when these things aren't tools I'm controlling but obsessions that are controlling me. Help me, Lord, to become aware of these times. Help me to become aware of the times I take back control and stop letting you be you. Help me to relax, to breathe, and to rest in your presence. Help me to live in your peace.

THE WORLD IS NOISY - GOD WHISPERS

There are times, Lord, (lots and lots of times) when I am so tightly wound; times when I am so consumed with doing things perfectly. I now surrender this perfectionism to you. Yes, I know that I am not, and will never be, perfect. I know there will be times when I fail. I know there will be times when I could have done things better. Help me to embrace these times. Help me to learn from them. Help me to laugh at myself and give myself permission to fall trusting that, when I do, the only place I'll be falling is into your loving arms.

Help me, Lord, to give myself permission to fall trusting that, when I do, the only place I'll be falling is into your loving arms."

Give me self-control, Lord. Give me a carefree spirit. Give me peace. Show me how to relax and *let you be you*, for you, my God, are much better at being God than I am. So, yeah, I would like nothing more than to quit acting like I don't know this is true.

Prayer

Come into my life, Lord, and show me. Show me how to use the gifts you are giving me for you glory. Show me how to let go and let you take control. Show me how to live in your peace.
I love you! I thank you! I praise you!

Read, Think, Pray: John 13:16

THE EASY YOKE

2/20/2014

It seems like so much time has passed since I've picked this journal up. Have I really *not* been inspired by you, Lord, once in the last ten days? No, that's unlikely. What's more likely is that I just didn't take the time to write about your inspirations. Yeah, what's more likely is that I just let myself get too busy and distracted by the things you haven't asked me to do.

Why, Lord, is it so easy to get distracted and consumed with worldly things? Why is it so easy to get lost in the noise? The truth is, it's easy for me to take a few minutes to write; to take a little time to put my thoughts on paper. It's really not a time-consuming or difficult process, I guess it's just easier not to do it.

Yeah, it's easy to pray, Lord, it's just easier to run from one thing to the next. It's easy to read your Word and good spiritual books, it's just easier to watch TV and mentally check out. It's easy to go to Mass, it's just easier to stay in bed. It's easy to engage in the Mass, it's just easier to get distracted. Yes, Lord, it's easy to do the things that help me become the saint you created me to be, it's just easier not to.

> It's easy to do the things that help us become the saints God created us to be, it's just easier not to.

Have mercy on me, Lord, for your yoke *is* easy and your burden *is* light (Matthew 11:30). I have just been looking for something easier.

Prayer
Help me to embrace the ease, Lord. Show me how to live a life under the ease of your yoke. I love you! I thank you! I praise you!

Read, Think, Pray: Matthew 11:28-30

BEYOND

2/27/2014

*"This world is not for you anymore."** I came across these words today in prayer, and they've got me thinking. I now wonder, is this world really for anyone?

I, my Lord, am after the abundant life (John 10:10). Yes, I desire the abundant life you came here to give us, but I will not be fooled into thinking that my earthly life will somehow "complete" me. No, I will not be fooled into thinking that this world is all there is. This world will never complete me, Lord, and I know it won't. You complete me, and this completion will only reach fulfillment in the life that is to come.

"This world is not for you anymore." Yes, I think I'm beginning to understand what this means. I think I'm beginning to experience the world that lies just beyond this one I can see. And, all I can say is, it's beautiful.

Prayer

Help me to see the beauty that lies just beyond this world, Lord. May my mind, heart, and soul always be rooted in and centered on you and on the life that is to come. I love you! I thank you! I praise you!

Read, Think, Pray: John 1:50-51

* I came across these words when reading a short reflection about the life of St. Gabriel of Our Lady of Sorrows (Also known as, St. Gabriel Possenti.) It is said that the Blessed Mother called out to his heart one day and that these words of hers are what finally encouraged him to leave the world and begin his religious life.

GREATER CONVERSION

3/3/2014

The season of Lent is upon us, Lord, and this year I feel you calling me to greater conversion. You can be sure I know what this means. Yes, I know this means that I will, without a doubt, be tested and challenged along the way. Since I know, Lord, that I am incapable of change, - yes, even the smallest change - on my own, I now turn to you for help.

Help me, Lord, to deny my bodily desires and make sacrifices (fast); to strive to use more of the time you give me doing good (pray); and to give more to those in need (give alms). Help me to unite my tiny sufferings and sacrifices to yours on the cross, and give me the grace to overcome any and all temptation to stay where I am.

Don't let me get discouraged along the way, Lord. Remind me often that the most lasting and significant changes happen slowly over time. Remind me often that true, lasting conversion comes from growing, little by little. Yes, remind me often that great sinners don't become great saints overnight.

Your desires for me, Lord, are my desires for myself. So, this Lent, lead me, as you desire, to greater conversion.

Prayer

Thank you, Lord, for the season of Lent and for your gift of salvation. Remind me often that there is no resurrection without the cross, and give me the strength I need to pick mine up daily and follow you. Help me to be a good steward of all you give me. Help me to die-to-self so that I may live-in-you. I love you! I thank you! I praise you!

Read, Think, Pray: Matthew 4:1-11

84

FREEDOM!

3/4/2014

The call to follow you, Lord, is a call to greater freedom. This kind of freedom isn't the kind that says, "Do what you want, when you want, with whomever you want." No, this kind of freedom is much greater. This kind of freedom means having complete control over the things that want to bind us to this world. This kind of freedom means being in complete control of our bodily desires and being able to say no to the things that we know are not best for us. This kind of freedom means things like money, power, pleasure, and control have no grip on us. They serve us; we don't serve them. This kind of freedom finds complete joy and peace in heavenly things and understands that this world is just a stepping stone to the next. This kind of freedom fears nothing, not even death, because its source of happiness and strength is you, and those free by these standards trust in you and in you alone. Those free by these standards "seek first your kingdom" and, as a result, receive all that they need (Matthew 6:33).

I've experienced this kind of freedom from time to time in my life, Lord. I've also experienced worldly freedom. When we are free by the world's standards, we may experience moments of happiness and moments of peace, but they don't last. They are just shadows of the real thing. When, however, we are free by your standards *no storm can shake our inmost calm*, and we are filled with true love, peace, awe, and joy.

We all want to be free by your standards, Lord, whether we consciously realize it or not, for you have designed us this way. What's sad, though, is that most of us look for this freedom in all the wrong places. Yeah, what's sad is that you want to fill us all with this freedom, - in fact, you came to set us free - but we reject it by rejecting you.

The call to follow you, Lord, does mean that we will have to give things up along the way, but why do we always think about what we have to give up instead of thinking about what it is you want to give us? Why do we always think about what we have to let go of instead of thinking

85

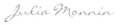

about what we will gain in the process? Why, Lord? Why? Why is it so easy for us to focus on what we're losing in the world instead of focusing on what we're gaining in the next? Why is it so easy for us to lose sight of what really matters?...You.

Prayer

Help me, Lord, to focus on what it is you want to give me. Help me to focus on what I will gain, including freedom from all my disordered passions, and not on what I must "give up" in order to receive it. The freedom is worth it, Lord, and I want to be free. Yes, I want to be free. Come into my life, and save me. Come into my life, and set me free. I love you! I thank you! I praise you!

Read, Think, Pray: Galatians 5:1

REFLECTION #52

DISCOMFORT ZONE

3/7/2014

Letting go is not easy. Being set free is not easy. As I work to do this in certain areas of my life, I'm realizing how weak I really am. I'm experiencing for myself how hard it is to actually let go and be set free. I once heard it said that discomfort is a necessary step on the road to change. Well, change must be on the horizon for me because I am quite uncomfortable!

As you know, Lord, this Lent I'm focusing on greater conversion. One way I am doing this is by attempting to become a master of my flesh. As I strive to become more and more like the person you created me to be, I'm realizing how many areas of my life are still in need of repair. My days are filled with a nonstop dialogue in my head between flesh and spirit. My flesh says, "Sleep longer." My spirit says, "Get up." My flesh says, "I need coffee." My spirit says, "Have a smoothie instead." My flesh says, "Tell others how you would do it because your way is obviously the right way." My spirit says, "Be Still." Yes, Lord, I'm finding these daily battles challenging, but I keep asking you to do the heavy lifting, and you keep proving to me that, though change is impossible for me, it's *not* impossible for you.

I'm finding it incredibly difficult to deny my flesh, Lord, but when I lay my head on the pillow at night I'm filled with joy as I call to mind the small battles I've won with your help. The spirit is, most certainly, a much better master than the body. The body, quite frankly, is a horrible master, and I'm sick of being controlled by it. Yes, I'm sick of being its slave. The flesh is stubborn and irritatingly loud, and it seems to me that the longer I've allowed it to control me in a certain area, the longer I need to persist in my efforts at denying it. That's been the biggest challenge for me. Yes, the biggest challenge for me has been shutting my body up long enough to allow the spirit to take over. Oh, Lord, I'm running to you in prayer more this Lent than ever before, and, even in this moment, I'm still calling out to you for help. Help me, my Lord! May these sacrifices and sufferings bring me closer to you by setting me free from these disordered desires of the flesh! May this temporary pain lead to eternal joy!

On this journey towards greater conversion I've found that denying my flesh is just part of the equation. The temptations are real, and I am weak. It is, therefore, inevitable that I will fall along the way, and that's why I've found that the other (and I would argue more important) part of all of this is repentance. Yes, my pride often gets in the way of my good intentions, and I find myself needing to turn back to you frequently. It's during this repentance that you give me the hope I need to keep going, the strength I need to continue, and the grace I need to actually take steps forward. I have learned, Lord, that I will lose without you, and this is, perhaps, the greatest lesson of all. Yes, this is, perhaps, the big idea. This is perhaps the very thing you are trying to get me to realize; how completely dependent I am upon you.

You know, my God, that much like denying the flesh, I, too, find the repentance uncomfortable at first. I, for one, never like to admit that I've messed up. You have shown me, though, how to embrace the discomfort of repentance because of what it leads to. Yes, you have shown me that the discomfort always leads to growth; the discomfort always leads to freedom; the discomfort always leads to the resurrection. And this is why I sought out your mercy in the confessional yesterday. As I poured out my heart to your priestly servant about the many ways I've fallen short this month, I was, once again, filled with your love, mercy, and peace. I told this man how frustrated I've been with myself because of how frustrated I've been with others, and he challenged me to resist the temptation to blame and point fingers. He challenged me to resist the temptation to make this about "them" and instead encouraged me to turn the question in. "Stop thinking so much about them," he kindly suggested. "Instead ask God how He is calling *you* to change. You are simply avoiding the work you know you need to do on yourself when you spend your time thinking about how others need to change." As I recall these words today, I am reminded how true they really are. Yes, Lord, I know how often I ignore the call to change. I know how often I point fingers and compare and say, "Well, I'm not as bad as them, so I guess I'm doing just fine." Yes, I certainly have much more work to do on myself, so I pray that, from now on, I spend my time doing just that.

You don't ask much of me, Lord. You only ask me to love, and that's what all of this self-denial and repentance is about to begin with. Yes, it's meant to show me how to love. Help me, therefore, to love others as you love me. Help me to deny the temptations of the flesh and to win this war between it and the spirit. Help me to remove the wooden beam from my own eye before even looking at the splinters in someone else's (Matthew 7:1-5). Lead me out of my comfort zone, Lord. Lead me to greater conversion. Lead me on the road to something more.

Prayer

Show me how to become the person you created me to be, Lord. Show me how to become a master of my flesh and how to live freely in the spirit. Show me how to love more like you. I love you! I thank you! I praise you!

Read, Think, Pray: Galatians 5:13-18

THE NOISE

CLEANSED

3/11/2014

So much has happened since I last wrote. I mean, not on the outside. No, on the outside everything looks the same. On the inside, though, things have changed. My mind is clearer and sharper. My energy is up. My soul is more alive. I have no doubt these changes can be attributed to the nutritional cleanse I started a week ago. (A cleanse which I fought to start and struggle to stick with every day.) Yes, I have certainly seen the fruits of it in my life. It's not just helping me physically. It's helping me mentally and spiritually, too. I can see now how attached my body is to certain foods and how saying "no" to those foods detaches me from them and attaches me more to God. Yes, I can see now how my spirit gets a little stronger each time I tell my body "no." It's as if I can feel myself being freed. It's as if I can feel myself becoming detached. It's as if I can feel myself learning how to live in the spirit.

As my mind becomes more centered and focused, I seem to be putting more and more together. In a way, everything just seems really clear. I'm amazed at how cleansing the body cleanses the mind, too. I can finally feel my spirit taking the upper hand and calling out in victory, "Step aside, flesh, because I'm taking over!" Yes, the fog is lifting, and, now that it is, it's easy for me to see God at work in my life.

I, you see, had been doubting again. Yes, I had been doubting that the work I've been doing is producing any fruit. I had been doubting that what I've been doing is actually making a difference. I've been trying to tell myself that all I can do is "bloom where I'm planted," but no matter what I've done to grow in Christ's love and to share this love with others, there has always been a nagging voice inside telling me it wasn't enough. But now that my mind and body are in this state of clarity, I realize, once again, that I *am* doing exactly what God has been asking me to do. Yes, I realize, once again, that I *am* on the right track. So, I will continue as is. Yes, I will continue down this road the Lord has me on remembering that sometimes it's the tiniest seeds that produce the largest fruit.

Prayer

You, my God, never cease to amaze me. You are so good, so loving, and so in control of everything. May I never again doubt the good I can do (and am doing) right where I am, and may I always remember that it's the smallest things that often mean the most.
I love you! I thank you! I praise you!

Read, Think, Pray: Mark 4:30-32

REFLECTION #54

JOY IN THE CROSS

3/15/2014

Though I am inspired and enlightened, though I am excited and joyful, though I am hopeful and optimistic, I have a cross. Yes, just like everyone else, I, too, have a cross. There are lots of women, (and men) for example, carrying the cross of infertility. I am one of them. Yes, I, too, long to be a mother and am waiting on God's perfect timing to be one. Even with this cross, though, - yes, even with this large and heavy cross - I am filled with more and more joy with each passing day. I know this seems impossible to those feeling the pain of a heavy cross, but I

have learned over the years that true joy comes from God and that this joy can be found at all times. Yes, even while carrying a cross.

If it ever seems like I'm forgetting this, - yeah, if it ever seems like I'm losing my joy in the cross - God has a way of reminding me. He did this again yesterday at a funeral. As the Mass came to an end and the family processed out of church to lay their loved one to rest, I was suddenly brought to tears by the hymn we were singing. The words, *"Should you turn and forsake Him, He will gently call your name. Should you wander away from Him, He will always take you back"** leapt off the page and into my heart. As they did, God quickly reminded me of my journey back to Him, and I was immediately overcome by His love..."How could I ever doubt your love?" I then found myself asking Him as tears streamed down my face. "How could I ever question your wisdom?"

Oh, God, how miserable our lives are when we live them away from you! How empty and incomplete everything is! Sure, we might have a moment of joy here and there, but it's nothing compared to the immense and complete joy of living in your grace. It's true, Lord. Yes, it's true. I never knew what happiness was until I found you. I never knew what peace was until I welcomed you into my life. Now, Lord, even in my crosses, I find you. Yes, now, even in my crosses, I find peace. Now, even in my crosses, I find love. Now, even in my crosses, I find joy. Thank you, Lord! Thank you for gently calling my name and for taking me back even though I was wandering from you; even though I was turning away from you by questioning your will for my life. I love you, my Lord, and I thank you. Yes, I thank you, even for the cross.

Prayer

I know, Lord, that you put my husband and I together to do something we could never do alone, and I pray that, whatever that is, we do it and do it well. Open the doors around us and give us the courage to walk through them. Guide us, protect us, and shower us with your blessings. May we be filled with great joy, - yes, even in the cross - and may you use us as your instruments to bring new saints to heaven.
I love you! I thank you! I praise you!

92

Read, Think, Pray: 1 Peter 1:3-9

* These lyrics are from the hymn *Though the Mountains May Fall* by Dan Schutte.

REFLECTION #55

BLESSED

3/21/2014

I did some reflecting today on the question, *"What is your favorite prayer during Mass?"* I've thought about this question before, and, yes, without a doubt, the 30-something-year-old me has a favorite prayer during Mass. I wonder, though, what the 20-something-year-old me would have answered. Oh, I'm ashamed to admit it, but my favorite prayer then was probably the final blessing. (You know, the part where the priest says, "The Mass has ended.") Yeah, that was probably my favorite part because those words meant that Mass was over, and that meant I could get back to doing whatever it was I wanted to do. Oh, how much has changed in just a few short years!

Yes, thankfully, life has changed much for me since then. Now my heart is lifted to God from the moment I step into church. There are times I get distracted, sure, but, for the most part, I am consumed by what is happening from the moment I enter and bless myself with Holy Water to the moment I leave doing the same. I am consumed by the prayers, by the songs, and by the Word of God. I am consumed by those things I can see, like my brothers and sisters surrounding me in the pews and the priest making the sacrifice on the altar, and by those things I can't see, like all of the angels and saints who are there praising and worshiping God with us. Yes, I am consumed. There is so much happening throughout the entire Mass that touches my soul, from the opening hymn to the closing one, that choosing a favorite prayer seems like an impossible endeavor. Oh, but I have one. Yes, I have a favorite prayer. I wonder, though, did I choose this favorite prayer or did God "choose" it for me?

Regardless, I definitely have a favorite prayer now. Yes, since being enlightened by the Spirit one part of Mass stands out to me above the rest.

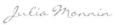

This one part makes me quiet myself and pay attention. This one part pierces my heart and speaks to my soul. This one part fills me with love, joy, peace, gratitude, humility, and awe. In a way, I guess this one part is "it" for me. Yes, *it* is what reminds me how much I am loved. *It* is what reminds me how much I am blessed. *It* is what reminds me how much I am chosen...

The priest genuflects, takes the consecrated host holding it slightly above the chalice of Blood and says, "Behold the Lamb of God, behold him who takes away the sins of the world. <u>Blessed are those called to the supper of the Lamb.</u>"

Yes, Lord, *"Blessed are those called to the supper of the Lamb!"* Blessed am I to have been called to your table! You and I both know I am unworthy of receiving this blessing; unworthy of receiving you. You and I both know I am unworthy of holding you, the Savior of the World, in my hand; unworthy of eating your Body and drinking your Blood. Oh, but you have called me to your table, Lord, and I am so very blessed because of it. So, yes, Lord, this is "it" for me. *"Blessed are those called!"*

Prayer

I am blessed, my God; blessed to be called to your table, blessed to be a member of your Church, blessed to be your child. May I never tire from running to you at Mass, and may my love for you grow deeper and deeper with each Holy Communion. I love you! I thank you! I praise you!

Read, Think, Pray: Revelation 19:9

REFLECTION #56

HUSBANDS AND WIVES

3/23/2014

As my love for Christ has grown, so has my work in ministry and in service to the Church. Now, these are, of course, great undertakings and, no doubt, one of the reasons the Lord has inspired me to begin with, but I just realized I've gotten a little lost in my newfound zeal and excitement. How do I know? Simple: I just noticed my husband has been riding in the back seat.

The time has come for me to remind myself of my list of priorities again: *My name is Julia. I am, first and foremost, a child of God. I am also a wife. Everything else comes next.*

Yes, the Lord has called me to the married life, and I can see now how selfish I've been in this area. I have been putting my husband at the bottom of my list when he should have been at the top, right after my relationship with God. I have worked so hard at our marriage for so many years that I guess I thought I could just let it go and it would take care of itself. What a mistake! My poor husband has not been getting the best of me. He, instead, has been getting the leftovers, and I now know this has to change. Yes, I now know that, no matter how busy I get serving Christ and his Church, my priorities have to stay in check: my relationship with God comes first; my relationship with my husband second.

Prayer

I have a tendency to overdo everything, Lord. Help me instead to live in a spirit of temperance. Bless my marriage. Bless my family. Bless the work you are calling me to and the people you are bringing into my life. May I be your living voice in the world, and may my marriage always be at the top of my priority list.
I love you! I thank you! I praise you!

Read, Think, Pray: Ephesians 5:21-33

ONE THING

3/29/2014

I am reminded today, Lord, of your call to *be* and not *do*. You know me, though, and you know I love a plan. Yes, you know I love order. You know I love efficiency and organization. I know these are not "bad" qualities. In fact, I know it is because of these qualities that you can accomplish much through me, but I constantly need reminded that rigid prayers and tightly-wound schedules are not what bring me closer to you. Yes, I constantly need reminded that it is not "doing" that you desire, it's love.

Lord, you know all things; you know that I love you. Help me to show my love for you in the ordinary moments of my day. Help me to remember that prayer and study are necessary and important but that there are millions of ways to do both. Help me to live my life out of love for you and to always be open to the promptings of your Spirit. Soften my heart, Lord. Take control of my schedule.

Today I have nothing planned. I have no appointments. I have no meetings. I have no lengthy to-do list, and yet today I struggle to *be*. I am tempted to find things to *do*; tempted to find ways to order my day. It is as if I seek happiness in a well-ordered, structured schedule, but I know, Lord, that this doesn't bring me true happiness. Yes, I know that you, and you alone, are the source of my happiness and that you only desire one thing: love.

God is the source of our happiness, and He only desires one thing: love

Prayer

Free me, Lord, from the trappings of my life that prevent my openness to you. Free me from the enslavement to doing. Show me how to be. Show me how to love. I love you! I thank you! I praise you!

Read, Think, Pray: Revelation 2:2-4

RECOMMITTED

3/30/2014

As I end one week and begin another I come to you, my Lord and Savior, to adore you, once again, in the Blessed Sacrament. As I sit and reflect, I wonder how I ever functioned without this weekly one-on-one time with you. Oh, and I wonder how much more my life would change if I would just commit to being in your presence in this way on a more daily basis. The answers always come during these times, Lord. Peace, clarity, and joy are always its fruit. What, then, is stopping me from coming to see you at church every day? My own selfishness and obsession with *my* to-do list and *my* schedule, that's what!

Right now, in your presence, Lord, I recommit myself to you. And, in so doing, I vow to come to see you, even if for only 10 minutes, in one of your holy churches every day for the remainder of Lent. Help me to avoid distractions and excuses that will try to keep me from being with you in this way, for I am certain I will be able to find reasons *not* to stop by. Break the cycle of my life, Lord. Help me to overcome the temptation to stick to my same old routine. Guide me into your presence. Lead me to places I have never gone before. Show me what I am missing.

As I pray and recommit myself to you, young students fill the church on the other side of the door. I can hear their excitement as they prepare for an upcoming play. As their noise level increases and chaos ensues, the teacher lovingly disciplines them in an attempt to calm them down. As her gentle guidance calls them back to order, I hear her say, "You know, you guys can be so good when you want to be." Oh, and I can't help but think that the same is true for me. Yes, Lord. Yes. I, too, can be good when I want to be. It's just that I can be lazy, undisciplined, and prideful when I want to be, too.

You can be so good when you want to be."

97

Help me, my God, to always choose good. Help me to always choose righteousness. Help me to always choose love. Lead me into your loving presence, Lord, and do this on a more regular basis.

Prayer

Continue your work in me, Lord, as I continue striving towards greater conversion. Lead me in your ways. Guide me in your truth. Teach me. May my life bear great and lasting fruit. May others see you in me.
I love you! I thank you! I praise you!

Read, Think, Pray: Psalm 25:4-5

REFLECTION #59

THE NEW COMMANDMENT

4/1/2014

"Love one another as I love you" (John 15:12). This is your commandment, Lord. It is *the* Way, *the* Truth, and *the* Life (John 14:6). It is not a suggestion, or recommendation, or one man's opinion, and yet, how can any of us actually do it?

Although, as a human, I could never fully grasp the extent of your love for me, I know it's there. I can feel it. I can sense your presence. This is why I wonder, Lord, how I, with my many human limitations, could ever love like you. Yes, this is why I wonder, how *I*, a mere human, could ever love like *you*, the God who *is* love.

Certainly the virtues of love, mercy, and kindness have grown in me because of the love, mercy, and kindness you, yourself, have given to me, but it seems that I have so much more work to do to even come close to obeying this command. I guess this is part of the genius of this commandment. Yeah, I guess its human impossibility means that we will *always* have to come back to you, *always* have to seek your help,

98

always have to rely on your guidance, for no human, no matter how virtuous, could ever become capable of loving like you on their own. No, none.

Oh, on paper, Lord, this seems like such an easy thing to do. I mean, the message is simple: love. It is anything *but* easy to do at times, though. Yeah, we are constantly surrounded by hurt, sin, and pain, and our wounded nature often makes love the last thing on our minds (let alone in our hearts). Instead we want to look out for ourselves, judge those who are in any way different than us, and persecute those who seem, by our standards, to be in the wrong. Yes, Lord, the message of love is simple, but it's soooo much easier to hate.

I want more than anything else to love like you, Lord. Yeah, I *want* to love others as you love me, but I will need your help. Yes, Lord, I will need your help. Detach me from myself. Show me how to love more like you.

Prayer

I want my heart to know one thing, Lord: love. So, please, give me a heart of love; a heart like yours. Help me to be patient, kind, and understanding and to love others as you love me. I know, Lord, that I am incapable of this kind of love without your help, so I beg you, help me! Teach me what it means to love like you. Teach me what it means to love like a saint. I love you! I thank you! I praise you!

Read, Think, Pray: John 13:34-35

UNANSWERED PRAYERS

4/6/2014

Today I am reminded again of your goodness and of your constant presence in my life, Lord. I know you have heard my prayers. I don't doubt they are reaching your ears. And, so, I wait, month after month, year after year, for your perfect timing. Although my prayers aren't necessarily being answered in the ways I thought for sure they would have to be, you are, without a doubt, answering them. Yes, you, my Lord, *are* answering my prayers even if the answer is "No" or "Not yet" or "Take this instead." Although these answers may not be what I thought I was asking for, I find that they are always exactly what I need (and even what I want).

Yes, each month that passes that I find out I'm not pregnant, each month that passes that I find out I have not been chosen to be used in your creative miracle, a small weight gets added to my cross. Although I certainly feel the pain, I never, - no, not even for a second - doubt your love for me. I never, - no, not even for a second - doubt your hand in it. I never, - no, not even for a second - question your will. It seems, instead, that each month comes with a simple question: the question of, "Do you trust me?" Well, this month I will take the time to respond.

Yes, Lord, I trust you. Yes, Lord, I love you. Yes, Lord, I believe. Let it be done to me (or not done to me) according to your will.

Prayer

I trust you, my Lord. I trust you. I trust you. I trust you. I know you hear me. I know you love me. I know you are in control. May I never lose this hope and confidence I have in you. May I never doubt your goodness and mercy. May I never question your will. Most importantly, Lord, may I never question your love.
I love you! I thank you! I praise you!

Read, Think, Pray: Luke 18:1-8

REFLECTION #61

SURVIVAL MODE

4/13/2014

I must admit, I thought I knew better. Yeah, I thought I was smarter than this. I thought I was farther along on my journey to recognize the error in my judgment. I guess, if I'm honest with myself, I *did* know, and I *didn't* forget, but knowing and doing are two different things. Yes, knowing and doing are two different things. Now it is with great humility that I turn back to God and seek His mercy.

"I'm sorry, Lord," I call out in heartfelt contrition. "Please forgive me. Oh, and thank you for waking me up. Yes, thank you for showing me what I was doing wrong. Thank you for showing me the way back to you. I needed a wakeup call, Lord! I needed a huge wakeup call. Thank you for giving me one!"

Yes, last week I got out of my routine a little. I was needed at the office all day, and I had lots of meetings scheduled in the evenings. I was just "busier" than normal. There was much on the schedule, and I ran around trying to squeeze it all in. I knew this time of busyness was coming, and I thought I was prepared for it, but I wasn't ready. No, I wasn't ready. When the time came to put to the test all I had been learning, I failed miserably. I focused on the wrong things and forgot the obvious answers.

It all happened so innocently. Since my days began a little earlier than normal, I just fell out of my morning routine a little. Instead of calmly sitting in prayer for the first several moments of my day, I quickly prayed as I ran out of the house. Instead of mindfully inviting God into my day and seeking His guidance, I spent time in quick prayer here and there throughout my day as I could fit it in. I didn't forget about God. He was still very much on my mind, but I didn't take the time to just be with Him, to just sit in His presence, to just listen to His voice. He, you see, was on my mind, but He was *not* in my heart.

Though I knew I was out of my routine some, I thought I would be OK. I thought I would be able to handle my schedule with ease and stay on top of my tasks peacefully. After all, I hadn't neglected prayer all together. I was still going to Mass, still swinging by church for 10-15 minutes as I could, still listening for God's voice in the ordinary moments of my day. So, yeah, I thought I would be OK. I didn't think I would notice. I thought my life would just keep heading in the right direction. I was wrong. I, you see, tried to work God around my day instead of working my day around God. And this, as I quickly learned, makes all the difference in the world.

After a day or so of falling out of my routine, no one (including myself) noticed much. After a few days, though, I began to notice. Yeah, I just didn't seem to have the same peace and joy I had grown accustomed to; something just wasn't quite the same. After a few more days, those closest to me began to tell something was different, too. Yes, as I became short-tempered and impatient with them it was clear to them that I wasn't myself. I, you see, was in survival mode, so the smallest inconveniences and surprises sent me into panic and shock. I was stressed out and anxious and began to sound a lot like the girl I knew a few years ago. (You know, that selfish, demanding, pushy girl I have worked so hard to overcome.) When I noticed this girl showing back up, I quickly realized I didn't like the way I was acting, but I couldn't seem to shake her. I couldn't seem to re-center myself and get my focus back on the right things. I couldn't seem to escape the noise.

Oh, thank God it only took me a week to wake up! (That's right, all of this changed so drastically in less than a week.) Thank God this life of survival was so uncomfortable that I knew something needed to change. Thank God this life got so uneasy that I knew something was wrong. Thank God this only lasted a week! Yes, thank God I didn't spend years watching my life pass me by in this way. Can you imagine how miserable I would have been? Even worse, can you imagine how miserable my misery would have made those around me? Oh, thank God He gave me a wakeup call! Yes, I am so grateful He called me back into the silence.

Prayer

I am nothing without you, Lord. The world swallows me up without you. To be honest, I am an ass without you; a prideful, stubborn ass. May I never again try to fit you around my day. May I instead always fit my day around you. It is not enough for me, Lord, to just have you on my mind. I want you in my heart. I need you in my heart. I long for you to be in my heart. So, come, Lord Jesus! Come, live in my heart. I love you! I thank you! I praise you!

Read, Think, Pray: Matthew 7:24-27

AN UNDESERVED GIFT

4/17/2014

On this, my dear Jesus, the holiest week of the year, I am, once again, beside myself thinking about your passion, death, and resurrection. After all, *this* is what it is all about. Yes, *this* is why you came into this world to begin with. What could I say that could ever really give you the thanks you deserve? What could I do that could ever really repay you for what you did for me? You and I both know the answer to this is "nothing," for I am nothing but an ordinary human being with what seem like extraordinary flaws. I know, though, that my weakness is not a hindrance for you. Yes, I know that all you really want from me is belief, acceptance, and love. Belief in you and in what you have told us, acceptance of your great love in spite of my obvious unworthiness, and my love in return no matter how weak and imperfect it may be. How, then, could I turn this down? How could I pass this up? How could I tell you, no? Oh, Lord, my mind wants to tell me there is a catch to all of this and that you are too good to be true, but my heart knows the truth. Yes, my heart knows you, and it knows that you are good. It knows that you are mercy. It knows that you are love. That is why I am often in awe when thinking about you. Yes, that is why I am often filled with indescribable joy, gratitude, and peace at the beauty and mystery of what your life means for me; of what your life means for all of us. That is why I just can't put into words the bigness of what you did for us while you were here and of what you left behind to help us until you come again.

Yes, Lord, one of the things I am most grateful for now is the Church; your Church. I can easily call to mind the sights, sounds, and smells that fill the church every Holy Week. I can easily call to mind the "sense" with which these sights, sounds, and smells fill my entire being. It is during such moments that it sometimes feels as if my body is on earth, but my spirit is in heaven. Oh, but I know this wasn't always the case. Yes, I know this wasn't always the case. How many years, Lord, did I show up to church and just go through the motions? How many years did I attend out of obligation without realizing the gift, without hearing

103

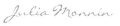

your Word, without recognizing your presence? How many years was I more concerned about what I was wearing and where I was sitting than I was about Who I was receiving? More years than I would like to admit, that's for sure. Yes, more years than I would like to admit.

I'm so grateful you woke me up when you did, Lord. Yes, I'm so grateful I finally "heard" your message. The message I had been listening to my whole life but had never really "heard" until a few years ago. By your grace, Lord, I have discovered that life with this sharp hearing is much different than a life of mindless listening. Oh, yes, by your grace, Lord, I have discovered that life is much different. Without this awareness life was chaotic, stressful, and meaningless. Without this awareness life was empty and unfulfilling. Without this awareness life was, quite frankly, miserable. Without this awareness "religion," fit into a tiny category on my ever-increasingly-demanding pie chart of life. Without this awareness I often found myself thinking things like, "Who cares?" Yes, I often found myself thinking things like, "If it works for others to squeeze religion in, then good for them, and if it doesn't, then what does it matter? I mean, my life is miserable and I go to church every week, so who am I to tell anyone that the answers they need are inside those church doors when I, myself, can't seem to find them there? Who am I to tell anyone what is 'true' when my life feels like one big lie? Who am I to even *care* what others do when, to be honest, all I really care about is myself?" Oh, Lord, it's painful to admit, but without this awareness the thought becomes, "Who needs God? Who needs church? Who needs any of this? I don't need anyone. I am perfectly capable of taking care of myself. Besides, anything that isn't something I want to do is obviously a complete waste of my time."

I know now, Lord, that life with you is different. Yes, I know now that life with you is better. Way better. I have lived the other life, - the life where religion fit into a tiny category, the life where I cared only about myself, the life where I was nothing but a rat in the rat race of life - but you have opened my eyes and now I see. Yes, now I understand the bigness of why we are here, of what we are here to do, and of where we are going next, so I never want to go back to that other life again. No, never! I know, Lord, that you gave us - your undeserving children - the gift of the Church out of your great love for us to help us on our journeys to you. I know that inside this gift is every tool we will ever need to find the narrow path, to do our best to stay on it, and to get back on it when we (inevitably) realize that our best just comes up short without you. Yes, I know you didn't give us the Church to just give us something to do. I know you didn't give us the Church to just feed your own ego. I know you didn't give us the Church to just pass on a bunch of rules and regulations. Yes, I know. I know this is all far from your reasoning. I know it is in your goodness that you have given us this gift. I know it is in your great love that you have given us people to commune with, the Sacraments to nourish, strengthen, and restore us, and places where we can all come together to worship you as one. Yes, I know. After all, what loving parent wouldn't give their child everything they need to thrive in life? It's obvious you are doing the same.

Sure, Lord, life requires discipline. Sure, life comes with a cross. But if you, my God, *chose* to carry your cross, then who am I *not* to pick mine up? Who am I *not* to drink from the cup of which you chose to drink? Who do I think I am to run from the very things that you so obediently ran to? After all, it's not like you're leaving me alone to fend for myself. No, of course you're not! That's why you gave us the Church!

"If you, my God, chose to carry your cross, then who am I not to pick mine up?"

Yes, you, my God, are here with me every step of the way rejoicing with me in my joys and crying with me in my sorrow. I have nothing to fear, I have nothing to worry about, and I certainly have nothing to run away from. No, nothing. With you, Lord, all of this makes sense. For you, Lord, I can do whatever it is you ask. In you, Lord, I will find the strength to move forward, one small step at a time. So, thank you! Thank you for your passion, death, and resurrection. Thank you for Holy Week. Thank you for your gift of the Church.

Prayer

May my life honor and praise you, Lord, and may I never again take for granted any of the gifts you have

> *given me, especially your gift of the Church.*
> *I love you! I thank you! I praise you!*

Read, Think, Pray: Matthew 11:25-26

THE DESTINATION

4/24/2014

I sit now in an airport terminal watching as my flight becomes delayed longer and longer. As my mind starts to imagine the worst case scenarios and my emotions begin to rise as a result, it's tempting to allow frustration and anger to take over. I mean, why are we delayed in the first place? Why doesn't anyone know? Why does it seem that in situations like these information is being withheld and there are always more questions than there are answers? Somewhere in the midst of this inner anxiousness, though, I am reminded of God. I feel His hand at work. I see Him around me. I hear Him speaking to my heart.

Now that I am centered on my Father and not on my frustration, the truth has become obvious. The truth is, traveling never brings out the best in people. We are overloaded with luggage, uncomfortable, tired, and sometimes even dirty. These aren't usually things that put people at ease. In fact, they are usually things that lead to disaster. It's not surprising then that when we're traveling even the smallest inconveniences push us over the edge opening the door for our worst selves to take over. When this happens, all kindness goes out the window and our inner turmoil becomes externalized. We feel wronged, personally attacked, and taken advantage of. As a result, our anger and frustration seems justified, and we walk around with attitudes of entitlement yelling, (or at least thinking) "Get out of my way! I have places to go! My schedule is more important than yours! The people I am heading to see are way more important than the ones you are! I don't care what has to happen just fix it, and do it quickly! Get out of my way!"

As I reflect on this idea and on the discomfort of traveling, I look up to see that my flight has been delayed even more. It is now painfully clear that I will miss my connecting flight, and, as a result, I am tempted, once again, to let it upset me; to let it push me into becoming one of those "entitled" people kicking and screaming on the inside and on the out. I don't want to give in to this temptation, though, so I take a deep breath, call it out for what it is, and center myself back on God. As I do, the Spirit enlightens me. Now things make even more sense. Now life finds yet another whole new meaning.

Yes, we are all on a journey. We are all on a journey home. Our ultimate destination is heaven, so our lives here are really just one big trip there. As we know, though, traveling isn't effortless. No, as travelers we are consumed, bombarded, stressed out, overwhelmed, and constantly drawn off course. I mean, we just want to get to where we're going! We just want to arrive at our destination! But, since we are not there, even the tiniest inconveniences can throw our emotions into states of major turmoil. If this happens, then we're simply not our best. If this happens, then our worst selves rear their ugly heads. And therein lies the constant struggle. You see, we are travelers on a journey trying to make the best of things, trying to find peace and happiness, trying to enjoy the ride, but nothing we do here completely fulfills us. Nothing we do here completely nourishes us. Nothing we do here completely perfects us. Why? Because we are *not* home; because this is *not* our final destination.

It now makes sense to me why it feels so uncomfortable here on earth sometimes. It now makes sense to me why living a life of virtue is sometimes such a difficult thing to do. Yeah, as I now see it, home really *is* where the heart is. It's just that our home is in heaven.

Prayer

I will never know when my flight to you will take off, Lord, so help me to wait with patience and work with diligence until that time comes. In your perfect time bring all my traveling

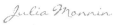

*to an end, and grant me the grace to arrive at my final
destination in peace. Help me to make it home.
I love you! I thank you! I praise you!*

Read, Think, Pray: 2 Corinthians 5:1-10

REFLECTION #64

UNWORTHY

4/26/2014

I sit, Lord. I ponder. I meditate. I wonder...Who am I that I should receive the gifts and blessings that you have given me? Who am I that I should be born into your Church? Who am I that I should be blessed with a loving husband, a supportive family, and wonderful friends? Who am I to be chosen?

I feel so unworthy. Yes, I feel so unworthy. Nothing I could ever do or say could make me worthy of these gifts, for I deserve nothing that you have given me. No, nothing. Nothing I could ever do or say could make me "earn" any of this, for my own merits grant me nothing. No, nothing. Yet you, my Lord, continue to shower your blessings upon me. You, the Great Giver, continue to give, continue to inspire, continue to enlighten, continue to provide. What else can I say but, thank you? What else can I do but sing your praises? What else can I do but love?

Prayer

*As I take this moment to sit and be with you, Lord, I am humbled
and filled with gratitude. Though unworthy, I am grateful. Yes, I thank
you for your many gifts. May you, my good God, be known and loved,
and may your goodness shine through me all the days of my life.
I love you! I thank you! I praise you!*

Read, Think, Pray: Romans 5:6-8

THE TRUE ENEMY

5/14/2014

My day-to-day duties have multiplied in the last few months. As a result of these increased demands, the busyness of the world has often consumed me. Yes, I have often gotten lost in the noise. Though I have had moments of peace here and there, - brief, short moments - most of the time my world has been filled with chaos and confusion. Most of the time I have been in survival mode which, of course, never leads to any sort of peace or joy. Because of this, it feels like I have not made any progress in any area of my life. It feels like I am running as fast as I can but getting nowhere. I hate that feeling. Yeah, I hate the feeling of being on a treadmill.

Though this busyness (and my less than saintly reaction to it) has caused me much pain, I am thankful that the constant running from one thing to the next feels so uncomfortable. I am thankful that the unending noise sends me into a panic. I am thankful that the mindless racing throughout my day leaves me feeling empty because I never want this chaotic state of "doing" to ever become my normal again. No, I never want this unending busyness to feel OK, and it is because it doesn't that I recently realized I needed help.

"Forgive me, Lord, for falling again," I cried out in prayer after coming to my senses. "Forgive me for refusing to learn any way but the hard way. Show me what I'm missing. Show me what I need to learn."

"There is a reason for all things," I eventually "heard" God reply in the stillness of my heart. "I can bring good out of everything. Yes, I can even bring good out of those things that seem like nothing but a big mess to you. You just have to let me. You just have to cooperate. Find my still, silent voice and remember the true enemy, my child. The true enemy is not 'out there' like you think it is. The true enemy is somewhere inside."

"What is this true enemy, Lord?" I asked.

"Pride," He replied almost immediately. "The true enemy is pride. The true enemy is *always* pride."

And, so, there you have it. Yes, I have, once again, given in to the demands of that prideful voice living inside. In order to try to keep this from happening again, I am going to take this time to give myself another little reminder. So, here goes...

Dear Julia: You are nothing without God and can do nothing without Him. Yes, you are completely dependent on Him. Without Him, life is meaningless. Without Him, you lose. Without Him, you fail and fail miserably. You need help, Julia. Yes, you need help. Truth be told, you need a Savior. Yes, you need a Savior. Please, I beg you, don't forget that again. You can't do this without God. Stop acting like you can.

Prayer

My pride wants me to believe that I don't need you, Lord. It wants me to believe that I can do all of this on my own, but you have shown me what a lie that is by letting me fall. Thank you! May I never again forget how completely dependent I am on you. I love you! I thank you! I praise you!

Read, Think, Pray: Proverbs 16:18

REFLECTION #66

CONSIDER IT ALL JOY?

5/17/2014

Sometimes we just need to *"hold on for one more day."* (And, yes, I am a product of the Wilson Phillips generation.) Sometimes we just need to trust that there is a reason for the pain. Sometimes we just need to believe that God has not left us and that His love for us hasn't changed. Sometimes we just need to let Him help us by accepting help from others. And, yes, this all requires humility; an area in my life that is in constant need of improvement.

As I have already mentioned, over the past few months I have felt super-consumed by the world and by my duties in it. I have spent more time praying, and going to church, and receiving the Sacraments, and, in those moments, I have found great peace, but that peace was quick to leave as I went back out into the world. I've heard it said, "It's easy when you're at church," and I was living that reality. I longed to feel God's presence and find His peace in the world around me, but it seemed the more I "worked" for it, the more chaotic my world was.

In the midst of this chaos and stress I know (and even knew at the time) that God was with me, but I wondered why I couldn't "feel" Him like I had in the past. It seemed that in the moments I felt I needed Him the most, He had left me to work through things on my own. This, of course, was not the case. In fact, I'm certain He was carrying me through these times, but this is what it felt like. Look, I know we're supposed to "consider it all joy" (James 1:2) and not prefer health over sickness or joy over sorrow, but I am still working on my sanctity, so I, for one, hate these moments of growth because they are so painful. Initially I always prefer joy over sorrow and health over sickness. Who doesn't? But I guess there is some part of me (the saintly part I know is in there, but that gets tuned out so often by the not-so-saintly part) that does "consider it all joy" because in the same breath I could say that I love these "desert" moments because of the growth and freedom and peace that comes through them. Perhaps I'm "holier" than I first thought because I know that, although change is hard and painful, it's often necessary and always worth it. Perhaps I'm "holier" than I first thought because I'm unwilling to stay where I am and always allow myself to be led (although sometimes, admittedly, reluctantly) to places I don't really want to go. Yes, perhaps I still have much more work to do on myself, but perhaps I'm getting better.

I think we would all agree that, as much as we may not want there to be, crosses, pain, and suffering are a part of every authentic Christian life. In fact, one slogan could be "Christianity: Crosses Guaranteed." But that's not where our story ends and that's why so many people "choose" to be Christian. (I say "choose" because we know it is God who is choosing us and not us who are choosing Him, right? (John 15:16))

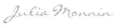

Anyway, yes, as Christians we believe and hope in what is to come. We know that God's grace is sufficient. We know that He is the one getting us through the struggles. We know that in His perfect timing we are led into, and then out of, the desert. We know that in His perfect timing we rise from the dead. In my own life it was seemingly out of nowhere when this happened; when He finally calmed the storm. I now feel more alive than I have felt in months. I guess you could say that *"I can see clearly now, the rain is gone."* (OK, OK. That one is a little before my time, but it's still relevant!)

It shouldn't surprise you then that I am, once again, reminded of God's presence, love, and goodness. As I reflect on these moments of pain, sorrow, and anxiety, I can see now how God was present in the people around me. I can see now how He sent people into my life to pick me up. I can see now how He worked through these people (mostly my husband) to comfort, support, and help me in my time of need. (Hindsight is always 20/20, right?) Yes, I am filled with gratitude for all God has given me and shown me during this time. I feel like I have gained knowledge of myself, and of Him, in the past two months that would have otherwise taken me years to discover. See how much God loves me? He knows how incredibly impatient I am, so He allows me to be put in situations where I'm forced to learn quickly (even if at first glance it seems like it's nothing more than intense suffering). All I have to say is, praise be to God!

After a period of great change God has a way of just bringing things together, of just making sense of the chaos, of just clearing the rubble. I was blind, but I can now see His hand in it all. I can now see the good that was brought out of the struggle and pain. I can now see more of the person He created me to be and less of the person, through my own fault, I had become. So, I guess what I need to say is, thank you. Thank you, Lord, for the cross. Thank you, Lord, for the struggle. Thank you, Lord, for the pain. I really do consider it all joy! Why? Because it all led me closer to you. And this, as it always is, was worth it. Yes, this, as it always is, was kind of the goal.

Prayer

I was blinded by my pain, Lord, but now I see! Thank you for

those people you sent into my life who helped me remove the blindfold that I, myself, had put on. Thank you for calming the storm and for proving to me how much you love me because of it. Thank you for allowing me to carry this cross for you and for allowing me to feel the weight of my sin. I have never felt more loved!
I love you! I thank you! I praise you!

Read, Think, Pray: James 1:2-4

REFLECTION #67

UNCHANGED

5/22/2014

In this ever-changing world, Lord, there is one thing that's constant. One thing that never changes. One thing I can always count on...You.

My world seems messy right now. Things seem to be all over the place. I seem to be all over the place; constantly changing, constantly jumping from one thing to the next. In reality it's probably not as bad as it seems, but in terms of how I feel, it's a mess. In this moment, though, in front of your True Presence, you remind me that no matter how much things, people, and situations change, you remain the same. You remind me that you are the only constant in this inconstant world.

I don't know why, but I'm filled with great peace as I ponder this reality. It's comforting to know that, no matter what, you don't change. You are always with me. You love me without ceasing.

I pray, Lord, that you help me to be your constant presence in the lives of those around me. I pray that I, like you, am always dependable, always merciful, always loving. Teach me, my God, to love others as you love me. Teach me to be merciful as you are merciful. Teach me to be more like you.

I know it, Lord. Yes, I know it. I know that you are *the* Way, *the* Truth, and *the* Life (John 14:6). Now, show me how to live it.

Prayer

My soul thirsts for you in the noise of my day, Lord. Thank you for these moments of rest in your arms. Thank you for these moments of silence in your presence. Help me to serve you in my daily duties and to seek you always. May my heart never stop longing for you. I love you! I thank you! I praise you!

Read, Think, Pray: Psalm 102:26-28

REFLECTION #68

LIFE LESSONS

5/30/2014

In just a few short months I went from having three employees to one, obviously increasing my personal workload and stress level. This was not an easy transition for me, and there were many times I became overwhelmed and defeated in the process. Yes, there were many times I became a human "*doing*" instead of a human "*being.*" Now that this time is coming to an end, though, I have to ask: *"What have I learned during this time of excessive busyness?"*

First and foremost, I've learned that you can't put a price on peace of mind. Whatever we do and wherever we go, we need to make sure we're finding time for what is truly important. We need to make sure we're finding time to be with our families. We need to make sure we're finding time to nourish our minds with good books, our bodies with good food and exercise, and, most importantly, our souls with prayer, Mass, Adoration, and Reconciliation. I've also learned that I am weak. I've learned that even my best, most purest-intentioned efforts are fruitless without God. Yes, I've learned that I am nothing without Him. I've learned how easy it is to say "I trust you," and how hard it is to prove that you do. I've learned that things on earth can be as they are in heaven, as long as we get out of the way and allow them to

"Dreams and goals and plans and to-do lists are good, but God's dreams, goals, plans, and to-do lists are better."

be. I've learned that dreams and goals and plans and to-do lists are good, but that God's dreams, goals, plans, and to-do lists are better. Most importantly, I've learned that in those moments of deep struggle and pain, those moments when it seems like God is nowhere to be found, those moments when it feels like we are all alone, God is still very much present. Yes, I've learned that God never changes.

I pray that I always remember the lessons I've learned from this experience. I pray that I always remember how easy it is to get lost in the world and how quickly everything falls apart when you do. I mean, as much as I want to achieve my goals and succeed, I am not, in any way, willing to sacrifice my soul in order to do so. After all, "What profit is there for one to gain the whole world and forfeit his life?" (Mark 8:36) There is *no* profit, I tell you! None! And these past few months have reminded me of that.

Prayer

I thank you, Lord, for all of the lessons you've taught me over these past few months. Now, I ask you to remove all the obstacles around my heart that are preventing my openness to you. Better yet, reveal to me what these obstacles are so that I can work with you to remove them. Help me, Lord, to see everything as you see it. Help me to live and experience life in the ways you desire. Help me to take rest in you. I love you! I thank you! I praise you!

Read, Think, Pray: Mark 8:34-38

THE PEP TALK

THE FEAR OF CHANGE

5/31/2014

When I first started opening my heart up to God and inviting Him into my life, change was really scary to me. In fact, it was the biggest obstacle. I can remember in the beginning only wanting to give God bits and pieces of my life. I mean, sure, I wanted all the good things He promised to give me, but I didn't want to have to give anything up in order to receive them. There were just certain things in my life I didn't want to let go of; certain things I didn't want to stop doing. Yes, my bad habits! When I thought about what it meant to live a "holy" life I wondered if I would even enjoy that kind of life if it meant I would have to stop doing all the things I had grown accustomed to. I wondered if I would even enjoy that kind of life if it meant I would have to stop doing all of the things I had come to enjoy. My not-so-holy habits seemed like so much a part of me that I couldn't imagine a life of joy without them. I couldn't imagine a life of joy without my many vices and guilty pleasures. I guess to me, being "holy" meant cutting out anything and everything that gave me any happiness. It meant picking up the cross and following Christ, and, in the beginning, I wasn't sure I was ready for that kind of change. I wasn't sure I was ready for that kind of commitment. I wasn't sure I was ready to walk away from the world.

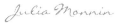

Well, thankfully, we don't have to be "ready" in order for God to start to go to work in us. Yes, thankfully, He meets us right where we're at. Thankfully, He loves us right where we are. Can you imagine if He didn't? I mean, if we were required to be "holy" before we could ever start to make our way to Him, then no one would ever make their way to Him; no one would ever live a life of virtue; no one would ever make it home. The truth of the matter is (as I have heard it said) "we don't have to change to love God, loving God changes us." He doesn't force us to give things up, we naturally give them up because the things that aren't good for us start to make us feel empty. He doesn't force us to rid ourselves of our unhealthy desires, we naturally lose our unhealthy desires as our healthy desires grow. He doesn't make us live strict, disciplined lives with no joy, we find great joy in doing His work; in doing things that have great meaning and purpose. (Yes, even the things the world tells us are a waste of time and completely unnecessary.)

So, you see, we don't have to change to love Him because loving Him changes us. And you know what else? We don't have to change to love her, either. That's right, loving her changes us, too. (And, yes, I am talking about Mary, the Mother of God.) We can start all of this by starting with her. We can start all of this by inviting her into our lives. We can start all of this by loving her.

I first heard these words, *"you don't have to change to love her, loving her will change you,"* in Fr. Donald Calloway's book, *No Turning Back,* and my life is proof that they are true. My life is proof that a "Yes" to Mary is a "Yes" to God because when I was lost and in trouble I didn't go running back to my Father. (I mean, who does that? Seriously, what child, when they know they are in trouble, goes to find their dad?) So, no, when I was lost and in trouble I didn't turn to my Father. I turned to my Mother. I hid myself in her comforting arms and let her wipe away my tears, and, in time, she showed me there was nothing to be afraid of. In time, she showed me what I needed to do. Yes, in time, she did exactly what God gave her to us to do: she took my hand and led me to her Son.

Now, as I reflect on all the changes that have happened in my life since reaching out to Mary for help, I often find myself wondering as Elizabeth did, "How does this happen to me, that the mother of my Lord should come to me?" (Luke 1:43) Seriously, how does this happen to me? Who am I that she came to me? Who am I that she picked me up, dusted me off, and then stood next to me as I, the prodigal daughter, returned to my Father? Who am I that she, with such ease, gently and lovingly took my hand and placed it so securely in her Son's? Seriously, who am I? How does this happen to me? Why did she ever come to help me?

Prayer

I love you, my Mother, and I thank you for showing me the way to the Father. I thank you for showing me the way to your Son. May my life do the same for others. May my life show others the Way. I love you! I thank you! I praise you!

Read, Think, Pray: Luke 1:39-45

REFLECTION #70

NO STRINGS ATTACHED

6/5/2014

There is nothing comparable to the peace and joy that comes from Christ. Period. Although this world is filled with much beauty and millions of things to be grateful for, it is nothing compared to what awaits us in the next. I'll say it again. It is *nothing* compared to what awaits us in the next.

From time to time, in moments here and there, it is as if I am somehow transported into this world that awaits us. The joy and peace that come in these moments is indescribable. I am not blissfully ignorant during these times. The challenges don't somehow disappear. The problems don't just vanish and go away, they just have absolutely no hold on me. I am free from them, and with this freedom comes the true peace that Christ promises us. The peace the world cannot give (John 14:27).

I don't know what I did to deserve the life I have or to deserve this relationship I have with God. I am humbled by it all. I guess none of us can really do anything to deserve any of the gifts He gives us. Yeah, I guess none of us can really do anything to earn His love. He just loves us freely and continuously gives to us without fail; no strings attached.

Maybe this is one of the reasons why so many of us struggle accepting His love, for we are damaged people with all sorts of baggage. Baggage that tells us we aren't loveable. Baggage that tells us we aren't deserving of love. Baggage that tells us no one, not even God, can love us unconditionally. But things are different for God than they are for us, and as I learn, little by little, to open my heart up to Him, to let my walls down, and to die-to-self, I am becoming more and more convinced of His unconditional, "no strings attached" kind of love. With that being said, I'm left with really only one question. If God loves me, with no strings attached, then what exactly is there to be afraid of?

Prayer

May the whole world come to know your love
for them, Lord, and may I learn to give this love in the
same way you do; with no strings attached.
I love you! I thank you! I praise you!

Read, Think, Pray: Psalm 27:1

MARTHA AND MARY

6/6/2014

I love the story of Martha and Mary. To be honest, it's one of my favorite passages in the whole Bible. The reason I love it is simple: I'm a Mary. Yes, I'm so much a Mary, in fact, that if Jesus were coming to my house for dinner, the actual dinner would be the last thing on my mind.

120

I've thought a lot about this passage over the years, and, although I originally thought that Mary was "right," which in my mind meant that Martha had to be "wrong," I now understand that it wasn't *what* Martha was doing that day that was the problem, it was *how* she was doing it. It was where her heart was *while* she was working. Yeah, the work wasn't the problem, it was getting lost in the noise of it that was, and I think all Jesus was doing was reminding Martha (and, of course, us) of this. I think all he was doing was reminding her (and us) how noisy the world can get.

I've learned through this passage that, ideally, we would be a healthy combination of these two holy women. Yes, I've learned that, ideally, we would live lives of active contemplation. (You know, lives in which we do the work God asks us to do without letting it stress us out; without taking our minds, hearts, and souls off the reason we're doing it.) Since I'm such a Mary, though, the temptation for me is to neglect my "Martha" duties, (yes, especially when it comes to my duties in the kitchen) but I know I can't give in to this temptation. Yeah, I know I must learn how to be more of a Martha without losing my Mary mindset.

I've been struggling to live this kind of life, though. Yeah, I've been struggling to work and pray in balance. It seems, instead, that I'm always taking one, or the other, to the extreme, and I've been wondering for awhile now why I've been finding it so hard not to. Well, today I got an answer. Yes, today, when I asked Jesus the question, "Why can't I just sit at your feet and think about you all day?" I "heard" him quickly respond, "Because you're not in heaven, yet!" I mean, Yes! Of course! Duh! Sure, my soul is made to be with God, and I need to spend much time here "sitting at His feet," but, no, I'm not in heaven yet. I'm in exile, and while I'm in exile my contemplative life has to be more balanced with my active one. Oh, and I know what this means. Yes, I know this means I'm going to have to start helping out more in the kitchen!...Ugh!

Prayer

I invite you into my life, Lord, and into all of my duties here on earth. Work in me and through me. Think in me and pray in me. Help me to fulfill all of my duties well, like Martha,

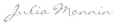

but in a spirit of peace and serenity, like Mary. Teach me
how to live my active life contemplatively.
I love you! I thank you! I praise you!

Read, Think, Pray: Luke 10:38-42

ONE FLESH

6/7/2014

In the past few years the Lord has opened my eyes to so much. Nothing in my life looks the same. To be honest, I feel like I was living under a rock for the first 25 years of my life just going through the motions of what I consider to be the minimum requirements of a practicing Catholic. My husband feels the same way. Although we are both cradle Catholics, we just didn't get it. We were disengaged at best.

It's probably no surprise then that, until very recently, neither of us really understood the purpose of marriage or the beauty of our vocation. I mean, I can't speak for him, but after we were engaged I thought more about the wedding than I ever did the marriage. I now understand the genius of the marriage prep that the Church required of us before entering into the Sacrament, but then, like the rest of my faith life, it was nothing more to me than an obligation.

If you think about it, seminarians prepare and study for years before entering into their vocations as priests and the call to married life is certainly as important as the call to the priesthood, so it makes sense that the Church "requires" a certain amount of prep work before entering into the Sacrament. But, for us, little time was spent actually preparing for the marriage. Sure, we spent lots of time preparing for the wedding, but those are two different things. One lasts a day, the other a lifetime. As you can probably tell, I had my priorities a little messed up back then. To be sure, I still would have married my husband had I understood then what I understand now, I just would have saved us years of heartache and struggle as we worked after the wedding day to figure it all out.

Marriage, of course, is so much more than the dress, the flowers, and the wedding bands, but to be honest I didn't think much about that until the father/daughter dance at the reception. Look, I know I should have thought about things a lot sooner than that, but it wasn't until that time came that I actually "got it" for the first time. As we were dancing my dad gave me some words of wisdom. "Marriage isn't easy," he told me. "You are going to have ups and downs, and you are going to have to work at it." As soon as I heard these words, I knew I could no longer ignore the obvious call-to-action. Tears filled my eyes as it finally hit me that if I wanted a strong marriage, a marriage like my parents, then I had a lot of growing up to do. Yes, it finally hit me that if I wanted a strong marriage, a marriage that could weather any storm, then I was going to have to start putting my wants at the bottom of my priority list. Oh, and this came as shocking news to the girl who was used to putting herself at the top of her list (and assumed she was on the top of everyone else's lists as well).

Time, of course, has shown me that my dad was right. Yes, marriage is filled with highs and lows, and our marriage is no different. It seems to us, though, that all the lows, struggles, and challenges have led to a greater trust in God and a greater commitment to each other. Yeah, it seems to us that all the hardships, confusion, and disappointments have caused this fusing of two separate people into one body in Christ. And, well, now that I think about it, I'm guessing that's been God's plan all along. After all, in marriage you learn pretty quickly what it means to die-to-self, to love like Christ, and to forgive, and that kind of is the point of all this, isn't it?

Prayer

Thank you, Lord, for the gift of marriage and for my husband; a man who loves me in such a Christ-like way that it makes it easy for me to understand your love for me. May I, too, be your presence to him. May he, too, come to know your love because of the way I love him. Give us a strong marriage, Lord; a marriage built on honesty, mercy,

Julia Monnin

> and compassion; a marriage filled with mutual respect, patience,
> and kindness; a marriage that is proof of your great love.
> I love you! I thank you! I praise you!

Read, Think, Pray: Mark 10:6-9

REFLECTION #73

A LEAP OF FAITH

6/11/2014

I am well aware of my perfectionist tendencies. I am well aware of how easy it is for me to go from organizing to obsessing. That is why when I found myself praying this morning that God would "perfect" the gifts of the Spirit in me so that I would be more confident in myself when I'm out in the world attempting to do His work, I quickly realized the error of my thinking.

Sure, it's true that I can do nothing without God and without His Spirit, but thinking that I should *wait* to do His work until I'm completely "perfected" is incredibly foolish. I mean, what would ever get done if we waited to do it until we felt like we were completely ready and 100% prepared for every possible scenario? Nothing, that's what!

Yes, I'm learning that we never have it all figured out and that the more we learn, the more we realize how much we don't know. I'm learning that no matter how much God enlightens us, we still have to remain open for what's to come. I'm learning that no matter how much God has prepared us, we still have to trust in Him to work out all of the details. I'm learning that no matter how much God has proven His power in us, we still have to embrace our weaknesses.

On top of that, I'm learning that God, as He says He is, is most perfectly revealed in those with meek and humble souls. Well, I pray that I am one of these meek and humble souls, not worried about what I have yet to learn but trusting in what I have learned so far. Not worried about how much more I could have prepared but trusting in how much I already have. Not worried about my many weaknesses but trusting in His power to work through them. May I embrace the call of authentic discipleship remembering that this call will likely mean that I'll have to take a leap of faith before I'm done looking.

Prayer

Increase my trust in you, O Lord! May I know and believe in what you have told us: that you will guide us and direct us at the very moments we need you to and that the weaker I am, the more powerful you become. May the hope I have in you and the belief I have in your promises far outweigh the fear I have of myself. I love you! I thank you! I praise you!

Read, Think, Pray: John 14:25-26

"O Heart of Love, I place all my trust in Thee; for though I fear all things from my own weakness, I hope all things from Thy goodness." - Prayer found in the book *The Seven Capital Sins* published in 2000 by TAN Books, an Imprint of Saint Benedict Press, LLC, Charlotte, NC

REFLECTION #74

THE SEARCH

6/16/2014

Have you ever lost something only to find it in the very first place you should have looked? I can remember, for example, looking all over the place for sunglasses only to find them sitting on top of my head. I can also remember looking for car keys only to discover I had been holding them in my hand the whole time. How does this happen? Seriously, how? I mean, in the midst of the search you're certain you've looked in all of the obvious places. As you continue looking, though, frustration sets in because you know they should be right where you left them.

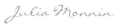

After all, it's not like they got up and walked away! Maybe it's at this point that you begin pointing fingers and placing blame because you know you didn't move them, so that can only mean someone else must have. Finally, though, after searching for what seems like forever, someone points out the obvious. Your glasses are on top of your head. The keys are in your hand. After this, what else is there to say? I mean, how could you have been so blind?

I'm just now realizing that this search is comparable to my search for God. Yes, as I grew and gained my independence as a young adult, I "left the nest" and went out into the world "searching." I was searching for my place in it, searching for love, searching for happiness. Oh, and I was certain these things weren't where I left them. Yeah, I was certain they weren't back home. So, that's why I stopped looking there and started looking everywhere else.

Over the course of my search, I spent lots of time looking in bars and at parties. Not surprisingly, I never found anything there. (Though that didn't stop me from going back and looking there again.) I also spent lots of time looking in shopping malls. That search always left me empty-handed as well. I mean, I'd find new things that made me "happy" at first, but those new things soon became as disliked as the old ones, and the "happiness" I received from them wore off as quickly as it came. I spent lots of time looking for these things on TV and in magazines and in movies, too, but, again, I'd find nothing. I'd think I had found the "love" and "happiness" I was so desperately searching for, but I'd soon find out it was nothing...a whole lot of nothing.

I looked and looked and looked and my search kept leading me nowhere. It kept leaving me disappointed, hurt, and angry. Yes, at some point I even began pointing fingers and placing blame. Eventually, though, after years of struggle and confusion someone kindly and lovingly pointed out the obvious. Someone finally showed me the Way. Someone finally reminded me of the Truth. Someone finally taught me how to Live. And, much to my surprise, the answers I was looking for weren't "out there" like I thought for sure they would have to be. No, they were right where I left them: right at home in the pews of the church I had been sitting in my whole life. My search, you see, led me back to where I started, and after years of desperately looking, I finally realized I had the keys in my hand the whole time.

Prayer

*Help me, my God, to not lose sight of the gifts you have
given me. If I ever begin a search in the wrong direction please
remind me that what I'm seeking might be right where I left it.
Please send me back home to look again. May I never again take
my eyes off you or take for granted your gift of the Church. Yes, Lord,
your Church is a gift and your love an even greater one, and I thank
you for them both. (Oh, and I also thank you for sending Mary
into my life when you did, for I know that she was the one
kindly pointing to the keys that were in my hand when I
was out searching for them in all the wrong places.)
I love you! I thank you! I praise you!*

Read, Think, Pray: John 14:4-7

*"We will not cease from exploration, and the end of all our exploring will
be to arrive where we started and know the place for the first time."* – T.S.
Eliot

REFLECTION #75

ONE'S TRUE SELF

6/18/2014

For years now I have been praying, meditating, contemplating, studying, learning, and growing, and, through it all, the Lord has been increasing my knowledge of Him by increasing my knowledge of myself. Today it is as if all of this is coming together in a new way. Today it is as if it is beginning to make sense on a whole new level. Today it is as if a seed is starting to sprout.

Yes, today I was given the wise advice to meditate and reflect upon the girl of my youth. I was encouraged to ask myself questions like: Who was this girl? What motivated her? What did she love? What did she do? This reflective meditation has proven to be very fruitful for me

127

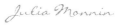

because it has helped me gain a better understanding of my true self: the real, pure me that was more clearly present in this young girl.

One thing I realized about my true self is that I have always been a giver. More specifically, I have always been one who loves to give gifts; one who loves to search for, find, wrap, and give away the perfect gift. Up until now I've always looked at gift giving in a strictly physical sense, but reflecting in this way has helped me see this in a new light. I mean, what more is the Christian life than a call to go out and share God's gifts with others? And, well, if I have always been one who naturally loves to give gifts, then perhaps this is part of my mission. Yes, perhaps finding and giving the perfect gift is as much of my calling in the spiritual realm as it has been in the physical one. Perhaps I am one of the people God has designed to search for, find, wrap, and give away His perfect gifts. Yes, perhaps.

Oh, and as if that wasn't enough, in addition to gaining a little insight about what the girl of my youth naturally "did" and tying that into what the adult me is here to "do," this reflective meditation has also helped me realize who I really am at my core. You see, before today, I had never really thought about my "true self" in this way. I guess I have been focusing too much on my not-so-true self and doing so has made it impossible for me to see the pure self that's still somewhere inside. I mean, I have always been quick to beat myself up and to magnify my many imperfections. I have always been really hard on myself for any and all my mistakes, but reflecting on this girl of my youth has shown me that these "mistakes" aren't really stemming from the real me. No, they aren't really a reflection of my true self. I have been getting mad at myself for years for not living up to my own expectations of who I should be, but this reflecting has shown me that I have been blaming the wrong person because the real me, the pure me, isn't the one "failing." No, the real me *is* virtuous. The real me *is* simple, easy-going, honest, fun, loving, creative, and full of life, faith, and hope. The real me *does* enjoy being around other people. The real me *does* value other people. The real me *does* love life and all those she is sharing it with because the real me *does* know that we are all children of God. The real me *is* patient, kind, and loving. The real me *is* gentle, compassionate, and caring. The real me *is* selfless and giving. Yes, the real me *is* a saint. This sinner in me isn't actually the real me. It isn't even some lesser version of me because it isn't any version of me. It's just not me! It never has been, and it never will be. To be honest, this "impure self," this "sinful self," isn't even a shadow of who I really am.

I, you see, am a child of God, created in His image and likeness. My true self, my pure self, is perfect just as my heavenly Father is perfect. This, of course, is true not because of anything I have done or anything I will ever do but because of who God is and because of who He created me to be. This "voice" in my head telling me otherwise isn't actually me. This "voice" in my head trying to convince me that "this is just the way that I am" and that "I will never be able to change" isn't actually *my* voice. I am finding that the challenge isn't to shut this voice up, the challenge is to ignore it. The challenge is not to believe the lies. The challenge is to rise above, overcome, and move past this voice of torment, remembering that I am *not* the sum of my sins. The challenge is to let my true self shine through remembering that I, in my inner-most being, am a saint; a saint who was put here to share God's perfect gifts.

Prayer

Remind me often, Lord, that I am your child, that I was created in your image, and that you live in me. Give me the grace and strength to tune out the voices that want to tell me otherwise. Help me to live in and through the Spirit so that my true self shines through the darkness that surrounds me. Help me embrace this true self; this self that is pure; this self that is a gift-giving saint.
I love you! I thank you! I praise you!

Read, Think, Pray: Genesis 1:27

REFLECTION #76

THE BEST GIFTS

6/18/2014

129

I was recently reminded of a childhood memory: The year was 1989. It was my mom's 31st birthday. I was 5 (almost 6) years old. I can remember being excited about it being her birthday. I loved parties! I can also remember wanting to give my mom some kind of gift. (See, I told you. I've always loved to give gifts. Besides, what is a birthday party without cake, ice cream, and presents?)

Anyway, I remember wanting to give my mom the perfect gift. There were, of course, just a few problems: (1) I was 5. (2) I had no money. (3) Even if I had money to buy something, I was 5. It's not like I could go anywhere to get it. So, I had to get creative. I found (or, what is more likely, made) a card and filled it with as much money as I had, which I believe was $1.10. (I remember taping the dime inside the card so it wouldn't get lost. The gift would have somehow felt incomplete without it.) I then joined forces with my little sister as we searched the house for more to give. Our search led us to the bathroom where we found things we knew mom would love because they were the very things she used all the time. After finding what we needed, we grabbed some boxes and wrapping paper and got to work wrapping up her bath towels and hair curlers and other such household items. By the time we were finished, we were really proud of our gifts and excited to give them away.

I can remember sitting around the kitchen table with my family as Mom opened her gifts and cards. The room filled with joy as she unwrapped her presents. You could see it on her face. You could hear it in her voice. You could feel it in her laughter; her laughter that wasn't *at* us but that was at the simplicity of our gifts. (You know, the laughter that comes when you experience for yourself the pure heart and true innocence of a child.) Yes, it was the kind of laughter that comes from pure bliss, and I can still remember how happy it made me to see her so happy.

I bet if you asked my mom today she would tell you that that was one of her best birthdays and that those were some of her most favorite gifts. In fact, she still laughs when thinking about unwrapping those things that were already hers to begin with.

And that, you see, is my point. Yes, this memory reminded me that sometimes the best gifts anyone can give us are the very things we already have.

Prayer

When I'm tempted by the things of this world, Lord, when I'm tempted to fill a void with something new, when I'm tempted to want more and more and more, fill me with gratitude for all that I already have. I know, Lord, that what I have now is all I really need because all I really need is you. Yes, you, my God, are the best gift I could ever receive, and I've had you all along. May I never take this for granted again! I love you! I thank you! I praise you!

Read, Think, Pray: James 1:16-18

REFLECTION #77

AN AUDIENCE OF ONE

6/19/2014

Do you know what's exhausting? Trying to be someone you're not. Seriously, so many of us think and behave inconsistently. Why is this? Why have we stopped trying to please God and started trying to please everyone else?

Oh, it's easy, Lord, to want to be validated by the world and by those around me, but it's exhausting trying to keep up. I just can't win. Help me instead to turn my gaze heavenward and to do all to please you; to do all to be validated by you and you alone. When you are the source of my validation, - when I find my identity in you as your child and not in my earthly roles, duties, or career - life makes sense; things are easier; I am a much happier person. Why? Because you are much easier to please, and it is in pleasing you that my soul truly finds peace.

Yes, Lord, you know me. You know the real me. There is nothing I can hide from you, nothing that you don't know, and no reason to pretend otherwise. And you know what? This is freeing! I mean, who am I kidding anyway thinking I can be everything to everyone? I can't! But

131

what I can do, is be everything to you, which I know I'm doing just by being me. Yes, Lord, I know you love me, and that is all I really need to know. So, from now on, may I seek to please the only audience that really matters: the audience of One.

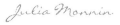

Prayer

Give me the courage to remove my masks, Lord. Give me the courage to let others see the real me. Remind me often that your opinion of me is the only opinion that matters. Remind me often that your validation is the only validation I need. May I live my life seeking to please you, and only you, and may my clear conscious be proof that I am doing just that. I love you! I thank you! I praise you!

Read, Think, Pray: John 5:44, 1 Peter 3:3-4

REFLECTION #78

THE SIMPLE LIFE

6/20/2014

Yesterday I had to venture out from my small-town home and head to the city. It was like a tale of two days. My morning started out like it always does: wake up, grab a cup of coffee, head to what has become my prayer chair, and spend time with the Lord. After finishing my morning routine, I jumped into the car and prepared for the 90-minute drive. The drive ended up being a continuation of my prayer. It was peaceful and calming. I spent time saying some devotional prayers and was brought to tears as I felt the Lord speaking to me through some lyrics of some of the songs I was listening to. Ultimately, I arrived at my destination filled with peace.

After my appointment, I headed out to do a little shopping and run some errands. That was when, like flipping a switch, the day seemed to change completely. All of a sudden everything got really noisy. People and cars were everywhere. Chaos ensued. I found myself heading to aisles of the store that I thought no one would be in, and yet every time I turned the corner someone seemed to be pressing up against me. Don't get me wrong. It wasn't the people I was bothered by. No, they were doing nothing wrong, so there was no reason to be bothered by any of them. It was just the noise in general that seemed to put me in panic-mode; this feeling of, "go, go, go!"; this feeling of constantly being "pushed." My insides began to scream and my mind headed into an irrational state as my emotions reacted to the environment. Although I was able to keep my composure, this constant chaos was all around me for the duration of the trip. When I finally headed home, I breathed a huge sigh of relief as I traveled farther and farther away from the city and closer and closer to the farmlands.

It was interesting to take a step outside of myself as all of this was going on. It was interesting to see how much I had changed on the inside as I reacted internally to what was happening on the outside. Once I was back in the silence I began to wonder how anyone surrounded by that type of nonstop chaos ever heard the voice of God. I began to wonder if some people become content with this type of life because the constant noise distracts them from ever taking a deeper look in. I mean, I'm sure this isn't the case with everyone.

Yeah, I'm sure there are lots of people living authentically-Christian, fast-paced lives who are constantly on the go, but the lesson I learned today remains the same: I need to take time to slow down, to sit in the silence, to just be. Why? Because the answers I'm seeking aren't in the noise, they're in the whisper.

The answers I'm seeking aren't in the noise, they're in the whisper."

Prayer

I can't always avoid the chaos, Lord. I can't always avoid the noise. In fact, sometimes that's exactly where you ask me to go. Yes, sometimes that's exactly where you need me to do your work. So, no matter what is going on around me, let your peace live inside me.

> *May I always be your calming presence in the noisy, busy world.*
> *I love you! I thank you! I praise you!*

Read, Think, Pray: Luke 5:15-16

REFLECTION #79

DENSITY

6/21/2014

Matthew Kelly reminds his readers often that the Law of Osmosis states that what is more dense will filter through what is less dense. He then goes on to point out that we are either more dense than the culture, or the culture is more dense than us. His point with this is that if we are more dense than the culture, then we filter through it. If this is the case, then nothing the culture promotes pulls us away from the Truth. (Capital "T.") If, on the other hand, the culture is more dense than we are, then it filters through us. If this is the case, then we absorb the lies of the world and they become our truth. (Lowercase "t.") Once this happens, once our minds have accepted the lies of the culture as truth, our behaviors become more and more "culture-influenced" and less and less "Christ-influenced." This is when bad habits start to take root.

A great example of this is with the typical American teenager. Most teenagers are less dense than the culture. Because of this every TV show, every movie, every peer-pressure situation can quickly become truth in their minds. (Again, lowercase "t.") Once this happens, once their truth becomes what they see on TV, they, too, become like the people they see on TV. As this cycle continues they slowly (without ever intending it) become the people they, as children, vowed they would never become. This, at least, is my story. Yes, this is what happened to me.

Simply put, there was a time in my life when I was not very dense. Looking back, I can see how easily I was influenced by the world around me. I can also see how this influence negatively impacted my behavior slowly, over time. So slowly, in fact, that I didn't even realize it was happening. Life is different for me now, though. Yes, now instead of using the culture as a compass showing me what I should do, I use it as a compass showing me what I shouldn't. Now the things that popular culture laughs at and dismisses are the very things I run to. These are the places I want to go, the things I want to see, the people I want to spend my time with, the stuff I want to "waste" my time doing. Oh, I'm swimming upstream. Yes, I'm swimming upstream. But I have never felt more alive and more at peace in my life. And you know what? I think that just proves I'm getting more dense.

Prayer

Give me the courage to continue my swim upstream, Lord. Help me to recognize the lies of the world for what they are and to hold fast to your Truth. Fill me with your light and wisdom. Make me more dense. I love you! I thank you! I praise you!

Read, Think, Pray: 1 John 2:15-17

THE TEMPER TANTRUM

6/22/2014

Have you ever witnessed a toddler in the midst of a tantrum? Even if you don't have children yourself it's likely you've been around a child throwing a fit. For lots of children these tantrums are the result of a missed nap, a change in their normal routine, a large intake of sugary foods, or some combination of these things. Once a child enters into one of these unpleasant states, it's difficult to say or do anything that makes them happy. They are loose cannons! Even when you give them the exact thing they're screaming for that doesn't necessarily end the tantrum. As a result, chaos ensues, and the parents (and all others

135

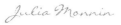

involved) are left feeling helpless. If, however, the tantrum comes at the end of the day after a missed nap rational adults know they had it coming because rational adults know an exhausted child never leads to a pleasant situation. So, we give the kid a break. We know this wailing child we see on the outside isn't the real child on the inside. We know the real child is happy and full of life not miserable, grumpy, and inconsolable, so we put them to bed, forgive them, and try again.

Well, I would argue that we aren't really much different than the toddlers in our lives. Yeah, I would argue that we, too, are pretty good at throwing temper tantrums. I mean, we might not literally kick and scream to get our way, but we do give impatient stares and blurt out unkind words, and, on the inside, these really are the same thing, aren't they? Even so, I don't think the fact that we are throwing lots of tantrums is the saddest part of all this. No, I, instead, think the saddest part of all of this is the fact that for most of us, most of the time, our overreactions could have been avoided. Simply put, I think too many of us are setting ourselves up to fail. I think too many of us are showing up to the party without a nap and crashing by the end of it.

Think about it. We spend our days running from one thing to the next. We wake up early and stay up late. We fill our bodies will all sorts of garbage; sugary drinks, salty snacks, and processed junk. We rarely take time to breathe. When we do take time to relax, we don't actually relax. Instead of sitting in silence and spending time with God, we tune out our lives by sitting in front of the television. We might take time doing things that matter like going to church, reading good books, and spending time in prayer, but we do them just because we feel like we have to. We are indifferent and distracted. Our hearts are hardened, and we aren't really ready or willing to make any changes, so we continue the rat race. We continue jumping from one thing to the next. We continue "surviving." We never rest. We never recharge or refuel, and guess what? We eventually crash just like the toddler. We cry. We scream. We push. We shove. We stomp our feet and cross our arms. We give others the silent treatment and throw a fit, and nothing anyone says or does makes it better because we are drained. Yes, physically, emotionally, mentally, and spiritually we are drained.

But, you want to know the good news? The good news is, just like the loving parent who looks past the tantrum of their worn out toddler and offers them love and mercy, our heavenly Father looks past our tantrums and offers us this, too. Yes, just like all good parents, our Father in heaven loves us unconditionally and knows that our actions in these situations don't accurately represent who we really are, so He, too, is always ready and willing to forgive us. He, too, is always ready and willing to give us another chance. Instead of seeing what looks like a crazy person throwing a fit on the outside, He sees the person He created us to be; the saint He knows is inside. And this image of us as His inwardly perfect children fills Him with love and mercy. So, you see, God doesn't say to us, "Pull yourself out of this or else!" No, He instead says, "Come to me all you who labor and are burdened, and I will give you rest" (Matthew 11:28). Yes, God invites all of us to take a nap; to fall asleep in His arms. Perhaps it's time we start accepting the invitation.

Prayer

We are a tired people, Lord; a tired, worn out people struggling to find and maintain balance in our lives. Help us to remember that, without you, none of this makes sense. Help us to remember that, without you, we are just rats in the race. Soften our hearts, Lord, and give us the grace to accept your invitation to take rest in your arms. I love you! I thank you! I praise you!

Read, Think, Pray: Psalm 127:1-2

REFLECTION #81

LEARNING TO WALK

6/24/2014

Today I was asked the question, *"How has the Lord shown His love for me?"* Mercy immediately came to mind. But this then got me wondering, "What, exactly, is mercy?"

Well, to me, mercy is love and love is mercy. They are one and the same. Mercy is forgiveness, sure, but it is much more than that, too. Yes, to me, mercy is kindness and compassion. To me, mercy is patience, understanding, and encouragement. To me, mercy is welcoming and inviting. As I see it, the mercy of God draws us towards Him, and when we are merciful as He is merciful, we do the same. We invite others to look towards Jesus and to run into his open arms.

I can picture the scene so easily. It's like the young child learning to walk. Someone stands behind the child, lifts him to his feet, and stays there stabilizing him. This person doesn't move. She is just there offering her support when needed. This, as I see it, is us. This is our role with our fellow brothers and sisters. We pick them up when they need picked up, we help them get their balance when they lose their footing, and then we let them go. We are always there, always cheering them on, always giving them our hand if they slip up, get shaky, or fall while on their journey, but we let them go. We have to. In order for them to get to where they're going, we have to let them go. That's the exciting part, though; the person/place they're heading. In this scenario, let's imagine it's the boy's father.

The father sits just a few steps ahead of the child, holding his arms out to him with a warm, gentle smile encouraging his son with the words, "Come to me. You can do it!" As the child moves forward, eyes locked on the eyes of his father, the whole room waits with joyful anticipation as he takes a few steps forward. When he finally reaches his destination, - when he finally reaches his father - everyone cheers ecstatically as dad takes him into his arms and lovingly embraces him. All are filled with joy at what the boy has accomplished. All are excited for the child who has just learned to walk.

I'm sure you've seen this story play out before. I'm sure you've seen a child learning to walk. Perhaps you're even reliving it at this very moment. If not, I encourage you to do so. Do you remember how you felt when that child took those first steps and made it into your arms? Do you remember the joy you had when he or she finally reached you? Well, this, as I see it, is comparable to our journey to God. The only difference, of course, is that the man waiting for us at the end of our journey isn't just any ordinary man; it's our Savior, Jesus Christ.

Jesus stands just a few steps ahead of us with his arms outstretched, looking at us with kind, compassionate, loving eyes. He patiently waits on us as we stumble through life, but he never takes us out of his sight or leaves us alone. No, he, instead, surrounds us with a room full of cheerful supporters encouraging us along the way. He places strong, trustworthy people like Mary, the angels and saints, and our own earthly parents, family members, and friends within our reach to pick us up, help us find our balance, and redirect us when we get off course or take a wrong turn. These people are always there, always cheering us on and helping us put one foot in front of the other, but Jesus is the one we are heading to, and he never moves. He waits, with arms wide open, encouraging us every step of the way. Imagine the joy we give him, and, of course, ourselves, when we finally make it into his arms; when we finally make it to home.

Although we may slowly crawl to Christ as we begin our journey to him, we should, in time, find ourselves moving in his direction with greater and greater ease. Some day we might even find ourselves running to him without much thought or effort. Yes, this, as I see it, is the journey of the spiritual life. We start out barely crawling and by the end we sprint without blinking an eye. This walk may never get "easier" as we journey through life, but along the way our footing becomes more and more stable; our focus becomes more and more clear. It's true, though, that if you're just starting out on your journey, if you're just learning to walk, then sprinting sounds impossible. If this is the case, if life seems to be overwhelming you and things seem to be piling up on top of you, then I invite you to do what I do in these situations: I invite you to look ahead. Place your gaze in the direction of our Lord. Lock your eyes onto his, and keep moving forward one small step at a time. He is there at the destination patiently waiting on you to find your way to him. He isn't judging. He isn't questioning your decisions. He isn't doubting your abilities. In fact, he understands it all better than you could ever understand it yourself, but remember, he won't push you. No, our Lord is not pushy. You have to take the steps. You have to decide to move towards him. You have to make the effort. You have to try. If you do, though, I think you'll discover what I have discovered: Jesus is madly in love with you, and he is always there mercifully waiting

"Jesus is madly in love with you."

on you to make it to him. "Come to me," he calls out with his arms extended. "You can do it!"

So, yes, to me, mercy is kindness and compassion. To me, mercy is patience, understanding, and encouragement. To me, mercy is welcoming and inviting. As I see it, the mercy of God *does* draw us towards Him, and when we are merciful as He is merciful, we do the same. We invite others to look at Jesus and run into his open arms.

So, I guess my answer to the question I was asked is pretty simple. *"How has the Lord shown His love for me?"* He has taught me how to walk.

Prayer

Teach me how to walk, Lord, and when I'm ready turn my walk into a sprint. Help me to move forward one step at a time always seeing you, my merciful Savior, with your arms wide open at the finish line. I love you! I thank you! I praise you!

Read, Think, Pray: Proverbs 4:10-13

REFLECTION #82

THE WATERS OF REBIRTH

6/26/2014

It has become a recent habit of mine when entering and exiting church to mentally renew my baptismal promises (in an abbreviated way) as I bless myself with Holy Water. Yesterday was no different. I entered church for Mass, placed my fingers in the font, and thought to myself as I made the sign of the cross, "Lord, you make all things new. In this moment, I recommit myself to you. Make me new." What was different yesterday, though, is that all throughout Mass I kept thinking about my Baptism and about that moment when I became an adopted child of God and a member of His Church; a gift that I am now most grateful for each and every day. The thought of this "rebirth" lingered in my mind as I made my way home. I wondered why. What was different about today? Why were the thoughts about it still there? This eventually got me thinking about the anniversary of my baptism. I knew it was some time in June, but I couldn't remember the date, so I did a little searching. And, well, my search did not disappoint! After a few moments of looking for an answer, I finally realized why the Spirit wouldn't let me stop thinking about my Baptism, for the anniversary of it was that very day!

I was overcome with joy as I put it all together and ran to get my baby book. In it I found a few pictures from the day and my baptismal certificate. Tears filled my eyes as I realized, for the first time in my life, the importance of the Sacrament of Baptism. As I continued looking at the pictures, my eyes were drawn to the words from Scripture printed at the bottom of the certificate (Ephesians 4:1-7). I had never noticed them before, but in that moment they spoke directly to my heart. I finally understood their great meaning. I finally understood their purpose. I finally understood the "why."...*Yes, Lord, we are called and chosen and are sent on a mission, and I thank you for it! I thank you for all of it!*

Needless to say, I was super-excited the rest of the day. I was much more excited about this "birth" day than I have ever been about my earthly one. You know, in the past, I've heard about families celebrating the anniversary of their baptisms, and I now understand why. From now on I, too, will celebrate this day with Christ, for it was the beginning of new life for me, and it is certainly worthy of a celebration. Yes, June 25th may not be my birthday, but it is my "Re-Birthday," and I assure you, I will never forget it again!

Prayer

Thank you, Lord, for calling me to the waters of rebirth. Thank you for adopting me as your child. Obviously, I could never repay you for this gift, but, please, don't let that stop me from trying! I love you! I thank you! I praise you!

Read, Think, Pray: Ephesians 4:1-7

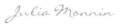

THE GOOD WOMAN

6/26/2014

I often find myself in a state of awe as I witness the workings of God in my life and in the lives of those around me. During these times I have a hard time putting into words the amazing wonders of the omnipotent God. Quite honestly these are those times when I am left speechless; something that, everyone who knows me knows, doesn't happen much!

One of these moments happened recently when I was brought to tears as I recognized God at work in the lives of those around me. His love and power was made evident as I read an email from a dear friend; a friend who has been held captive and tortured by lies, deceit, and hurt for years; a friend who, for most of her adult life, has been chained to the past. Today, I can tell by her words that a rope is being loosened, a link on the chain is being shattered. This realization of her being set free from these many years of anguish reminded me of God's goodness and of His constant presence in our lives. It was an answer to many years of prayer and, as always, He delivered! Yes, time and time again, He proves to me that what seems impossible for us is *not* impossible for Him.

I like to call moments like these "God Moments." These are the times in my life when I can clearly see God at work; the times when I am fully aware that He is the One who has made something happen. Because of the timing of this particular event, though, I was also reminded of the hand that is behind these moments; the hand that takes ours and connects it with the hand of her Son. This, of course, is the hand of the Blessed Mother; our great intercessor, our humble Queen. She has proven to me, once again, that she meets us right where we're at and takes us to Christ.

"Go to him," she calls out. "He has the answers you are seeking. 'Do whatever he tells you'" (John 2:5).

And, so, my Mother, I thank you again for these many gifts, for your many prayers, and for your constant intercession. I've heard it said before that behind every good man is a good woman. That woman is you, isn't it?

Prayer

Pray for us, Mary, our Mother. May your Son be glorified.
May God's will be done. May we become saints.
I love you! I thank you! I praise you!

Read, Think, Pray: John 2:1-11

REFLECTION #84

PERFECT TIMING

7/1/2014

I was recently asked the question, *"As you imagine yourself as an older person, what five aspects do you like best about yourself?"* After some short reflection, I gave the following answer:

(1) My priorities are in order.
(2) I am full of knowledge and wisdom.
(3) I have a free schedule and am never in a rush. (There's so little to do, and so much time to do it!)
(4) I am secure in myself and know who I am. (I don't wear any masks!)
(5) I am no longer a rat in the race.

As the group shared answers similar to these, I found myself wondering why I have to be "old" before becoming this person. The more I wondered, the more I was angered by the thought. I mean, what a terrible way to live out the days of my youth! What if I never make it to these "older" days? After all, it's not like I'm guaranteed tomorrow!

Don't get me wrong, I know some of these things, like growing in wisdom for example, will come naturally as I mature, but shouldn't I start doing the other things now? What am I waiting for? Aren't we told to *Be Still* (Psalm 46:11) and to *Take Rest* (Matthew 11:28)? Aren't we told to embrace the *Abundant Life* (John 10:10)? Did I miss the part that says, "But wait to do it until you're old."?

This discussion gave me a serious reality check. It reminded me that *now* is the perfect time to get my priorities in order, to grow in knowledge and wisdom, to free up my schedule, to remove the masks, and to take myself out of the rat race. Seriously, I don't want to wait any longer. I don't want to waste another day. Yes, I am convinced that *now* is the perfect time to become that "older" person I dream of becoming. So, you know what? *Now* is the time that I will.

Prayer

I know I don't have to be "old" to find rest, peace, and happiness, Lord. Yes, I know you want to give me these things now, so show me how to weed through the noise and tune-in to your voice; the voice guiding me to freedom. Help me to make good use of everything you send my way. May I embrace the abundant life you came to give me (while I am still young)! I love you! I thank you! I praise you!

Read, Think, Pray: 2 Corinthians 6:1-2

REFLECTION #85

TRUE PEACE

7/8/2014

We, as human beings, are hard-wired for love. We are made to love and be loved, and everything we do and everything we are has love at its core. Seeking love and validation, therefore, isn't the real problem since, by design, we are made to love and be loved. The real problem is that many of us seek this love and validation in all the wrong places and from all the wrong people. The real problem is that many of us bypass

God and try to fill the holes in our hearts with anything and anyone else. The real problem is that many of us are miserable.

Not to pick on teenagers and young adults here, but this type of behavior is most obvious when we are this age. I mean, when we are young we feel an extreme amount of pressure to be liked, to fit in, to be part of the crowd. In my own life, I can look back and easily see how this was true for me when I was in school. Everything I did, said, and wore was an attempt to fit in and be liked. It has only been very recently that I have realized that this type of outside-in validation doesn't just go away when we enter adulthood. Yeah, as adults some of us still get a certain job, buy a certain car, build a certain type of house in a certain neighborhood, and have a certain number of children all because we want to be liked; all because we want to fit in. If we were wise, though, we would realize that this type of outside-in validation didn't make us happy in high school, it didn't make us happy in college, and it isn't going to make us happy in adulthood either. Yes, if we were wise, we would realize that this type of outside-in validation is a never-ending cycle of pain and disappointment; one that never fills us with true peace.

If we want true peace, sincere joy, and total happiness, then we have to start seeking love and validation from the only One who can actually give it to us. We have to start looking in. We have to start turning our minds, hearts, and souls towards God. We have to start living for that *Audience of One* remembering that God is the only one who has the answers we are seeking; remembering that He is the only one who can truly fill that void in our hearts; remembering that He is the only one who can really give us peace. (You know, that true peace the world cannot give (John 14:27).)

Prayer

Fill me with an even greater love for you, Lord.
Purify my heart, mind, and soul. Give me the peace I'm
really after; the peace the world cannot give.
I love you! I thank you! I praise you!

Read, Think, Pray: Colossians 3:23-24

ACTION!

7/17/2014

I've come to realize that sometimes we've already said all that needs to be said. I've come to realize that sometimes we already have the answers we're seeking. I've come to realize that sometimes we already know what we need to know. So, why do we keep talking? Perhaps we're afraid of moving forward and continuing to talk and ask questions delays our response to take action. Perhaps we welcome more talking and more questioning because it keeps us from taking the next step. Yes, perhaps.

After all, fear tells us it's better to do nothing than it is to mess up at doing something. Fear tells us we should wait to take action until we know we are completely ready; until we know we can move forward without making a mistake. This non-responsive attitude keeps us feeling "safe" because it gives us the impression that we aren't accountable for those things we've never tried. It gives us the impression that, as long as we don't mess anything up worse than it already is, then we are doing our job. This train of thought, though, couldn't be further from the truth.

God, of course, doesn't expect "perfection" from us, but He does ask us to try. And, yes, not trying is even worse than failing because God can perfect even our most imperfect attempts, but He can't do anything if we never move. Paralysis, by fear of the unknown or uncertainty about what is to come, is *not* how we answer the call of Christ. It only leads to more chaos, more confusion, and more misery, and any "comfort" or "safety" we feel by staying where we are is not real. It is a false security. We shouldn't doubt God's ability to work through us because He created us to do His work, and He gives us everything we need to accomplish whatever it is He asks us to do. So, maybe the time has come for us to stop asking so many questions and to start taking action.

The next time you find yourself in a conversation with God, I challenge you to stop talking so much. Sometimes our words just serve as

146

distractions and are delaying the inevitable. Sometimes we have said all that needs to be said. Sometimes it's just time to get to work, and, as I've learned, the sooner we do what it is God is asking us to do, the more everything else will start to make sense. The next time you find yourself in a conversation with someone else, I challenge you to stop talking so much. Offer an encouraging nod, a gentle smile, a heartfelt, loving glance. Have a conversation without words. Why? Because most people don't need advice. In fact, most people don't *want* advice. Yeah, most people don't need (or want) to be told; they just need (and want) to be shown.

You may be doubting that now is the time to move forward, but there is never a bad time to do a good thing. At some point, we all need to *prove* by our actions that we really do mean what we say. I mean, even God Himself chose to *prove* His love for us by dying on the cross, so we are certainly not exempt from "putting our money where our mouth is." Yes, actions really do speak louder than words; they always do. The time, therefore, comes for each of us to stop talking and to start taking action.

The time comes for each of us to stop talking and to start taking action."

Prayer

Help me, Lord, to speak less and to listen more. Help me to trust my inner most being and to overcome the fear that wants to keep me from moving forward. Increase my trust in you, my God. May the actions of my life prove my love for you. May the actions of my life speak for themselves. I love you! I thank you! I praise you!

Read, Think, Pray: Ecclesiastes 5:1-6, 1 John 3:18

"Who you are speaks so loudly we can't hear what you're saying." - Ralph Waldo Emerson

THE STEPS FORWARD

ATTITUDE CHANGE

7/22/2014

Something has been different for me, spiritually speaking, these past few weeks. I have spent some time traveling and vacationing with family and friends, and, although these are certainly good things, I have realized over the course of it that something inside me has changed in the process. I have spent time in prayer and have gone to Mass while I've have been away, but it is as if the Lord has somehow distanced Himself from me. I know He is still here, but I don't feel as "tuned-in" as I normally do. It's almost as if the world is moving around me, but I am numb to what is happening. Though I don't really know for sure what is going on, I decided to enter into my prayer today with a new attitude. Instead of praying so that I could "cross pray off my list for the day," I prayed for one reason and one reason only: to spend time with God. Instead of trying to take control of my time in prayer by saying the prayers I'm comfortable saying in the way I'm used to saying them, I let the Spirit guide the conversation. This attitude change opened my mind, heart, and soul to a whole new level of understanding, and, as it did, I realized several things.

First, silence is necessary. There's not a whole lot one needs to add to that. All prayer is important. Mass is, most certainly, important. Spiritual reading, too, is important, but if you never take these things to the silence, they will never produce the fruit they have the potential to produce. We must run to the silence. We must make it a priority. I am convinced that, in time, we can all learn to love it.

Second, God is only concerned with our best effort. He knows right where we are and what we are capable of. He knows our talents, our weaknesses, our past and our future, and He is not concerned with how these things measure up with others. No, He is not concerned with how we compare to the person sitting next to us. He only asks that we do the best we can with what we have been given and knows that for some of us our best is to attend Mass every day, for others it's to go every week, and for those who have been away from church for awhile it may just be to seriously think about going. Yes, God knows that we all have to start somewhere, and just like the coach who likes to play the players who always do their best instead of the most talented players who have a bad attitude, I think He is more pleased with the person who is honestly discerning making changes in their life than with the person who, although is filled to the brim with talent and potential, just shows up every week expecting to get something in return. The spiritual life, therefore, is not a competition with others, it's a competition with ourselves. Our individual best is all that really matters.

> *The spiritual life is not a competition with others, it's a competition with ourselves. Our individual best is all that really matters."*

Lastly, it's important to take time to recognize and celebrate any and all progress we are making in our lives. Although my poor attitude in prayer while I was away reminded me that I am nowhere near where I am striving to be, the fact that I even made an attempt to pray while I was gone shows me that I'm further along than I was a year ago, and, in the end, that is what matters because growth is always the goal. So, be patient, celebrate your wins, learn from your losses, and remember persistence is key.

Run to the silence, do your best, thank God for the work He is doing in you, and become a person who persists long after others have given up. This is what it takes to become the people God has created us to be. This is what it takes to become a saint. Who knew a simple attitude change would make such a difference in my life? Yeah, suddenly God doesn't seem so far away. Perhaps attitude really *is* everything.

Prayer

Thank you, Lord, for the time you give me to "get away."
Thank you for my family and friends and for revealing yourself
to me through them. Thank you for the dryness in my prayer while
I was away and for prompting me to change my attitude when I
returned home. Thank you for showing me how I was coming up
short and for humbling me enough to admit that I needed to make
some changes. May my prayer never again become a "head" thing.
May it never again become something I do to "cross off my list."
May my prayer instead always be a "heart" thing. May it always
be about spending some quality time with the One I love.
I love you! I thank you! I praise you!

Read, Think, Pray: James 4:8-10

REFLECTION #88

THE WHISPER

7/23/2014

The mysteries of God's Kingdom are all around us. Can you see Him at work in your life and in the lives of those around you? Can you hear Him in the sounds of nature and in the laughter of a child? Well, He is there. Yes, He is everywhere.

Perhaps you thought He would reveal Himself to you in "louder" ways, but God doesn't usually come to us in the strong and heavy winds, in the earthquakes, or in the fires. No, God instead usually comes to us in "a light silent sound" (1 Kings 19:12).

Maybe you haven't noticed Him yet because you assumed He would need to be "loud" to be heard and "big" to be seen, but that's not how God works. Start paying closer attention to the whispers, and you'll soon realize how present He really is. Yes, you'll soon realize how much He is at work in your life.

It is then that you will see Him at work in your neighbor who drops everything to come to your aid. It is then that you will see Him in the stranger at the grocery store who holds the door open for you as you walk inside. It is then that you will see Him in the onlooker who sends you a loving, understanding glance as you struggle to get your kids in the car. Yes, it is then that you will see Him in the ordinary moments of your day.

God is all around us. Sure, it's true that evil is, too, but you have the power to choose what you look at and what you pay attention to, so live in choice. *Choose* to see the good instead of the evil. *Choose* to see others at their best instead of at their worst. *Choose* to see the beauty of life instead of the culture of death. Choosing what you look at doesn't make you ignorant, naïve, or hopelessly optimistic, it makes you wise. Choosing to weed through the noise to find the whispering voice of God doesn't make you foolish, it makes you chosen.

> "Choosing to weed through the noise to find the whispering voice of God doesn't make you foolish, it makes you chosen."

The world is noisy. God whispers. Do you hear Him?

Prayer

Come, Lord Jesus, come. Reveal yourself to me in the people around me and in the ordinary moments of my day. Give me eyes that see and ears that hear. Show me how to find your light whispering voice in the noise of my life.
I love you! I thank you! I praise you!

Read, Think, Pray: 1 Kings 19:11-13

REFLECTION #89

HUMBLE PIE

7/24/2014

As I go through life striving to become all God has created me to become, I have found it helpful to dedicate each month to growing in a different virtue. So, since I have been working on humility this month, I wasn't surprised when I "just happened" to stumble across a prayer on it that I had never heard of before. Yeah, I have been asking God to show me how to become a more humble person, and He answered by showing me a prayer that drew obvious attention to an area in my life that is in great need of change.

I know that finding this prayer was not a coincidence. Yes, I know *nothing* in life is a coincidence. This ordinary event was proof of God at work in my life. It was God revealing Himself to me in the whispers of my day. Well, I heard His whisper. In fact, the message in His whisper was so clear, it was impossible for me to ignore. I now realize that I am far from being the humble person I am striving to be. I now realize that there is still more pride in me than I would like to admit. How do I know? Well, see for yourself. Here was my train of thought as I read the prayer for the first time:

"O Father, give us the humility which: Realizes its ignorance. *(OK, I do that.)* Admits its mistakes. *(Yep, I've learned how to do that. This was*

153

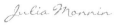

really hard at first, but with God's help I've learned to do this and do it quickly.) Recognizes its need. *(Absolutely! I'm never afraid to ask for help.)* Welcomes advice. *(Say what now? Welcomes advice? Are you serious? Is that something people actually do? I mean, if I ask for your advice, then I'll welcome it, but the thought of welcoming unsolicited advice is unfathomable to me. Who does that? Is that really a part of being humble? Well, as much as it pains me to admit, it obviously is, and due to my reaction, it's also obvious that it should be at the top of my "ongoing conversion" list. I must say, though, having an attitude of "welcoming advice" seems impossible to me right now. I will certainly need God's help in order to do it.)* And accepts rebuke. *(I'm sorry. I can't get past that last one! I'm sure this is an area I could improve in, but it will have to wait. I still can't wrap my head around the idea of welcoming advice. Aaahhh! I can't imagine!)*

So, yes, it's clear this is an area in which I have lots of room to grow. It's clear that when it comes to growing in humility, this is the place I should start. Oh, but this wasn't the only thing God showed me I needed to work on this month. No, there was another huge area of concern that He kindly made me aware of. I realized later that I not only struggle welcoming advice, I also find it incredibly annoying to have to repeat myself. Got pride, anyone? I mean, seriously. How have I never realized these are problems for me? Well, regardless, it's obvious now, and that is why the time has come for another reality check.

Dear Julia: Not welcoming advice and becoming annoyed with having to repeat yourself are obviously not character traits of a humble person. Quite honestly, they are pointing in the opposite direction. The time has come to wake up and make some changes. Get to work!

Prayer

I love you, Lord, and I thank you for showing me how much work I have yet to do. I thank you for showing me how far I have yet to go. I don't feel defeated or overwhelmed by the work I have left. No, I am not in anguish, and I am not going to beat myself up about the ways I have, and still am, falling short. I, instead, run to you. I fall on my knees and beg you for your mercy, your help, and your patience. Then I pick myself up, dust myself off, and try again. I know that,

*with your help, Lord, I can overcome these vices because, with
your help, I have overcome so much more. So, I love you, Lord,
and I thank you for the great big slice of humble pie!
I love you! I thank you! I praise you!*

P.S. - As I worked through these flaws in my character in the weeks that
followed, I went back and reread some of my past reflections so I could
get a better idea of what has been going on inside. I was shocked to
discover that there were multiple times over the past few years that the
lesson I learned about life was exactly the same. I would have told you
that, when I wrote about something, I was learning the lesson for the
first time. I would have never guessed that *God* was having to repeat
Himself to *me*, but this has made me realize what I should have realized
long ago: when it comes to us learning and growing, God does not get
tired of repeating Himself. No, of course He doesn't! It is with the same
loving, merciful patience that He points something out to us the first
time that He points it out to us again the 100th time. A prideful person
like me might grudgingly say, (or at least think) "I've told you this a
million times already! What don't you get?" but God wouldn't. No, God
would say, "I'm so glad you asked! Here is what you're missing. Here is
what you forgot. Is there anything else you need?" So, yes, this proves
it. If God doesn't get tired of repeating Himself to me, then I shouldn't
get tired of repeating myself to others. Oh, the time has definitely come
for me to shed my ego!

Read, Think, Pray: Philippians 1:6

*"O Father, give us the humility which realizes its ignorance, admits its
mistakes, recognizes its need, welcomes advice, and accepts rebuke.
Help us always to praise rather than to criticize, to sympathize rather
than to condemn, to encourage rather than to discourage, to build
rather than to destroy, and to think of people at their best rather than at
their worst. This we ask for Thy Name's Sake. Amen."* - Prayer for Humility by
William Barclay*

* I don't know much about William Barclay, but from the little I've read, it seems that many of his
religious views are much different than my own. Even so, his prayer above has been a great help to
me in my striving to grow in humility, and, for that, I am grateful.

Julia Monnin

BLIND FAITH

7/29/2014

I doubt too much, don't I, Lord? Yes, I must, for I hear you telling me often, "Trust in [me] with all your heart, on your own intelligence do not rely" (Proverbs 3:5). In fact, these are the words I hear you calling out to me the most. These are the words that seem to be on repeat in my mind and in my heart.

I feel like having complete trust in you should be easier than what it is. After all, I know that you are the master builder, and I am just a worker. I know that you see how it all comes together, and I only see one small piece at a time. So, how could I ever really think that I know what the next best move is? How could I ever really think that my way is better than yours? How could I ever really think that I should trust more in myself than I do in you?

The way I see and understand life, Lord, is not the way you see and understand it, and I know that some things just aren't going to make sense to me. Yes, I know that some things just aren't going to answer all of my questions, so I want you to know that I know I can trust you. Yeah, I want you to know that I *do* trust you. In fact, I want you to know that I trust you so much that, from now on, I won't even ask where you're leading. I'll simply follow you blindly wherever you go.

Prayer

Thank you, Lord, for another opportunity to prove to you that I trust you. May I never doubt you or your love for me. May I never question your will for my life. I love you! I thank you! I praise you!

Read, Think, Pray: Proverbs 3:1-6

156

"I know you are my Father! I feel secure in your protection. I do not ask the way you lead, I blindly follow your direction. And if you placed into my hands, my life that I myself direct it, I then would say: O, take it back, Your trusting child is well protected." - Prayer of Fr. Joseph Kentenich, founder of the Apostolic Movement of Schoenstatt

REFLECTION #91

A JOYFUL SURRENDER

7/30/2014

Who in their right mind finds it easy to "sell what you have and follow [Him]" (Matthew 19:21)? Is it just me or does this type of change seem frightening and impossible? Of course, it does! In fact, I think it's supposed to, for it is only when something seems impossible that we know for sure God had to be the one to do it. I'm realizing, though, that many of us don't look at life from God's perspective, so, when we read passages like this from Scripture, we are tricked into believing that a life centered on God must mean a life of misery. We read words like, "sell what you have," (Matthew 19:21) "take up [your] cross," (Matthew 16:24) "love your enemies," (Matthew 5:44) and think that God must just want all of us to be miserable. If we fall for this lie, (and sadly many of us do) we become paralyzed by fear, and, instead of taking any steps in the right direction, (even if they are super-small steps) we do nothing; we stay put; we "[go] away sad, for [we] had many possessions" (Matthew 19:22). Ah, but these lies are no match for God. Yes, God knows what we're up against, and He knows how to inspire and motivate us in the midst of it. He knows how to patiently guide us to make changes slowly, over time. So slowly, in fact, that we often don't even realize we're doing it. This, at least, is what I just realized happened to me.

Yes, I just realized I've never really thought about what I've "given up" to follow Christ. I simply ran back to Him begging Him for mercy, and, in the tiniest, most insignificant ways, I showed Him that I needed Him, that I wanted Him in my life, and that I loved Him. He did the rest. He gave me the grace I needed to do whatever it was He was asking of me

157

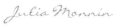

along the way. Sure, some of the change took months, some even years, some is, without a doubt, still in progress. But much of it was easier than I ever thought it would be and really just took a moment.

As I look back now on how I've changed, I realize some of the things I've "sold" on the road to following Him; things that I never would have let go of at first; things that had anyone "forced" me to give up I would have only held on to tighter. Yes, I have let go of some friends. Yes, I have let go of some material stuff. Yes, I have let go of some "free time." Yes, I have even let go of what I thought was my career; a career that I enjoyed, a career that I did well, a career that seemed so perfect and great that I never imagined myself leaving it. Yes, slowly, but surely, I let go and let God guide me into a new "career;" a "career" that is incredibly foreign to me, but that I am now certain is the very thing I was created for. Oh, and you know what else I've let go of? "My" fertility. That's right, I've let go of even the thought of raising a family because, as He's shown me, it's not a "right" to have children, it's a gift. And it's one that we don't all get. So, yes, I've "let go." I've "sold." I've "taken up my cross." And you know what? It's freeing!

I guess I've fallen so in love with God that none of this "letting go" scares me. Yeah, I guess the love of God is so complete and the taste of heaven so sweet that "letting go" of these things, - yes, even the "big" things - barely feels like the slightest inconvenience. Like the merchant who finds the great pearl and sells all he has to acquire it, (Matthew 13:45-46) I willingly - and with great joy even - let go of these things for even the chance of getting to know God better; for even the chance of one day meeting Him face-to-face; for even the chance of loving more like He does. And this, you see, is what makes this "letting go" feel like a blessing instead of a curse. This, you see, is what makes the pain of carrying the cross seem like an honor. Yes, this, you see, is what makes the surrender a joyful one.

Prayer

I love you, my God, and the more I come to know you, the more I love you, and the more I love you, the more I want to "sell" to get to know you better so that I can love you more. This is no accident. Yes, I'm certain this is by design; by your genius design. Thank

you! I would be lost without it. I would be lost without you.
I love! I thank you! I praise you!

Read, Think, Pray: Matthew 13:44-46

A STEPPING STONE

7/30/2014

I have spent much time reflecting on this journey we call life. I have spent much time reflecting on what it all means; reflecting on my massive failures, my tiny successes, and my never-ending strivings. There is still much that I wonder about, so I find myself asking God often, "What does it all mean, Lord? What does it all mean? Let me in on your Truth. Let me in on your goodness. Let me in on your plan. What does it all mean, Lord, and where do I fit in to it?" Well, in the midst of one of these question-filled conversations with God here recently, an image of a stream filled with stepping stones suddenly came to my mind. "Why?" my questions to Him continued. "What does a stream of stepping stones have to do with it? What are you trying to tell me? What is it, Lord? What is in the stream?"

"Oh, that's it, isn't it?" I thought a few moments later. "Of course, that's it! How could I have forgotten? How could I have doubted your presence? How could I have doubted your guiding light, your helping hand, your solid foundation? How could I have doubted you? My God, YOU are the stepping stones in the stream, aren't you? These stones represent your ever-present, helping hands in our lives, don't they? They are the people and the thoughts and the things that you surround us with to help us on our journey to you, and they are always there; always available for us to use. If only we step from one to the next, moving from right to left, always looking for the one you place in front of us, then we make our journey to you with relative ease, don't we? If this is the case, then I suppose we wouldn't even think about the

159

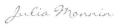

dangers that surround us, would we? Yeah, I suppose the dangers would never scare us because we would know they had no chance of hurting us as long as we stay on the path you've placed before us. Oh, but we, your sometimes prideful children, often make things more difficult than they need to be, don't we? We often venture off the perfectly laid out stones and believe the lie that we can do it on our own and that our path is better than yours, don't we? Yes, we do, and, in so doing, we willingly step off the stones of safety and step into the dangerous waters that surround us. What a mistake! What an awful mistake! I guess we don't always step off the trail intentionally, though. Yeah, I guess sometimes we don't want to step off. I guess sometimes we just don't know what we're doing; sometimes we just loose our footing and slip off out of ignorance. But regardless of how or why we fall the fact remains the same: we have stepped off the trail that you have laid out for us and so find ourselves in the worrisome waters that surround it. Now what? Now what are we to do?"

I think I know what you would say, Lord, because you say it so often. I think you would tell us, "Do not be afraid." Yeah, I think that is exactly what we would need to do first; we would need to remain calm. You never leave our side anyway, do you? There is never anything to fear, is there? Even in these situations where we have clearly walked away from you, you have not left us, have you? No, I am convinced that you are never the one to leave. I am convinced that we are, instead, always the ones leaving you; the ones giving up; the ones turning away. Oh, Lord, if we were wise, it wouldn't take us long to figure out the mistakes we've made and to climb back on the stepping stones. We would know the stones are always there and that all we have to do is make the effort to get back on them. If we were wise, we would realize we have fallen and would do everything we could to step back on before we get too far away. Oh, but how foolish many of us are, for how often do so many of us delay this action? We allow ourselves to float downstream and get farther and farther away from the stones; farther and farther away from the safety, security, and true peace that come with it; farther and farther away from you.

At some point in this drifting you try to wake us up. You try to bring us back into a state of awareness. You help us realize that we are in trouble and that we are drowning, but we ignore you. We are so far away from the stone-filled, peaceful waters that they are practically invisible. We may know deep down that they are there, - we may know deep down that *you* are there - but it all seems out of reach. It all seems too far way. Yes, it seems that we are too far gone and that it is impossible to get back. And, if we're not careful, it is at this point that we are led into despair; it is at this point that we lose all hope. We give up and just keep floating by waiting for the end, thinking, "What does it matter anyway?" Oh, Lord, if only we were paying closer attention! If only we would pull our heads above water just for a second we would see the life preserver floating in front of us waiting to save us and take us back to the peaceful waters; waiting to save us and take us back to you. Oh, if only we would look up! If only we would overcome the fear, and look up.

Perhaps that's the real problem. Yeah, perhaps the real problem isn't the dangerous waters, it's that we spend too much time looking at the danger instead of looking at the safety net in the middle of it all. Yeah, perhaps the time has come for us to look up. Perhaps the time has come for us to look at what has been staring us in the face; the thing that, though clearly visible, has somehow seemed invisible. Yes, of course! It's been there the whole time, we've just been overlooking it. It's seemed hidden because we weren't expecting it to be so obvious. Yes, we expected the path back to be more difficult, but there it is. It's so clear now, so crystal clear. How could we have overlooked it for so long? How could we have missed it for so many years? How could we have been so blind? It's never too late to reach out to you, is it, Lord? You never leave us, do you? You are always there, aren't you?

"Yes, my child," I can "hear" Him respond. "The world may think you are too far gone, but I don't. I never have, and I never will. Look up! Look to My Son. Look to Jesus, your Savior. He is your life preserver. He is your

safety net. He is the Way back. Reach out to him and let him lead you to calmer waters. Let him place you back on the path that leads to me; back on the path that I have laid out just for you. So you got off track a little bit. Get over it! My mercy is endless. My mercy is always there for those who seek it with a sincere heart. Do not, therefore, fear the danger that is lurking around you, just reach out and take my hand. I love you, and I will bring you home."

Prayer

Fill me with the deep humility that recognizes its need for a Savior, Lord. Show me how to take hold of the hand you have sent here to help me; the hand you have sent here to save us all. Come, Lord Jesus, come. Rescue me. Lead me back into restful waters, and keep me there all the days of my life.
I love you! I thank you! I praise you!

Read, Think, Pray: Proverbs 4:26-27

REFLECTION #93

NO QUESTIONS ASKED

7/30/2014

In case you haven't noticed, Lord, I'm feeling quite inspired today. Yes, you are certainly at work in my life, and, I must admit, I love days like these! Look, I know I'm supposed to "consider it all joy," (James 1:2) but let's be honest; some days are just easier to be joyful than others. I can never plan days like today, though. No, I can never *make* the inspiration come, and it often comes when I least expect it. (You know, on those days when my to-do list says I don't have time for it.) Oh, but you have shown me, time and time again, that my to-do list is a joke! Yes, you have shown me, time and time again, that the more obedient I am to your promptings, the more I am filled with the joy, happiness, and peace that you promise. (I know...Who knew, right?)

On days, Lord, when I'm feeling less inspired and more sluggish everything just seems a little harder. (And, in case you were wondering, no, I don't "like" days like these as much as I like the inspired ones.) I mean, I usually come to my senses and eventually "consider them joy," too, but it's human nature to hate the struggle at first, and I am, after all, human. I know, though, that I learn more through the struggle than I do through the ease, and that's why I've learned to be grateful for the "hard" days, too. Yes, the "hard" days remind me how weak I really am, and this always reminds me how truly dependent I am on you. (And you and I both know I am in constant need of being reminded of my dependence on you!) So, yeah, although I prefer the "fun" days, the days like today when I'm feeling super-inspired, (After all, you know I'm a Sanguine.* I like to have fun!) I also appreciate the days I have to work for it a little more; the days when it doesn't come so easily. (As you also know, I'm even more so a Choleric.* I'm not afraid of a little work!) Regardless, today is one of those "easy" days; one of those days I'm feeling super-inspired. So, today I will do what I have learned comes most naturally to me when this inspiration strikes; today I will write.

So, Lord, I turn my attention back to what has most recently inspired me in the first place, your Word; more specifically, your Word in Chapter 13 of the Book of Jeremiah. Now, I know I am *not* a theologian and, therefore, can't even begin to tell you I understand everything about this passage, but I couldn't help but be intrigued by it as I read it today. Yeah, I couldn't help but put myself in the story and wonder how I would have reacted had you been telling me to do the things you asked Jeremiah to do. After all, you must admit, Lord, you sound a little crazy in this story at first. I mean, to paraphrase, you say, "Go buy some underwear and put them on, but don't wash them. Just do it. I am God and I told you to." Then you say, (again paraphrasing) "Now take them off and hide them in those rocks." Only to then say later, "OK, now go and get them." You see what I mean? On the surface this seems like a bunch of crazy talk, and that's why after reading it I couldn't help but laugh! I mean, can you imagine what Jeremiah was thinking as he received all these instructions? Well, I know what I would have been thinking, anyway. I would have been thinking things like, "Will you make up your mind already, God? Why do I have to do all these things? These are ridiculously odd requests! What does this have to do with anything?" Unlike me, though, Jeremiah did what he was told, and we have no indication that he questioned any of it. Instead it seems that he followed your orders obediently with a no-questions-asked, "Yes, of course, my God, whatever you say" attitude. Oh, how different my response would have been! It's a darn good thing I'm not a prophet, huh?

It's obvious to me now, Lord, that this passage was meant to be just crazy enough to catch my attention. Yeah, it's obvious that it was meant to get me asking the questions it got me asking because these questions made me realize how much more I have yet to learn. Yes, these questions made me realize how often I am more concerned about figuring out the *whats* and *whys* behind what you're asking of me than I am about just doing what I'm told. They, once again, reminded me that some things don't, and just won't, make sense to me, but that *doesn't* mean they don't make sense to you. They, once again, reminded me that all things really *do* happen for a reason and that, no matter how silly or confusing or challenging they seem, they really *are* all part of your plan. So, yes, Lord, I have learned much today, and I thank you for all the grace-filled inspiration and guidance. From now on, I will strive to do whatever it is you ask me to do no matter how easily it comes or how ridiculous it seems. From now on I will just put the underwear in the rocks and then go and get them when you tell me to, trusting that there is a reason for it all.

Prayer

Increase my faith and trust in you, my God! I know that you know all and that there is a reason for all things. So, may I never again doubt you or question your plan. May I never again delay in doing what it is you have asked me to do. Inspired or not, Lord, may I always promptly obey...no questions asked!
I love you! I thank you! I praise you!

Read, Think, Pray: Jeremiah 13:1-11

* Sanguine and Choleric are two of the four temperaments identified by ancient philosophers and used for centuries by people looking to better understand human nature. (Temperaments help us understand our *tendencies to react* to situations. These *tendencies to react* influence our total personalities.) I, myself, have been studying the four temperaments for the past few years and have found this study to be incredibly beneficial to me in my personal and spiritual life. Knowing how I am designed has not only helped me better understand myself, (and those around me) it has also helped me better understand God, the Creator of us all. If you are interested in learning more about the four temperaments and how they tie into your spiritual life, I recommend Art and Laraine Bennett's book, *The Temperament God Gave You,* as a starting place.

UNVEILED

8/6/2014

"What am I here for? What does God want me to do? What is my mission?" - I've spent lots of time prayerfully reflecting on this idea of "mission" and, in particular, what my mission is, but I still don't know what I'm here to do. I mean, it's not that God isn't answering me or anything, it's just that He's been answering me progressively; unveiling things little-by-little, one small piece at a time. During the last few years, for example, He's been slowly revealing to me who I really am, - who He created me to be - and this increased knowledge of self has helped me put some of the pieces together about what I was created to do. But, I still don't really know *what* my mission is. Yeah, I still don't really know *what* I am here to do.

Up until this point, all I have known for sure about "mission" is that I have one. All I have known for sure is that I am here for a reason and that I am here to do something no one else is here to do. None of this, though, means I actually know *what* my mission is. Yeah, I guess to me, the hardest part has always been figuring the *what* out; the easy part has been doing it. Yeah, I guess the *hows* have just always had a way of naturally working themselves out once I figure out the *whats*, but it's the *whats* I'm so unsure of right now. It's the *whats* I have this inner desire to know more about. It's the *whats* I have been wondering about trying to put my finger on; the whats like, *"What am I here to do?"* and *"What is my mission?"*

Well, I'm happy to report that God recently unveiled another piece of my "mission" puzzle. Sure, there is still more I don't know about my mission than there is that I do know, but I now have a better idea of *what* I am here to do, and that is enough to keep me moving forward. Just how did God unveil this to me? Well, He showed me like He usually does, by revealing to me a little more about who I really am and tying that into what I am here to do. This time this increased knowledge of self came as I worked through some emotional struggles I was having. These struggles showed up after I began seriously thinking about

165

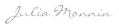

moving into a new "career." You see, though I now realize I'm here to do something other than what I've been doing and that the time has come for me to move on, I've been having a really hard time actually making it happen. Yes, I've been having a really hard time actually letting go and moving forward. Maybe it's because there is still so much I don't know about what is to come. Maybe it's because I still don't really know for sure what it is I'm moving on to. Maybe it's just because I'm scared of getting out of my comfort zone. Regardless, the fact is, this hasn't been an easy transition for me, and the discomfort has made me ask some better questions; questions that have led to an even greater understanding of who I am and of what that means in terms of what I am here to do.

As I worked through this emotional struggle, I realized that one of the fears I was having through this transition of changing "jobs" was the fear of not being needed. I guess I have always wanted to be needed. (I would bet that we all do.) As all of this was going on, though, it seemed like God was asking me to go beneath the surface of this want and figure out what it really meant, so I took it to prayer. And, after spending much time in prayerful reflection, I was still at a loss! It was at this point that I jotted down the following. *I don't know what this all means, but I know it means something. It bothers me not to know, but I will take a step back and just let it unfold on its own. When I'm supposed to know what it all means, it will be revealed. There's no need to worry or push. Just live.* And, so, I did just that. I went on living mindfully, paying close attention to what was happening around me and how I was reacting to it, and forty-five minutes later (yes, I realize how quickly this actually came) as I continued to wrestle with the doubts of, *What does it matter anyway? I want to be needed, but no one really <u>needs</u> me because all anyone really needs is God, so what do I really have to do with any of this? How could I ever really help?*, I "heard" God calling out, "You're right. No one really *needs* you because everything they really need they already have, but they don't realize this. They don't realize that I am all they need, and that is where you come in. Yes, that is what you are here for."

And, so, though I still have more questions than I have answers about what it is I'm here to do, this day of prayerful reflection has helped rid me of some of the doubt I've been having about what difference I can make in the lives of others and whether or not there is a "need" for what it is I'm doing. Yes, this process has helped me get one step closer to knowing who I really am and what it is I am really here to do and because of that, I'm grateful. Yes, because of that, I'm most grateful! Another piece has been unveiled. Thank you, my God!

Prayer

Thank you, Lord, for shedding some light on what it is you are asking me to do. Thank you for shedding some light on what it is you made me for. I want to know why I'm here, Lord. I want to discover my mission. Please strengthen me for my journey. May I never grow tired of the search. I love you! I thank you! I praise you!

Read, Think, Pray: Romans 10:13-15

REFLECTION #95

THE UNSPOKEN WORD

8/7/2014

I find great comfort in being understood. (I think most people probably do.) In recent months, though, something has changed in my desire to seek out this understanding. I don't really know why this change is happening or what is actually going on, but I've been noticing it for awhile now, especially these last few weeks. It has been during this time that I have found myself becoming more and more drawn to the inner life. It has been during this time that I have found myself becoming more and more drawn to God. It has been during this time that I have found myself becoming more and more drawn to the unspoken word.

Since I'm a talker by nature, I'm finding this inner desire for the "silent" life very strange. I mean, where did this even come from? Never before have I longed to live in a world where all is understood without saying a word. Never before have I desired to bring things to light without speaking. No, never before. I have always wanted to talk. I have always

167

wanted to explain. I have always wanted to externalize things. Something is changing, though. Yes, something in my inner life is being made new.

This change has been most evident in my prayer. Simply put, I have felt myself being drawn to God in ways that I have never been drawn to Him before. I guess I can't really explain what's happening, but there is a "completeness" I feel in my prayer that I don't feel anywhere else. In fact, I'm so comforted by His presence in prayer that I often find it difficult to leave it. I guess it just feels like no amount of time I spend with God is long enough.

Again, I don't really know where this is coming from, what is actually going on, or how to describe any of it. I'm just finding it more and more comforting to know that, sometimes, the unspoken word is all one really needs.

"Sometimes the unspoken word is all one really needs."

Prayer

Thank you, Lord, for proving to me that you are at work in the unspoken word in ways that far surpass anything you are doing in the spoken one. Show me how to embrace this inner life. Show me how to live like a saint. I love you! I thank you! I praise you!

P.S.* - It's true that as I advance in my spiritual life, I am finding myself living more and more contemplatively, and, now that I think about it, I guess that's to be expected. Yeah, I guess this is a somewhat natural progression in the spiritual life. Since, however, these deeper levels of contemplation are new to me, I'm finding it more and more challenging to capture what I'm experiencing on the inside in the written word because I now find great meaning in all things. Yes, even in the smallest, seemingly most insignificant, moments of my day. How could I ever write about them all?

Read, Think, Pray: 2 Corinthians 4:16-18

* The "P.S." section of this reflection was originally written on 8/13/2014.

JUST ENOUGH

8/13/2014

As I continue my search of discovering my mission, it's becoming more and more clear to me that God is a God of slow, progressive revelation. How do I know? Well, no matter how much I think I want it or how much I beg Him to show me, He never quite gives me the full picture. No, He never quite tells me the whole story. I guess that's just not how He works. Yeah, I guess that doing so is just not in our best interests. I guess that when it comes to us knowing and fulfilling our missions, God is a God of "just enough." Yeah, I guess "just enough" is all we really need.

Over the last few years God has been giving me "just enough." He has been giving me "just enough" to know where to look next. He has been giving me "just enough" to know what I should do next. He has been giving me "just enough" to keep me moving forward. Oh, and you can be sure that all of these "just enoughs" are always followed by that one, huge, reality-checking question. You know, that question of, "Do you trust me?"

"Do you trust me, Julia?" I can "hear" God ask me every time He gives me "just enough."

"Yes, Lord, I trust you. Yes, Lord, I believe," I faithfully respond.

"Well, then, prove it," He "says." "Prove that 'just enough' is more than enough. Prove that 'just enough' is all that you need."

"Ok," I tell Him. "I'll prove it. Yes, I'll show you that I trust you. But before I do, I've just got a few more questions. I mean, what if this isn't the right step? What if there is a better step? What if I misunderstood you? What if I don't really know? What if I screw it up? What if I'm wrong? What if..."

169

"Impossible," God lovingly interrupts. "My child, it is impossible for this next step to be the wrong step because, with me, every next step is the right one."

So, you see, God and I are in a huge game of trust right now. Yeah, it's obvious the time has come for me to stop *telling* Him that I trust Him and to start *showing* Him that I do. And you know what? I'm guessing He'll give me "just enough" to do it.

Prayer

Yes, Lord, I trust you! Yes, Lord, I believe!
Now, give me "just enough" courage to prove it.
I love you! I thank you! I praise you!

Read, Think, Pray: Philippians 3:12-16

REFLECTION #97

THE RESISTANCE

8/13/2014

Have you ever heard the expression, "the night is darkest just before the dawn"? Well, I don't know how true this is in a physical sense, but I have found it to be true in a spiritual one, and I think I'm in the midst of one of those "dark nights" right now. Yeah, I think that's why I'm feeling so tempted to quit. I think that's why I'm feeling so tempted to give up. I don't think this struggle I'm going through is unique to me. No, I don't think I'm alone. In fact, I think it happens to all of us over and over again throughout the course of our lives. Yeah, I think it happens every time we try to make a change; every time we try to move forward. It goes like this:

We, with whole-hearted determination, resolve to change and begin taking steps in the direction of our goal filled with this same steadfast attitude. Then, as the process of change continues and obstacles begin

170

to arise, (which they always do) we start to lose our motivation. We start to doubt and begin wondering things like, "Is this even what I'm supposed to be doing? I mean, who was I kidding? This isn't for me! I can't do this!" In the midst of all this doubt our stamina decreases, and the dark night hits, tempting us to give up; tempting us to stop, turn around, and go back to where we came from.

This, at least, is what is happening to me right now. Yes, rarely does a day go by when I'm not tempted to quit, but I know quitting would be the worst thing I could do because I know God will keep helping me as long as I keep trying. Yes, I know this is just part of the process. I know the "resistance"* is just proof that I'm on the right track, so I will keep putting my head down and going back to work. I will keep running to Christ and begging him for help.

"You're almost there," I can "hear" him call out. "The dawn is coming. Don't give up! Persevere! Finish Strong!"

So, that's what I'll do. Yes, I'll keep moving forward. I'll keep taking one tiny, (albeit agonizing) step at a time.

Prayer

It's tempting to give up, Lord. It's tempting to stop trying, but I know there is still more to do. Yes, I know I am not done yet, so I will keep moving forward trusting that you will give me every grace I need to do your work. "[Your] grace is sufficient for [me]," my God (2 Corinthians 12:9). Yes, your grace is more than enough. I love you! I thank you! I praise you!

Read, Think, Pray: James 1:12

* I first heard this inner battle referred to as "resistance" in Steven Pressfield's book, *The War of Art,* and I have found no better way to describe it, so I use this term often. Though Pressfield's book is not a book on Catholic spirituality per se, I recommend it if you're looking for tips on how to *"break through the blocks and win your inner creative battles."* (Which, by the way, just happens to be the subtitle of the book.)

WANTING

8/13/2014

The truth is inside. Yes, everything we need to know is "written on our hearts" (Jeremiah 31:33). And you know what else? Everything we need to be truly happy is there, too. That's right, everything we need is inside. Everything we need is within. I have to wonder then, why do so many of us still "want"?

Yes, we are a "wanting" people. Yes, most of us spend our lives "wanting." We "want" to be done with school. We "want" the job. We "want" the new car. We "want" the new house. We "want" the higher-paying job. We "want" the comfortable retirement. Why is this? Why are we always "wanting"?

I guess "wanting" isn't really a "bad" thing. Yeah, I guess "wanting" is really just a sign that we are spiritually alive. How so? Well, God made us to be fulfilled. Yes, He made us to be happy, so if we're not, then it's natural to "want." Yeah, it's natural to "want" to fill the void. The problem, of course, is that many of us make the mistake of trying to fill this void with things that are outside of us. Many of us make the mistake of trying to find happiness in the "stuff;" in the retirement, in the new cars, in the new homes, in the new toys, in the new careers, and, yes, even in the new spouses. But these things aren't what we're really missing, so these things aren't what are really going to make us happy. No, they can't because what we really "want" is inside.

An outside-in mentality makes us think that, "My lack of (fill in the blank) is the reason for my unhappiness, and when I get (again, fill in the blank) then I'll be happy," but this isn't how it works because none of us are really lacking anything. No, because everything we really need is inside. I'll admit, though, it's easy to fill the "wanting" void with things outside of us because these things give us a ton of pleasure, but pleasure is *not* happiness. Pleasure is short term. Pleasure comes and goes. Pleasure always leaves us "wanting" more. Happiness is different.

Happiness never leaves us "wanting." Happiness fulfills us. Happiness is what we're made for.

Yes, the truth is, happiness comes from God, (and from God alone) and it's when (and only when) we find this happiness with Him that we never "want" again.

Prayer

Teach me, Lord, how to turn to you in my times of great "want" instead of turning to the world. Open my mind and heart to see what's inside. Teach me how to seek the happiness that comes from within; the true and lasting happiness that only comes from you. I love you! I thank you! I praise you!

Read, Think, Pray: Proverbs 21:17

REFLECTION #99

FORGIVENESS

8/14/2014

"Forgive." This may be but a single word, but, as I see it, it's one of the most important in all Scripture. Yes, we are told over and over again to forgive. "Forgive not seven times, but seventy-seven times" (Matthew 18:21-22). "If you forgive others their transgressions, your heavenly Father will forgive you" (Matthew 6:14). "Turn the other cheek" (Matthew 5:38-39). "Blessed are the merciful" (Matthew 5:7). Etc., etc., etc. Though much of Scripture can leave us wondering, "What is God really saying here?" the passages on forgiveness leave little room for error. Yeah, they are quite clear, - painfully clear actually - and their message is simple: "Forgive. It's not an option." Doesn't this make you wonder, then, why so many of us walk around harboring grudges?

Forgive.

It's not an option."

173

I mean, I get it. Forgiveness is hard. It is, no doubt, more of a process than it is a single action, and it is one of the most difficult processes we will ever go through, but don't you think we should try? It is, after all, kind of a "requirement" of discipleship. I know, though. Yes, I know. I know it hurts. I know it seems unforgivable, but don't you think God knows that, too? Yeah, don't you think He knows how hard it really is?

I've heard people put it this way, "Not forgiving someone is like drinking poison and expecting the other person to die." I repeat, "Not forgiving someone is like drinking poison and expecting the other person to die." It really makes you think, doesn't it? Oh, and, yes, it is so very true. When we *choose* not to forgive (and, as hard as it is may be to do at times, it really *is* a choice) we set ourselves up to fail. We chain ourselves to the past. We drink our own poison. Christ, though, wants to set us free. In fact, he *died* so that we could have this freedom. And I think that's why he asks us to forgive in the first place. Yes, as I see it, the freedom he offers to each of us is in the forgiveness.

So, I guess what I'm really trying to say is this: All of us (myself included) should just forgive already. Why? Because if we want to be free, then it's really *not* an option to do otherwise.

Prayer

You died, Lord, so that my many sins would be forgiven, and when I choose not to forgive others, your death is a wasted sacrifice. Help me, therefore, to be quick to forgive. Help me to be merciful as you are merciful. Doing this is not easy, Lord, but I want to be free. So, show me how to forgive. Heal me from my past.
I love you! I thank you! I praise you!

Read, Think, Pray: Matthew 5:21-26

REFLECTION #100

FALSE PERCEPTION

8/14/2014

I had a friend join me this morning for my morning prayer session; a little bird that I couldn't help but notice. Unfortunately, this bird seemed to be having a rough morning. Yes, unfortunately, he seemed to be a little confused. I mean, I don't know much about the nature of birds, but I'm guessing there are times when they get a little territorial; times when they "fight off" other birds. Well, I think this bird was going through one of those times. The problem, though, was he was not attacking some outside enemy like he thought he was. No, the problem was he was attacking himself in, what we humans know to be, his reflection in the window.

This whole situation got me thinking about how we, as humans, act in this very same way. Yeah, it got me thinking about how we, just like this bird, pound our heads up against the wall over and over again without realizing we aren't perceiving the situation correctly; without realizing what we're doing isn't working; without realizing what we're thinking isn't true. Yes, we are often like this helpless bird. We, too, are often our own worst enemy. We attack ourselves by thinking things like, "I'm so stupid. I'm so fat. I'm not good enough and never will be. That person is better. I'll never be able to do that. If I could just have that, then I would be happy." And so on. And so on. And so on.

With that being said, I think it would be wise for us to take our gaze off our reflection and remind ourselves of the truth.

The truth is, the negative thoughts we have about ourselves are not coming from God. The truth is, these negative thoughts are lies of the true enemy. The truth is, we are created in God's image. The truth is, we are perfect and can do (perfectly I might add) whatever it is God asks us to do.

Look, I know we can't always turn the thoughts off all together, but we *can* choose how we respond to them. Yes, we *can* choose to ignore them. We *can* choose not to believe them. We *can* choose to fly away. So, yes, I think it would be wise for us to take our gaze off the reflection of false perception, and fly away!

Prayer

Help me to disregard the lies that want to tell me that

> I'm not good enough, Lord. Help me to come to know the
> truth; the truth that I am your beloved child, created in your
> image and likeness, and that you love me for me.
> I love you! I thank you! I praise you!

Read, Think, Pray: Ephesians 6:10-12

REFLECTION #101

ENEMIES

8/17/2014

Dear God: Thank you for my enemies...Now, let me explain.

I believe that God wants me, and everyone else for that matter, to one day join Him in heaven. I also believe that in order for us to get there we need be perfected; made holy; become saints. Well, I, for one, find myself most challenged to become the saint I was created to be when I am in the presence of an enemy. It is in situations like these that every instinct in my body wants to fight back. It is in situations like these that I find it incredibly difficult to be patient, kind, loving, understanding, and forgiving, but these are, of course, the very virtues I'm called to nourish and grow. Yes, these are, of course, the very virtues I need to work on developing the most. So, since my enemies clearly point to where my greatest vices are, I no longer see these people as obstacles I need to rid myself of. Instead I see them as gifts from God packed with lessons about life showing me what it means to love more like Him. And that, you see, is why I am grateful. Yes, my enemies train me in virtue, and I need all the training I can get!

My enemies train me in virtue, and I need all the training I can get!"

176

Prayer

Train me in virtue, Lord, and teach me what it is that I don't know.
May I learn from every situation you allow me to be in.
Yes, even in those situations with an enemy.
I love you! I thank you! I praise you!

Read, Think, Pray: Luke 6:27-36

"There is nothing annoying that is not suffered easily by those who love one another." – St. Teresa of Avila, *The Way of Perfection*

REFLECTION #102

THE HAPPY PLACE

8/17/2014

Can you imagine a day when absolutely everything goes exactly the way you want it to go? You wake feeling rested and ready to start your day, and, from that moment on, everything goes perfectly. You spend the day with the people you love and enjoy the most. (Or you spend it completely by yourself if that's more your thing.) The kids are on their best behaviors, your to-do list is empty, and all your time is spent in ways that make you the most happy. Your day is filled with complete and utter bliss.

Perhaps you've been blessed enough to have some "perfect" days like these in your life, but, even if you have, you probably know that perfect days in this world are scarce. Yes, we learn pretty early in life that most days here are, in all actuality, far from perfect. Imagine this though. Imagine there isn't an end to the perfect day. Imagine there isn't an end to the ecstasy. Imagine you have the perfect, joy-filled day, and tomorrow is exactly the same. Nothing can, or ever does, go wrong. Nothing is ever boring or incomplete. No one is ever upset, disappointed, discouraged, fearful, hurt, or confused. Everything always makes perfect sense. The work is always done. Your joy is always complete.

Well, this, as I see it, isn't just some made up dream world. This, as I see it, is heaven, and the thought of it is what keeps me moving forward. Yes, the thought of it is what gets me out of bed in the morning when I feel like sleeping in. The thought of it is what keeps me putting one foot in front of the other when I feel like giving up. The thought of it is what makes everything make perfect sense when all I see is imperfection. The thought of it is what gives my life purpose when it feels purposeless.

Take heaven out of the picture, though, and everything in life suddenly loses its meaning. Take heaven out of the picture, and everything in life is suddenly empty and incomplete. Take heaven out of the picture, and pain is just pain and suffering is just suffering. Take heaven out of the picture, and the imperfect world we live in is nothing more than that; imperfect.

"Take heaven out of the picture, and the imperfect world we live in is nothing more than that; imperfect."

So, when this imperfect world we live in starts to overwhelm me and I'm tempted to let it bring me down, I do what lots of people do. I "go to my happy place." My "happy place," though, isn't some fantasy land in a make-believe world. No, it's the happiest place of all; the home of the never-ending perfect day: heaven.

Prayer
May my mind and heart always be focused on you and on the life that is to come, Lord. May I hope all things and believe all things, especially in your promises of eternal life. I love you! I thank you! I praise you!

Read, Think, Pray: Psalm 27:4

TREASURE TIPS

8/18/2014

I just finished listening to a podcast of Fr. John Riccardo's radio program, *Christ is the Answer,* and his practical insight into the familiar passages of Matthew 6:21 ("Where your treasure is, there also will your heart be.") and Matthew 6:24 ("You cannot serve God and mammon.") has opened my eyes to a whole new level of understanding. (I say that a lot, don't I?) Anyway, I don't often take the time to journal about what I'm learning from my study in this way, but the advice I heard today was too good not to write down. I don't want to forget it! I feel like they were tips straight from God to help me "check myself" as I continue my journey to Him.

In this program, Fr. Riccardo said that if we want to know that our treasure is in God, then we should start paying closer attention to our thoughts in two specific ways. First, he suggested we pay closer attention to what is distracting us in our times of prayer, adoration, and/or during Holy Communion. He said that our repetitive distractions, especially during these times, could be a sign that our heart is focused on the wrong things. I agree. I can remember, for example, the Communion procession being like a fashion show in my mind when I was a teenager. There's no denying that at that time in my life my treasure was on my appearance and on how that appearance compared to others. Yes, my heart was far from God. I can also remember a time more recently when my prayer was constantly being interrupted by thoughts of money, finances, and business. It's clear now that money was where my heart was. Yes, as Fr. Riccardo suggested they might, these repetitive distractions were signs that my treasure was not in God.

His other suggestion was to pay closer attention to how we react to losing things. (Or how we react to even the thought of losing them.) He asked questions like, "How would you react (or how did you react) if you ruined your favorite shirt? Or wrecked your brand new car? Or broke the vase that was your great-grandmother's? What feelings come up

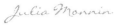

when you even think about losing your home and all that's in it?" Well, for most of us, feelings like fear, worry, anxiety, and maybe even anger come up, and he made the point that, although our feelings certainly aren't the "end-all, be-all," they can be a sign that we are overly attached to the things in our life. I agree. Here's why...

A year ago my husband and I had an accident with our boat a few weeks before a planned trip away with it. Boat mechanics are scarce where we live and often overbooked in the summer, so we both panicked. It felt like the end of the world. We were so excited about getting away that the thought of not being able to do so made us crazy. We were more than just disappointed; we were worried, anxious, angry, and frustrated. These emotions proved that the boat was controlling us. They proved that our treasure was far from being in God. Well, in a "coincidental" event a few weeks ago, (and, no, I don't think it was really a coincidence) the exact same thing happened. That's right, the *exact* same thing; same timing, same damage, same trip planned a few weeks later. This time, however, our reaction to it was completely different. Yes, this time the emotions seemed more appropriate. We were disappointed, sure, and perhaps even mad at ourselves, (and the inanimate object we ran into) but we weren't "panicked" like we had been the year before. No, this time it didn't feel like the end of the world. This time we recognized the accident for what it really was; unfortunate but certainly *not* a crisis. This time our treasure was not in our boat or in our trip away, so this time our world didn't feel like it was crashing down around us like it had felt the year before. (Oh, and on a side note, this accident actually came at the perfect time. I, you see, was in a place spiritually where I needed a little pick me up. Yeah, I needed some "proof" that the work I was doing on myself was paying off, and my opposite reaction to this identical accident proved to me that I was making steps in the right direction. It proved to me that I was, in fact, setting my heart on God and prioritizing my life better than I had been the year before. It was another gift from God; another whisper calling out to me through the noise of my day.)

So, yes, since the goal of the Christian life is for our treasure to be in God, Fr. Riccardo's tips to pay closer attention to our constant distractions, reactions, (and overreactions) has proven to be beneficial in my life. I guess his guidance just reminded me that, although most of us don't give much thought to our thoughts, doing so is one of the most simple and effective ways we can grow spiritually because it helps us gain a better understanding of ourselves and trains us to start separating the "ungodly" thoughts that enter our minds from the "Godly" ones. (I heard one speaker* even go so far as to say that we should go through our days imagining that we have a "thought bubble" over our heads displaying each and every thing we're thinking about. (You know, like in the cartoons.) He said that if we want to change, then we should pretend that everyone can see our "thought bubble." "After all," he continued, "God can.")

Prayer

Unite my heart more closely to yours, Lord. Make me yours and keep me yours forever. May my treasure always be in you, and when it's not, may you be quick to point it out and call me back into your loving arms. I love you! I thank you! I praise you!

Read, Think, Pray: Matthew 6:19-21, 24

* This "Thought Bubble" suggestion came from Matthew Leonard's talk, *Pray like a Saint*, available from Lighthouse Catholic Media.

REFLECTION #104

DIGGING DEEPER

8/20/2014

I'm going through a period of great change. Yes, I'm going through yet another period of great change. Every time I'm in the midst of such great change, I'm reminded that change is hard and that knowing it's hard doesn't make it any easier. Oh, but every time I'm in the midst of such great change, I'm also reminded that change is the only way we grow and, therefore, the only way we become the people God created us to be.

So, though the pain of change is pretty intense for me right now, I know I must be getting close to the end because the resistance, at least for me, always feels the heaviest at the end. And, well, right now the resistance is super heavy. It's so heavy, in fact, it feels like the world is screaming at me trying to convince me to give up and turn around. But if it's getting this desperate, then I know the finish line must be right in front of me, so I'm not going to let the noise scare me into quitting. No, I'm not going to let the noise scare me into turning around. It's not going to work! In fact, it's only going to make me dig in a little deeper.

One way I'm "digging in" is by making sure I'm looking at life through the eyes of faith. I'm doing this by reminding myself often that, although the resistance is heavy, the pain is real, and the temptation to quit is intense, God hasn't left my side. I mean, sure, there have been times I have found myself calling out to God impatiently saying things like, "Hello? Where did you go? Are you mad at me? You're not? Well, then, where the heck are you? I'm drowning down here!", but I know He hasn't really gone anywhere. Yes, I know He is very much aware of what is going on. I know this is all part of His plan, so I just keep asking Him for the strength I need to move forward. I just keep asking Him to show me what I should do next. I just keep asking Him to show me what I need to learn. Then I just keep trusting that He will show me the way through.

Another way I'm "digging in" is by constantly reminding myself that the problem isn't "out there with them." Yes, I'm constantly reminding myself that the problem is somewhere in me which means the solution is somewhere in me, too. Why am I doing this? Well, because the pride in me always wants me to point fingers and place blame, so I know I need to be on the lookout for the times I'm tempted to do this. I mean, I pray daily that God will make me a saint, and I really do want to become one for the right reasons, but sometimes I'm tempted to say, "Lord, make me a saint, but I don't really want to change, so can you just make me one by changing everyone around me? I mean, if they would just do what I want them to do, in the way I want them to do it, then I would have no problem loving them like you love me. It sure does seem like it would be a lot easier if you could just change them instead of changing me so much. Besides, don't you think they have a lot more to work on right now than I do?" This is such a joke, though, isn't it? I mean, when I put it this way, it's obvious that this is *not* the path to sainthood. Oh, but

182

the pride in me likes to try to make me believe it is, and that's why I need to be on the lookout for it. That's why I need to constantly remind myself that the only way for me to become the saint I was created to be is for me to actually continue on this path of change, no matter how rough it may get along the way.

And, so, change I have done and some more change I will do. Though my path right now is being met with heavy resistance, painful suffering, and an intense temptation to quit, I will keep moving forward relying not on myself, but on God to get me through.

Prayer

Though I am heavily tempted to quit, Lord, I will not do it. I know you are with me, and, with you at my side, there is nothing to fear. So, I will continue my race one small, but persistent, step at a time. Yes, even if it's a small, but persistent, painful one. I love you! I thank you! I praise you!

Read, Think, Pray: Psalm 23

THE END OF ONE CHAPTER...

GOD'S MEASURE

8/28/2014

I have a problem *not* overdoing things. Yeah, I'm always tempted to push for more. I'm always tempted to say things like, "That's not good enough, Julia! You can do better!" I'm always tempted to think that what I'm doing, no matter how "big" or how "good," is not "big" or "good" enough. Sure, this quality of striving keeps me moving forward and motivates me to always do my best, but I lose balance with it often. Yeah, I often take it way too far. How do I know? Well, instead of it motivating me, it often belittles me.

I know this belittling is not from God. Yeah, I know letting this healthy quality of being self-motivated turn into a disordered passion telling me my best isn't good enough is *not* a working of my Almighty Father. That's why, as soon as I recognize this negative self-talk, I quickly run to God for help.

"What's going on?" I ask Him. "Why does everything always have to be 'bigger' with me? Why does it always feel like my best is not, and never will be, good enough? Help me, Lord! Help me overcome this temptation to want to doubt you by doubting myself. Free me from the lies running through my head. Show me the truth that is in my heart."

Well, after conversing with God like this following one such moment of heavy temptation to beat myself up recently, two saintly stories* came to mind.

The first was of a young girl whose life powerfully influenced the great Archbishop Fulton Sheen. Her story meant so much to him that when he was asked late in his life who inspired him, she was the one he gave credit to. Yes, she, an 11-year-old girl, who was a "nothing" and "nobody" to the world around her, inspired the man who inspired millions. And just what did this young "nobody" do? Well, after witnessing our Lord in the form of consecrated Hosts being abused, thrown, and scattered on the ground during a time of war and persecution, she put her own life at risk by returning each evening to the place of desecration to lovingly adore him and properly consume each one. According to the priest who could see her doing this night after night from his cell, on the evening she consumed the final Host, she was spotted by the guard who then immediately put her to death.

The second is of a person who played an important role in the conversion of the great Saint, Ignatius of Loyola (the founder of the Jesuits). While Ignatius (then a Spanish knight from a noble family) was in his family castle recovering from a severe wound he had received while fighting in battle, he asked for something to read. Since no one could find a worldly book that interested him, someone handed him what was available; a book on Jesus and the Saints. That someone didn't write the book, or teach a class on it, or follow up with Ignatius after he had read it to discuss it further (not that we know of anyway). No, that someone just handed a recovering man a book, and that single action was enough for the Spirit to go to work in the life of the man who later changed the Church, and, therefore, the world She lives in, forever.

On the surface these stories may seem to be completely unrelated to the questions I was asking God in prayer, but, as I continued reflecting on them, I soon realized why they were the two stories that God brought to mind. You see, I had been doubting what kind of difference I could make in the world since I am just one lowly person whose actions, even if they were "great" and "saintly," would be nothing more than a drop in the bucket in the grand scheme of things. But God reminded me through these stories that we don't all have to be Doctors of the Church, or founders of religious movements, or great Popes to make an impact on the world. No, God's measure is different than ours. God doesn't measure our greatness by the size of our deeds but by the size of our love, and He, of course, can do great things with even our smallest, most seemingly insignificant efforts. And, well, this, (as you can probably imagine) is music to my over-achieving ears!

"God doesn't measure our greatness by the size of our deeds but by the size of our love."

Prayer

Help me to breathe and enjoy the journey you have me on, Lord. Remind me often that my mission, even if "small" in the eyes of the world, is great in your eyes. May I never again doubt the impact you can make through me whether what you ask me to do is as simple as handing someone a book or as noble as risking my life to honor you; whether what you ask me to do is as praiseless as changing a dirty diaper or as praise worthy as running a multi-million dollar company; whether what you ask me to do is as unnoticeable as praying silently at home for my family and friends or as noticeable as traveling the world to share your Good News with others. You are the master builder, Lord. I am your humble servant. May I trust that the purpose of my life will be great in your eyes, no matter how purposeless it may seem to be to me. I love you! I thank you! I praise you!

Read, Think, Pray: 1 Corinthians 12:4-11

* I can't remember where I first heard about either of these stories, but you can read more about the girl who inspired Archbishop Sheen by going to www.sign.org and searching for their 6/9/2015 article titled "How a young Chinese girl inspired Archbishop Fulton Sheen to make a Holy Hour every day." And you can read more about the life of St. Ignatius on the "Ignatius of Loyola" Wikipedia page.

THE MONSTER IN THE CLOSET

9/4/2014

What I'm about to say is really hard for me to say. I mean, I'm certain it won't come as a surprise to those who know me best, (especially to my mom and sisters who loved me unconditionally through the dark times and to my husband who, no doubt, suffered patiently as I worked through my "little" problem). Even so, what I'm about to say is not easy for me to say because this "little" problem was anything but "little" to me. It, you see, was one of the darkest, most tormenting parts of my "old self." It, you see, was one of the biggest "monsters" I have ever been enslaved to. Because of that, it's hard for me to bring it up. It's hard for me to talk about it. It's hard for me to think back and remember the pain. Still, my hope is that bringing this darkness into the light will call it out for what it really is and, in so doing, finally free me from it once and for all. So, although it's difficult, I refuse to let this "monster" control me another day by letting it scare me into not talking about it. So, talk about it I will.

What probably started innocently in my childhood playing dress-up and wanting to look like a princess turned into an obsession in my tween, teen, and early 20's. (And I don't use the word "obsession" lightly here. That is *exactly* what it was.) Yes, my "old self" spent countless hours worrying about, planning for, and working on my physical appearance. I couldn't shop enough, couldn't work out enough, couldn't diet enough, and couldn't spend enough time and money in the salon. Though I don't know for sure where all this obsessing about my looks came from, (I, jokingly, (but maybe not so jokingly) like to blame it on middle-child syndrome) it was there, and it was very real.

Since, during this time in my life, my happiness was *not* dependent on God but instead was dependent on how I looked, something as simple as getting dressed in the morning was agonizing to me. Yes, agonizing. Picking out what I was going to wear for the day could be an hour long process on its own and actually getting myself ready was usually at least another hour. (And that, of course, was assuming I was not having a "fat" day. You know, one of those days when absolutely everything in your closet looks terrible on, you feel like burning it all, locking yourself in your room, and never going out in public again. Well, that, at least, is what those days felt like to me.) Still, what was even worse than the obsession with my wardrobe, was the obsession with the number on the scale and the size on my pants. Yes, for so many years, my happiness was completely dependent on my "beauty." And, no, not on my true, inner beauty as God would define it, on my fleeting, outside beauty as the world would.

Although I tried for more than a decade to fit into the "beautiful box" of the world, I never did. No, never. No matter how much I dieted, how much I worked out, or how much weight I lost, I was never thin enough. No matter how many outfits I could put together, how many designer labels I would purchase, or how many closets I needed to store all my clothes and accessories, I still never had anything to wear. No matter how much time I spent looking through magazines, how much effort I gave looking at pictures online, or how much money I spent in the salon trying to match the new hairstyles I had discovered, my look was never "perfect." No, never. I never won. I never fit into "the box." I never looked "the right" way. I was never "perfect." And, well, though I didn't realize it at the time, it's clear now that I was on the slippery slope of addiction.

So, yes, it's hard to admit, but for several years of my life I had a very serious addiction. I was addicted to the number on the scale. I was addicted to diet and exercise. I was addicted to shopping. Thankfully, though, after years of slowly opening my eyes, God finally called me out of the darkness by sending someone into my life to wake me up by "afflicting me in my comfort." This someone blew my little world up when he told me, "You know, Julia, it doesn't matter. It really doesn't matter." He didn't have to say anything else. No, I knew exactly what He meant by those few simple words. What he was really saying to me was, "It doesn't matter what you wear, how much you weigh, or how stylish your hair is. It doesn't matter what box you fit into and what box you don't. It doesn't matter what the world wants you to look like and what you actually look like. No, it doesn't matter. None of it really matters."

This man's words, though simple and said in passing, were impossible for me to ignore. They stirred something in my heart and got my wheels

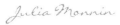

turning. Why? Well, for starters because they seemingly came out of nowhere. I mean, I didn't really know this man very well at the time, and, though I sort of brought the topic up, his words were just too "out of place" not to be noticed. More importantly, what he said hit me like a ton of bricks because I knew he was right. Yeah, I knew I *was* way too concerned about how I looked. In fact, I knew there were times when *all* I was concerned about was how I looked. So, yes, his simple statement, said to me in passing, stopped me in my tracks. We may have said much to each other during our conversation that day, but all I heard were the words, "It doesn't matter." And it was then, and only then, that I realized there is a big difference between taking care of ourselves by treating our bodies like the temples of God that they are and obsessing about our health, weight, and clothing. It was then, and only then, that I realized how enslaved I was to the obsessing. Yes, it was then, and only then, that I realized my innocent, and even healthy, desire to take good care of myself and look my best had turned into an addiction.

As soon as the Lord convicted me of the bigness of my "little" problem, I knew I needed to do something about it. Yes, His conviction immediately called me to action, and this call-to-action began the same way all the previous calls did: by me running to God in prayer and in the Sacraments. As I, little by little, worked through my "little" addiction in these ways I eventually took the next step by paying more attention to what I was thinking about during the actual moment of heavy temptation to overly obsess and buy more stuff. Once this temptation to obsess and shop showed up, I "counterattacked" by taking a deep breath and reminding myself of that man's afflicting words. "It doesn't matter," I would tell myself as the temptation to fall into old habits reared its ugly head. "It doesn't matter," I would tell myself as I stared into my closet wondering what I should wear for the day. "It doesn't matter," I would tell myself as I felt the urge to buy just one more pair of shoes or just one more handbag. "It doesn't matter," I would tell myself when my less than perfect hair style wanted to send me into a panic about how I didn't measure up with the world around me. Then I would follow up all those "It doesn't matter's" with a little statement about what did matter: Christ. "Just put on Christ," I would tell myself over and over again. "Just put on Christ. All that really matters is that you put on Christ. Be less concerned with others seeing your trendy outfits on the outside and more concerned with others seeing the saint living on the inside. That's right, be less concerned with others seeing how 'good' you look and more concerned with others seeing the good that lives in you. Just put on Christ, Julia. Just put on Christ. The rest doesn't matter."

And so, as the months passed and I continued this work to shed myself of this "old self" that was overly concerned with my appearance and put on the "new self" that was only concerned with putting on Christ, the temptations, torment, and agonizing self-mental abuse slowly began to lessen. Yes, the addiction slowly began to lose its grip. As it did, I found myself getting dressed for the day by putting on whatever I saw first. (Which, by the way, was a miracle in and of itself.) As it did, I found myself avoiding the monthly shopping trips to pick up that "one" little thing that was always missing from my wardrobe. (Yes, another miracle.) As it did, I found myself unsubscribing to all the fashion magazines, catalogues, and mass market emails I was receiving from my favorite stores alerting me, day in and day out, about every sale I "just couldn't miss." As it did, I found myself caring less and less about what hair style was "in" and about which one would look "perfect" on me. Yes, as it did, I found myself becoming more and more concerned about others seeing the saint living inside and less and less concerned about them seeing the "stuff" on the outside trying to cover the sinner up.

So, though I'll admit there are still days when this "old self" wants to reappear and send me into a panic by tormenting me about how I look and about what I have (or don't have) to wear, I am far from being that person whose closet "owned" her. Now, it's pretty easy for me to separate the lies from the truth. Yeah, now, it's pretty easy for me to see the person I really am; the person God created; the person God loves unconditionally; the person whose true, inner beauty will never fade away. And, you see, when this image is clear, - when I am clear about who I am as a child of God - then no "monster," no matter how big and scary it is, can touch me. And you know what that makes me? FREE!

Prayer

Thank you, Lord, for setting me free from the monster living in my closet. May I "Put on Christ," each and every day, never again doubting my true, - and only

important - identity; my identity as your beloved child.
I love you! I thank you! I praise you!

Read, Think, Pray: Proverbs 31:30

REFLECTION #107

BLINDING LIGHT

9/6/2014

Darkness can't survive in the light. Period. If we want out of the darkness, if we want set free from the lies around us that are tormenting us and keeping us from being the people God created us to be, then we need to turn on the light. In fact, we need to not only turn it on, we need to make sure it stays on. For those of us living in the darkness, though, this is always easier said than done. Why? Because after being in the dark for an extended period of time, the light, simply put, is blinding.

I can painfully remember what it was like living in the dark and being blinded by the light. At that time in my life, light seemed like the enemy, and the people God sent to me as "light-bearers" were the very people who bothered me the most. In hindsight, I'm now grateful for all those people, but at the time all I really wanted to say to them was, "You've got some nerve saying that to me! Who do you think you are? I didn't ask you for your opinion! I'm fine, thank you very much and don't need, or want, your two cents!" Or, if I wasn't in the mood to give them an angry, defensive response like this, I would just try my best to ignore them or cut them out of my life for good. So, yeah, I know what it feels like to be blinded by the light. I know how hard it is to hear words of truth. I know how painful it is to admit that "the annoying person who just had the nerve to say that to me" is actually right.

Well, in an "ironic" turn of events, (and, no, I don't really think it's irony) I just had the opportunity to be on the other side of this situation. Yeah,

I, a past slave of the darkness, just had the opportunity to experience for myself what if feels like to be on the other end of this light-bearing spectrum. And you know what I discovered? I discovered that it's just as painful and uncomfortable on this side! Yeah, I discovered that, as uncomfortable as it is hearing the truth, it's just as uncomfortable being the one to say it. This experience has reminded me that the truth really does hurt and the light really is blinding. (And the death-stare I received after shedding a little light into someone's darkened world just proved that to me!)

Look, I think there are times in all of our lives when the darkness creeps in, and we need reminded of the light. So, yeah, sometimes we are on the giving end of this light-bearing and sometimes we are on the receiving end, but, regardless of the position we are in, one thing is for sure: the unpleasant situations, hate-filled words of defense, death-stares, and silent-treatments could really just be proof that the light has been seen and that the darkness has been stirred up as a result. And, well, as I see it, this isn't something to run away scared from, to fight against, or to get mad about. It, instead, is just another reason to praise God. Why? Because seeing the light (even if it's blinding at first) is the first step to living in it.

> "Seeing the light (even if it's blinding at first) is the first step to living in it."

Prayer

Give me the courage to be the voice of truth to others when you are asking me to be, Lord. Give me the wisdom to know what to say, how to say it, when to say it, and when, of course, to say nothing and just keep praying. May I be an authentic Christian worthy of being persecuted for love of you, and, when met with resistance, may I remember that the darkness doesn't like the light and that an emotional reaction to it may just be a sign of a soul waking up and turning to you. Help me also, Lord, to have the humility to hear and accept the truth when you send others into my life to

> *reveal it to me. May I thank them, and you, for showing*
> *me the light and for helping me to live in it. May I*
> *walk always as your child; a child of the light!*
> *I love you! I thank you! I praise you!*

Read, Think, Pray: Ephesians 5:6-14

REFLECTION #108

THE JOURNEY FORWARD

9/14/2014

The obstacles in my life have increased drastically as I continue this process of making a "career" change. At this point, I have no doubt this is a change that God Himself has prompted me to make, but I'm still finding the task of actually leaving one job and beginning another slow and painful. The transition has been filled with resistance and has required lots of additional work on my end, both on paper and in me personally. Still, I'm certain that, in the end, it will all be worthwhile because I know (as well as anyone can know) that this is God's will for my life right now and that I'm on the right track. I must say, though, the resistance and obstacles I'm meeting on my way to get to where I'm going are real, and the temptation to quit is real, too. Yep, I'm back to that point again. I'm back to being tempted to quit. I'm back to being tempted to stop moving forward. Even worse, I'm back to being tempted to turn around.

Though it's hard for me to admit that I'm still struggling with some of the same issues I probably should have mastered by now, I picked up my pen today to remind myself of the truth. And the truth is, obstacles exist, and we shouldn't let them stop us. The truth is, obstacles exist, and sometimes we just need to take the extra time and go around. The truth is, obstacles exist, and they're not always a sign we're doing something wrong. The truth is, obstacles exist, and they're often a sign we're doing something right.

So, I can't let myself believe any of the lies swarming around my head right now in the midst of this temptation to quit. I can't let myself believe there's no way around, the complexity is too complex, or the work is too hard. I can't let myself believe I'll never make it to the end, and the pain will never be worth it. I can't let myself believe I'm better off quitting and turning around. No, what I need to do is simple. I need to remind myself of the truth. And the truth is, the journey forward is the only one that is ever worth taking; obstacles included.

Prayer

Thank you, Lord, for showing me the way through the obstacles in my life. May I be quick to move forward and slow to give up even when the resistance is heavy; even when the obstacles seem insurmountable. May I persist as long as necessary patiently, lovingly, and calmly moving around the roadblocks trying to keep me from you. I know, Lord, that nothing is more important than growing and moving towards you, so let nothing stand in my way of doing this. May I persevere, trusting not in my own strength, but in yours to get me through. I love you! I thank you! I praise you!

Read, Think, Pray: 1 Corinthians 10:13

REFLECTION #109

LETTING GO

9/16/2014

On paper, these last few weeks seem like steps back. My life has gotten really messy. My passions have, once again, become disordered. My good qualities of being driven, goal-orientated, highly motivated, hard working, and organized have, once again, taken over and turned into an obsession. Although I've been aware of the slippery slope I've been on, I haven't been able to flip the "off" switch. I haven't been able to change

195

the direction I've been heading. In fact, the more I let myself become consumed by the over-doing, the harder it has been for me *not* to over-do. And, well, after having an "all work, no play" attitude for months now, I, not surprisingly, crashed.

Yes, today everything came to a head. Today I'm at the point where I'm physically feeling the effects of the mental stress I've been putting myself under. Yes, today I officially crashed and suffered the effects of textbook "burnout." Now, I'm not going to sit here and play the "How did I let this happen?" game. I mean, what good would that do anyway? No, it's not worth it. This physical reaction is nothing more than a natural response to the unnatural (i.e. high stress) mental state I've been in. So, as I see it, there's no reason to ask, "How?" The only question really worth asking is, "What can I learn?"

As always, this experience has taught me much. First of all, it has proven to me that God is at work in my life and is answering my prayers. How so? Well, I've been asking God to make me a saint and overcoming these tendencies to over-do everything is obviously one of the changes that needs to happen in me (perhaps one of the biggest changes) in order for me to become one, so coming face-to-face with the weight of these not-so-saintly control issues is just part of the process of God freeing me from them. Yes, He is answering my prayers by shedding me of my old self and by putting on the new self, (Ephesians 4:22-24) and the pain I'm feeling throughout this process is proof. Secondly, this experience has reminded me how dependent I am upon God. (Apparently I need reminded of this often!) How so? Well, a fall is always humbling, and this humility has made it painfully clear that, in spite of my best efforts, I can't do all of this on my own. In fact, this humility has made it painfully clear that, in spite of my best efforts, I can't do *any* of this on my own!

So, though I hate that it seems like the best way for God to get my attention is for me to learn the hard way, I'm now grateful for this stressed out part of my journey (and for the crash that came at the end of it) because this situation has proven to me that, in my hands, everything gets messier than it needs to be. Now that I see how awful things get when I try to do them on my own, in my own way, and in my own time, I can happily let go and give the control back to God. (I don't know why I ever tried to take it back to begin with!)

Prayer

Be with me, Lord, as I move forward. Help
me to breathe and trust in you and in the process.
Help me to let go and let you do the work in me. I'm
trying too hard, Lord. Show me what I'm missing.
Fill me with your peace and joy. Shower me with
your love and mercy. Teach me how to let go.
I love you! I thank you! I praise you!

Read, Think, Pray: Exodus 18:17-23

REFLECTION #110

EXPOSED

9/17/2014

Earlier today, in a moment of deep emotional pain, I headed to the only place I knew could give me any sort of comfort: church. After receiving the Lord's mercy in the Sacrament of Reconciliation, I found a spot in a pew towards the front, knelt down in prayer, and locked my eyes on the crucifix. As I did, thoughts filled my mind.

"I am weak," I told Jesus. "I am angry, hurt, upset, and disappointed. I feel abused, neglected, and taken advantage of, and I'm mad at myself for letting it get this far. I'm vulnerable. My walls are down."

"My Lord, I'm constantly apologizing to you and to others for the ways I've failed, and, in so doing, I'm living a life completely exposed. It's frightening! This exposure makes me feel as though I'm stretched out hanging on my own cross with all my defenses down. No, my hurts haven't been physical, but I emotionally feel crucified by the words and actions of others. I can feel their words piercing my hands and feet. I can feel their actions puncturing my heart. Yet, in this moment of deep pain I find you, and I know I'm not alone. I know it is not in vain. I know there is great power in the cross and that I must trust in this power."

"I want so badly, my Lord, to be like you, and in your moment of deep pain and vulnerability, in your moment of humiliating exposure, you chose forgiveness. You chose love. You begged our Father to have mercy on those very people who were hurting you. Well, I want to choose these same things, so I echo your words. 'Father, forgive them, they know not what they do'" (Luke 23:34).

"Though in my weakness I want justice, Lord, I accept and pick up my cross knowing it is only hurting me to harbor a grudge; knowing it is only hurting me to hold on to the pain. I let it go, Lord. I forgive. I love them as you love them. I love them as you love me."

"I have been beaten and scourged, Lord. I am bruised and battered, but I thank you for it. Yes, I thank you for the cross. I thank you for pouring your healing grace into my heart and for helping me unite my suffering - my tiny, incomparable suffering - to yours. I know, Lord, that your love is greater than any evil in this world and that forgiveness is the greatest act of love I can show, so I forgive. Yes, Lord, I forgive. Help me to do so again and again and again...even when it hurts."

Prayer

Help me to trust in the power of the cross, Lord, for I know there is no resurrection without it. Fill me with the joy that comes from carrying the cross for you, and grant me the peace, healing, and freedom that comes through forgiveness. Increase my love for you, Lord, by increasing the love I have for those who have hurt me. I love you! I thank you! I praise you!

Read, Think, Pray: Luke 23:33-34

REFLECTION #111

UNICORNS

9/21/2014

I love children! I love their stories. I love their emotional roller coasters. I love their honesty. Children have a way of calming me down when I'm stressed, a way of comforting me when I'm discouraged, a way of filling me with joy when I'm feeling sorrowful. Yes, children help me make sense of the confusion. They show me what life is really about and remind me how to have fun. They teach me how to love more perfectly. They help me keep my priorities straight. They remind me what is simple and what is true, and, as I work through this stressful time in my life right now, I need all the reminders I can get.

I got such a reminder here recently when one of my young nephews told me, completely out of nowhere and very matter-of-factly I might add, "You know, Aunt Julia, if God wanted to, He could make a unicorn." I immediately responded with a, "Yes, of course He could!" but as we drove away I thought more about my response. Did I really believe it, I wondered? Did I really believe that if He wanted to, God could make a unicorn?

After some honest reflecting I realized there was much about my life I didn't believe anymore. I realized there was much about my life I had given up on. I realized I had lots of "unicorns;" lots of things that I thought were, although nice ideas, just make-believe and unattainable. Then I had a reality check. How could I place my problems in a box marked "unsolvable" when my God is the God of it all; the One and only; the Creator of heaven and earth? Sure, it's true that God's Will is supreme, but who am I to decide what His will is and what it isn't? Who am I to assume that what is impossible to me is impossible to Him? Who am I to tell God He can't make a unicorn?

So, as it turns out, my nephew was right that day. Yes, through his one, off-the-wall statement, I was reminded that childlike trust doesn't put limits on God. I was reminded that childlike trust doesn't question God's abilities. I was reminded that childlike trust doesn't doubt God's plan. I was reminded that childlike trust knows that, without a doubt, if God wanted

"Childlike trust knows that, if God wanted to, He could make a unicorn"

to, He could make a unicorn. With that being said, I'm done thinking so small. Yeah, I'm done putting my adult-like limits on God.

Prayer

Increase my trust in you, my God! May I have the faith and trust of a child knowing that you are in complete control and that nothing is off limits for you. Help me to believe in you and in your limitless power. May I always remember that with you, all things really are possible. Yes, even unicorns. I love you! I thank you! I praise you!

Read, Think, Pray: Jeremiah 17:7-8

REFLECTION #112

LEAVES FROM HEAVEN

9/28/2014

"I want to give God a message...Thank You!" - These were the words of my 4-year-old nephew today (yes, the same "God could make a unicorn" nephew) after we witnessed the somewhat supernatural sight of a beautiful fall day. Oh, who am I kidding? It wasn't a *somewhat* supernatural sight, it *was* a supernatural one! There is no other way to describe what he and I, and a few of my other family members, saw. I mean, we have all seen leaves falling from trees before, but today's witnessing of this ordinary fall event was anything but ordinary because today's leaves weren't falling from just any tree, they were falling from a tree in heaven!

Look, I know how hard this little story is going to be to believe, but there is no other way to explain what I saw. Though it would be natural to doubt what I'm telling you here, (after all, I, too, doubted at first, and I was the one seeing it) I assure you, I'm not making this up. So, believe it or not, here's what happened.

Today started out as an ordinary fall Sunday at my parents' house. (We are there most Sundays with the rest of my family.) But as we sat outside enjoying the beautiful fall weather, the day quickly became extraordinary; one that I will never forget.

As a few of us sat outside in the backyard, we slowly began to notice some leaves blowing all around us. This, we knew, was somewhat odd because there are no trees at my parents' house that could account for the amount or type of leaves we were seeing. So, as the "strange" leaves continued to fall, we eventually started asking some questions. "Where are these leaves coming from?" we wondered as we searched for their source by tracing their direction backwards. It was then that, much to our surprise, (and, unfortunately, our disbelief) our eyes were drawn heavenward, and we saw what none of us were expecting to see: leaves raining down from an opening in the clouds above.

Once we realized where the leaves were coming from, we, the adults witnessing the event, immediately tried to come up with some sort of earthly explanation. (Yes, we were at first unbelieving.) As we struggled to come up with some rational reasoning, I finally asked one of the kids to go in and get their dad; my older brother, the science teacher. I thought for sure he would know what was going on, but after showing him what we were looking at, he, too, stared in wonder. After thinking about it for awhile, he looked at us, shrugged his shoulders, and said "I don't know." (He is a man of few words.) As we continued to rack our brains, one of the kids (yes, my 4-year-old nephew) finally chimed in. He, too, saw what we were looking at, but he wasn't desperately searching for answers like we were. No, he understood exactly what was happening without having to know "how" it was taking place. He knew in the first moment he saw it what our adult-like doubts wouldn't let us believe: the leaves were falling from a tree in heaven.

It took us a little while, but we all eventually came to the same conclusion that, at first glance, my nephew had come to. As we sat in amazement staring up at the leaves raining down from the clouds above, his wise, childlike response said more than any of us ever could.

"I want to give God a message," he said with great joy.

"What message is that?" I asked him.

"Thank You!"

And so, my God, I would like to take this time to repeat the words of my nephew. Yes, I, too, want to give you a message. I, too, want to tell you with great joy and complete amazement, "Thank You!" You really are who you say you are, aren't you?

Prayer

Thank you, Lord, for the gift of life, for the wonder that surrounds us, and for the beauty of the seasons. Thank you, too, for the children in my life and for the constant lessons you teach me through them. I am now convinced that you don't give us children so that we can teach them, you give us children so that they can teach us. So, please make me more like the children in my life. Show me how to trust more like them. I love you! I thank you! I praise you!

Read, Think, Pray: John 20:24-29

REFLECTION #113

REPAIRMEN

9/29/2014

In case you haven't noticed, I've recently found my way out of a spiritual battle. I'm not sure my writing has been able to capture the intensity of the battle I was just in, but I assure you, I've been at war. It looks like I'm on the other side of it now. Yeah, it looks like there's been a cease-fire, but I'm still not ready to move on. No, I'm still not ready to put this little battle in the "finished and over-with" box. I don't want this time in the darkness to go to waste. I don't want this suffering to be in vain. I want to learn everything I can from it so that it bears great fruit, and that's why I'm not walking away from it just yet. Yeah, that's why I'm spending some time today taking another look at the struggle.

In order to learn everything I can from what I just went through, I've got to ask myself a follow-up question: *"Was my battle plan the best it could have been?"* Well, thankfully, my strategy this time was good enough to get me through the fight victoriously. What was this strategy? Prayer, Mass, Reconciliation, and Fasting. Yes, in the midst of the struggle I didn't let go of God and run away, I held on tighter and ran closer. I did this by remaining faithful to my habits of prayer, Mass, and Reconciliation even though they weren't producing the same "feel good" feelings they once had; even though they weren't really giving me any "relief." I held on to my faith knowing that God was with me even though I couldn't feel Him; knowing that He was carrying me through the struggle even though it felt like He had abandoned me. Towards the end of the battle I remembered I had another weapon I hadn't yet taking advantage of: fasting. (I always "forget" about fasting until things really get ugly. Fasting is hard!) But, once I remembered it, this spiritual weapon, like all the others, gave me another advantage to come out on top. It sent me back into the battle armed and ready to fight.

Looking back, there's no doubt this strategy is the foundational battle plan I will always need, but I suspect the war I'm in is far from over and that future battles are only going to get more intense, so I'm wondering if there is anything else I can do to help myself in a fight. Yes, I'm wondering if there are any other resources at my disposal that I can take advantage of in the midst of a battle. This wondering got me asking myself another question: *"Is there anything <u>anyone</u> <u>else</u> can do to help me? Is there anything <u>anyone</u> <u>else</u> can do to help ease the pain?"* Well, after some prayerful reflecting, I came up with two answers: "Yes" and "No."

The "No" part of this answer is pretty simple. I mean, as loved ones in other people's lives it's natural to want to "fix" all their problems. It's natural to want to take away the pain. It's natural to want to help, but the truth is, none of us can take away the pain our loved ones sometimes feel. For the most part, we all need to work through our problems on our own and in our own time. We need others for support, sure, but the "fixing" can't come from outside of us. No, the "fixing" has to come from within. The "fixing" has to come from God. The pain of spiritual warfare is something we need to work through, something we need to learn from, something we need to feel, experience, and come to understand because this is how we learn, this is how we grow, and this is how we are set free. So, yes, the first part of the answer to this question is "No." No, there isn't really anything *anyone else* can do to take away the pain of the fight. It's something we have to work through with God.

The "Yes" part of this answer is pretty simple, though, too. I mean, although it's true that God is the one doing all the "fixing," He has put us here together to live in communion with one another, to lighten each other's loads, and to bear each other's burdens, so, yes, we can, most certainly, help others in their fight. We must remember, though, that the help we need from others (and the help others need from us) never comes in the form of "fixing." No, "fixing" is never what we need. In fact, "fixing" usually only makes things worse and prolongs the situation. What we need instead is what we always need: love. We need those around us to love us through the good times and the bad. We need a listening ear, a shoulder to cry on, a hand to hold. We need companionship. We need to know we're not alone. We need encouragement to persevere in faith. We need some sort of response, but usually not advice. In short, we need friends, not repairmen.

So, back to my battle plan, back to my strategy. Knowing what I know now, *"is there anything <u>anyone</u> else can do to help me in the midst of a battle?"* Well, "Yes" and "No." Yes, they can help by loving me through it. (And this help is no small thing!) But, no, they can't help by "fixing" it. With that being said, the next time I find myself in the midst of a battle, I will do exactly what I did this time, but with one minor addition: I will seek out more friends and less repairmen.

Prayer

May I remember what it's like to be at war, Lord, so that I'm patient, kind, and understanding when others find themselves in one. May I be your healing presence to those who find themselves in a similar situation. May I come from a place of understanding, not of a place of fixing. May I be a friend, not a repairman. I love you! I thank you! I praise you!

Read, Think, Pray: Galatians 6:1-5

THE GRACIOUS GIVER

10/6/2014

For the past few weeks, a common theme has been coming up in my life: love. In particular, God's love for us.

Though I, myself, struggled for years to let go of my guilt and accept God's love and mercy, this father-daughter love I now share with Him is so real, so all-encompassing, so true that I often forget what it's like to live without it. Yeah, I often forget what it's like to live in the darkness filled with the hurt and pain. Recently, however, I was reminded of how real that pain is when I came face-to-face with someone who, like me for so many years, was seeing God as a God of judgment and condemnation instead of seeing Him as the God He really is; a God of love and mercy. As I watched the darkness that I, too, was once consumed by consume this other person, I found myself in complete awe at God's work in my life. I then asked Him a simple question, "Why me? Why am I out of the darkness, and they are still in it? Why is it so easy for me to see when for others it seems that all their trying is in vain? Why am I here, and they are there? Why me?"

"My daughter," I "heard" God call out in the midst of my questioning, "remember my words: 'to everyone who has, more will be given'" (Matthew 25:29).

"OK," I answered, "but what exactly does that mean? This has never made much sense to me. Please, help it make sense."

"Love me," He answered back. "Invite me into your life. Call on me, and let me be your Father. Let me save you. Then you will be free to receive all it is I want to give you. My child, those who have are always given more because they are always open to receiving more, and they are always open to receiving more for one reason: they let themselves be forgiven."

And, well, with that being said, I guess I need to be less concerned with *why* I have been chosen and more concerned with *what* I'm going to do about it, don't I?

Prayer

I love you, my Lord! I love you in a way that I didn't know was possible. I love you in a way that no human love could ever compare; in a way that no human words could ever describe. I miss you, Lord, when I'm away from you; when my pride and arrogance pull me away. You are my God, my loving Father, the author of my life. You know me, all of me, and you love me, all of me. Your arms give me comfort. Your presence fills me with peace. Your love makes me whole. May my heart always be open to receiving your love, and may my life always remind others that this unconditional love is being poured out on them, too. I love you! I thank you! I praise you!

Read, Think, Pray: John 14:22-23

REFLECTION #115

FRUITS OF PRAYER

10/8/2014

I was recently asked the question, *"What has the Father given to you through prayer?"* Well, the answers, they seem, are as numerous as the stars in the sky, but the first thought that popped in my head (and is still stirring in my soul) was, "the ability to pray."

I'm certain as children we know how to pray innately. (Not our memorized, vocal prayers, of course, but praying in a sense of turning our hearts towards God.) It seems, however, (at least for me) that as we grow and slowly stop praying in this way, we somehow "forget" how to do it. (And, as my younger brother once pointed out, "Once you forget it, you'll never remember it.") In any event, I found it incredibly difficult as an adult to make prayer a part of my life. It took many years of "practicing" before I ever felt comfortable with it. To be honest, in the beginning vocal prayers seemed boring, meditative prayers seemed confusing, and contemplative prayers seemed impossible. As with anything, though, we get better by practicing, and the more I "practiced" praying, the "easier" it became.

I'm sure God doesn't really care how we pray. Yeah, I'm sure He takes even our most simple efforts at doing so and increases them ten-fold. I'm sure He is less concerned with the *whats* and *hows* of prayer and more concerned with just being with us. I'm also sure, however, that the more we spend time with God, the easier it is to spend more time with Him. After all, that is how all healthy relationships work.

The more we spend time with God, the easier it is to spend more time with Him."

So, as I have slowly grown in my relationship with God over the years, praying, (i.e. conversing with Him, spending time with Him, and seeing Him at work in my life and in the lives of those around me) has become more "natural." I no longer have to "try" like I first did, and that is why one of the biggest fruits of my prayer is, simply put, "learning how to pray."

So, yeah, my answer to this question is simple. *"What has the Father given to me through prayer?"*: the ability to pray!

Prayer

*I need you in my life, Lord. I am nothing without you.
I can do nothing without you. Life is nothing without you.
And prayer has taught me this. Thank you for calling me to
you each and every day. Thank you for welcoming me into your
presence day in and day out. Thank you for allowing me to take
rest in your arms. Thank you for revealing yourself to me in our
time together. In all ways, Lord, teach me to pray!
I love you! I thank you! I praise you!*

Read, Think, Pray: Luke 11:1-13

Julia Monnin

REFLECTION #116

HONEST CONVERSATION

10/9/2014

I have a tendency to over-complicate things. Perhaps I've mentioned that before. (In fact, I'm sure I've mentioned that before!) Regardless, this little "trait" of mine likes to show up in all areas of my life. Yes, even in my spiritual life. How so? Well, in the beginning of my spiritual journey I over-complicated my prayer. (I wonder now how that is even possible. I mean, prayer is just talking to God, just recognizing each other's presence, just spending time together. There's no "right" or "wrong" way to do it, so how could I complicate it? Well, impossible as it may seem, I did!) Yes, I slowly made my prayer more and more "adult-like" and less and less "child-like" by convincing myself that it made sense to order my prayer just like I order everything else. I thought things like, "From this time to this time, I'll say this chaplet. For this 15 minutes, I'll recite this devotional stack of prayers. At this time, I'll pray for those people." As I grew spiritually, though, I soon realized that my most fruitful times in prayer were the times I resisted the temptation to "control" it and instead let it be guided by the Spirit. (I know...Who knew, right?)

After spending more time than I should have making my prayer "harder" than it needed to be, I finally realized that it's our raw, honest, childlike prayers that are often the most heartfelt. These are the times in prayer when we don't "sugar-coat" things; the times we just tell God like it is. For me personally these raw, honest, childlike prayers happen most naturally when I first wake up in the morning. It's at these times, in the first moments of my day, that I'm not quite "with it" enough to be able to string together beautifully crafted sentences, so I just talk. I just tell God whatever comes to mind and remain still enough so that I can "hear" His response. And you know what I've found by doing this? I've found that prayer like this is not only OK, it's really all God wants from us. Yeah, I've found that all He really wants from us is honest conversation.

Don't get me wrong here. I love the vocal and devotional prayers of the Church. I mean, in no other place in the world will you find such rich, beautiful prayers. (And these prayers really *are* the foundation of our

208

spiritual lives.) But I'm learning there is much more to our spiritual-selves than just memorizing and reciting someone else's words. Yeah, there is just something different about praying from a "script" and talking to God in an honest, open-hearted way. Again, don't get me wrong! I love the Church and all of Her rich prayers! I say lots of chaplets, rosaries, and novenas and love praying in this way, but, as I've heard it said before, "there is a vast difference between saying prayers and praying," and I'm learning we would be wise to learn what that difference is. After all, sometimes it's more than OK to go to the store, buy a greeting card for someone, and have it capture what it is you want to say to them, but most of the time it's just a few words from our heart jotted down on a scrap piece of paper that would really mean the most. Why would it be any different with God?

Prayer

Give me the wisdom, Lord, to know which type of prayer my heart is longing for and the humility to allow myself to be guided there. May I never be afraid of "being real" with you. May I never feel like I have to filter myself when it comes to you. May I never feel like my prayer has to be "ordered." Help me to trust in your constant, loving, and understanding presence. Help me to be open with you at all times and never try to hide or keep anything from you. Lead all our conversations, Lord, and make them honest ones. I love you! I thank you! I praise you!

Read, Think, Pray: Philippians 4:6-7

REFLECTION #117

DETAILED PLANNING

10/14/2014

I'm at a crossroads in my life. I'm in a period of great change. (Great as in "big" and "a lot," but great as in "awesome" and "wonderful," too.) As with all change, I'm finding the process uncomfortable. You see, I know

what I'm doing where I'm at now. There are systems and procedures and plans, and I like systems and procedures and plans. Yes, I like a well thought-out, highly-structured, detailed, organized plan. I don't know why. I guess a plan makes me feel like I have some sort of control over the outcome, and, even though I know it's a false-sense of control, I still like to have a plan. Yeah, I like a "Plan A" and a "Plan B" and a "Plan C" and a "Best-Case Scenario Plan" and a "Worst-Case Scenario Plan" and a "Troubleshooting Plan" because, as you can clearly see, I am a planner! To be honest, the thought of not planning makes my skin crawl.

As I move through this period of great change, though, I'm learning that, as much as I want to and as much as I try to, things at this point are just too unknown for me to actually plan anything. As you can imagine, this has been sending me into panic-mode on a somewhat regular basis. Today, however, it seems I've had some sort of breakthrough. Yes, today it seems God has shed some light on a solution to these endless high-stress days that are beginning to consume me. This solution came after I found myself in "unscheduled" prayer after a melt-down.

"What's going on?" I asked God after realizing the problem had to be with me. "What do I still need to let go of? What am I still holding on to? What am I still trying to control?"

"Your plan," He quickly responded. "Give up your plan and receive mine. I will give you direction along the way, just look for the open doors, and trust that I will give you the grace you need to walk through them. Proceed whole-heartedly but with peace. Proceed calmly, sure of my presence and guidance, and know that I am with you always. You ask me, my child, what you are still holding on to, but the answer is right in front of you. You are still holding on to your plan. Give up your plan and receive mine."

And, so, I can no longer deny what's staring me in the face. I have, as God so lovingly (and directly) pointed out, been holding on to my plan. In fact, I'm now convinced it's the death grip I've had on it that's been the very thing strangling me these past few months. As always, I'm grateful for God's redirection because, as always, I've learned much from it. I've learned that the abundant life (John 10:10) He calls us to isn't one with detailed instructions. I've learned that this abundant life requires a certain level of trust; a level that doesn't need to see the entire picture; a level that willingly accepts the minute-by-minute game plan disclosures, constant reroutes, and endless detours; a level that says "Yes" without knowing how it's all going to work out. Most importantly, I've learned that even if the destination of this abundant life is clear, the journey there can't be planned. And, well, for a planner like me, this is a life-changing lesson; a life-changing lesson that can only lead to one thing: FREEDOM!

"Even if the destination of this 'abundant life' is clear, the journey there can't be planned."

Prayer

I'm tired of driving, Lord. Attempting to drive is stressing me out and making me do stupid things, so I'm giving up control. Yes, I'm turning everything back over to you. Here, take the keys. You drive! I don't need to know where you're taking me. I don't need to know how we're getting there. I don't need to know when we'll arrive. Just tell me what you need me to do along the way. The rest, as I now know for sure, is up to you. I love you! I thank you! I praise you!

Read, Think, Pray: Proverbs 19:21

REFLECTION #118

TIME THIEVES

10/15/2014

"My time is more valuable than my money." - I told my sister this a few weeks ago, and I meant it. Yeah, my time *is* more valuable than my money. And you know what? Just like money, it's always at risk of being stolen. Yes, "time thieves" are real, and they're way more dangerous and way more prevalent than any other kind of thief. They break into

our schedules daily without so much of a trace eating up 20 minutes here and 20 minutes there, and, if we're not careful, they make us look back and wonder, "Where did the day go?" Or, worse yet, "Where did my life go?"

Yes, time thieves exist, and I have, for some time now, been very aware of their presence. In fact, I've been so aware of them that, until today, I would have told you I had a really good handle on them. Yep, until today, I would have told you I had outsmarted the majority of them, but I just realized I have some more work to do. Yeah, I just realized there are still many I have not yet conquered. One of them, in particular, is the time thief of "meaningless conversations."

I became aware of this one after reading a short bio* on St. Teresa of Avila that said that before her major conversion she "wasted time every day in long, foolish conversations." This little blurb quickly made me realize that I, too, have been the victim of this same thief. And, well, now that I know it, I'll be more on the lookout. Yeah, now that I know it, I'll be better on guard. After all, there really *are* some conversations that are just nothing but "long and foolish," - conversations that are just nothing but "meaningless" - and I don't want to waste any more of my time having them. Why? Because I really do believe my time is more valuable than my money. I just need to start acting like it.

Prayer

Time is a gift, Lord, and I want to use it more wisely.
So, when I'm tempted to waste time online or in front of the television or on my phone, remind me of the many times I've made the excuse not to do something because I didn't think I had time. When I'm tempted to gossip, remind me of my own sinfulness. When I'm tempted to listen to gossip without trying to redirect it, remind me that I'm not only accountable for what I do but for what I fail to do. Teach me how to be a better steward of your great gift of time, Lord. Come into my life, and help me make the most out of each moment.
I love you! I thank you! I praise you!

Read, Think, Pray: Ephesians 5:15-17

* I read this bio on the Cantcha, Inc. *iMissal*™ app in the *Saint A Day* section on 10/15/2014.

212

MAKING ROOM

10/15/2014

Have you ever met someone who is unwilling to get rid of anything from the past? Over time the old mixes with the new, clutter is everywhere, and all that's left are piles of unneeded stuff. Well, it's becoming clear to me that God doesn't let our souls fill up with junk the same way we sometimes let our homes. In fact, it's becoming clear to me that the only way we can have room for the new He wants to give us is by letting go of some of the old that has already served its purpose. Yeah, it's becoming clear; crystal clear. In order to receive, we have to give, and by give I mean "let go."

Letting go can be scary, though. I mean, the future is always unknown and the unknown can be frightening, but, whether we want it to or not, life is always moving forward. There is no pause or rewind button. We can't stop time where it's at or make it go backwards. Do you ever wonder, then, why so many of us try?

I guess for some of us our lives now (or our lives "back then") could seem so '"good" that we have a hard time imagining the future being any better. If this is the case, maybe we fear letting go of the old because we mistakenly believe that since life can't possibly get any better, then it's going to get worse. But this, of course, isn't true. I mean, sure it's true that the future is always different, but different

"Different doesn't have to mean bad. Different can actually mean better."

doesn't have to mean "bad." After all, God always wants to give us more. He always has greater things in store. He always wants the future to be more fulfilling, so different can actually mean "better." And you know what? I think I'm finally ready to receive this "better."

213

Yes, for month's now, God has been encouraging me to let go. He's been encouraging me to take the next step, telling me things like, "You think that was good? Just wait until you see what I give you next! I have things in store for you beyond your wildest imagination. Let that stuff go, and I'll show you." And, well, it took me awhile, but I'm finally here. Yeah, I'm finally ready to respond to His invitation, so here goes...

"I'm letting go, Lord. I'm making room. Show me what it is you want to give me next."

Prayer

It's hard to start a new phase, Lord. It's hard to begin a new chapter. I mean, just when I think I'm figuring one out, you invite me to move into another one, but I trust you. Yes, I'm ready to move on. Help me, therefore, to turn the page. Help me to let go. Help me to make room so that I can receive the new you want to give me. I love you! I thank you! I praise you!

Read, Think, Pray: Ecclesiastes 7:10

...THE BEGINNING OF ANOTHER

THE INNER DESIRE

10/16/2014

Over a year ago I felt an inner desire to write; to start a journal. The words I wrote in this journal were just my thoughts on paper, nothing more. I wasn't writing them for anyone else. They were meant for just me and God. A few months ago, however, I felt an inner desire to not only write but to share. Sharing my writing, though, has never been part of my plan. No, I have never thought my words would mean anything to anyone else, but it's becoming more and more clear that God's plans are different than my own. Yes, the doors seem to be opening all around me to share my writing, and, I must say, it's scary to even consider! I mean, what will people think? Who am I to do this? What can I say that hasn't already been said a million times before by millions of other people? Still, though the fears about sharing are real, the desire to share is real, too, and, try as I may, I simply cannot ignore it any longer. I can't help but think that if even one person is helped by reading my journal, then it will be worth sharing. I also can't help but think that this inner desire to share is, in fact, coming from God. I mean, where else would it be coming from? It certainly isn't coming from me! No, I have been quite happy with my little life and career. I have been quite happy hanging out in my nice little comfort zone. To be honest, this whole "mission" thing has turned my life upside down!

Yes, I'll admit it. I have been content sitting in the background. I have been content having "my thing" and letting others have "their thing." In fact, "You do your thing, I'll do my thing, and we'll all be happy," was kind of becoming my motto, but something inside tells me this isn't the life I'm called to live. Yeah, something inside tells me this "writing thing" is a huge part of why I'm here, and I can't just keep ignoring the feeling. I can't just keep pretending like I'm not seeing all the people around me struggling. I can't just keep looking past those people searching for more who are lost on their way when I know God has given me the knowledge and the ability to help. Still, I've come a long way from the girl who would do anything to be the center of attention, so the thought of making my private journal public goes against everything in me. Even so, faith tells me the reason this desire to share won't go away is because doing so is part of why I'm here. I guess time will tell if I'm right. In the meantime, I won't let the fear paralyze me. I trust God. I know His timing is always perfect, and, as certain as I am that this inner desire to share is coming from Him, I'm equally certain the fear I have about doing it is not.

As always, in this time of inner conflict I have found comfort in Scripture. In it we read, "My grace is sufficient for you, for power is made perfect in weakness" (2 Corinthians 12:9). So, since doubt stemming from my many weaknesses seems to be the main cause of my fear of sharing, I, too, cry out, "I will rather boast most gladly of my weaknesses, in order that the power of Christ may dwell with me...for when I am weak, then I am strong" (2 Corinthians 12:9-10).

As I continue thinking about God's power and my many weaknesses, my mind is led to the cross. I see Jesus stretched out, crucified, and mentally, physically, and emotionally weaker than any human could ever be. Yet in this moment, - in this single moment - God's power was made perfect. In this moment Christ's human weakness was so meek, so humble, so pure that it was powerful enough in God's hands to save the world; to redeem us all. May this be all the proof that I need. Yes, may the power in Christ's death on the cross be my sign to embrace my weaknesses. Besides, this is all about him anyway. This has nothing to do with me. If this were about me, it would have blew up in my face a long time ago.

Prayer

*Fill me with courage and strength, Lord. May your power
be made perfect in my many weaknesses, and may my writing
become whatever it is you have made it to become.
I love you! I thank you! I praise you!*

Read, Think, Pray: Isaiah 55:10-11

*"My daughter, be at peace; do as I tell you. Your thoughts are united to
My thoughts, so write whatever comes to your mind."* - The words of our Lord,
Jesus Christ, to St. Faustina as recorded in her Diary, *Divine Mercy in My Soul*, 1605.

REFLECTION #121

A CRY OF THE POOR

10/21/2014

In the past week I have heard the same cry from three different people. This tells me two things: (1) that God wants me to take note of it and (2) that it is a cry of many. What is their cry? They tell me that the more "religious" they become, the more confused, fearful, and even distrusting they become as well. They say, "I pray more, I attend Mass more, I study more, I go to confession more, but I feel farther away from God. I am more fearful. I trust Him less." Though I am somewhat surprised by their cry because this is in no way what I have experienced on my "religious" journey, I have no reason to believe any of these people are lying to me. I mean, why would they? No, I'm certain they are, in fact, feeling this way, so I have to wonder, what is actually going on. Yeah, I have to wonder what (besides the obvious fact that they are at war with evil) is actually happening. Is there anything anyone can do to help?

As I pondered the answers to these questions I was reminded that Christ gave us the Church, and everything in it, to help us on our journeys home. In a way, therefore, the Church is like a giant tool bag with every tool we could ever possibly need inside. The problem with this, of course, is that tools can be misunderstood, and, as a result, misused, and if we misunderstand and/or misuse a tool, then it could create issues for us. It could make the work we have to do harder than it needs to be. I mean, a screwdriver isn't a hammer, so if we try to use it as one we will make the job harder. Likewise, a novena isn't a magic lamp, so if we're using it as something to make wishes on, then we're probably going to be disappointed with the results. Yes, there is *more* to prayer, study, Mass, and Reconciliation, and this cry has made me realize that many of us need a better understanding of what that "more" is.

> "A novena isn't a magic lamp, so if we're using it as something to make wishes on, then we're probably going to be disappointed with the results."

To me, the "more" with all of this is love. Yeah, to me, the "more" is that Catholicism is meant to be a "heart" thing. The tools of the Church are meant to transform our hearts. They're meant to comfort, heal, and strengthen us. They're meant to show us the Way, the Truth, and the Life (John 14:6). Prayer, therefore, should be about getting to know God. Reconciliation should be about humbling ourselves and receiving God's mercy so that we can be set free. Mass should be about worshiping as a family and receiving God's life-restoring, life-changing, and life-giving Word and Eucharistic Meal. Self-sacrifice, pain, and suffering should be about dying-to-self so that we can live in Christ. If prayer, suffering, and the Sacraments aren't about transformation, deeper conversion, growth, and worship, though, then Catholicism can easily become a "head" thing. If this happens, then religion can seem like nothing more than burdensome rules, meaningless suffering, and countless obligations. And you know what? "Head" things like these breed indifference and relativism. They breed confusion, fear, and distrust. They breed selfishness and pride. That's why Catholicism isn't meant to be a "head" thing. Yeah, that's why it's meant to be a "heart" thing. And I'm guessing this cry was God's reminder to me to make sure it remains just that.

Prayer

It's easy to live from my head, Lord. My head is not a vulnerable place; it's a "safe" place where I can logically and rationally make sense of the world. My heart, though, is a different story. Yeah, my heart can't be clearly defined or turned into a "safe" zone. My heart is completely vulnerable, and that's why it's such a scary place to go. I know, though, that the truth is in my heart, Lord. Yes, I know that you live in my heart, and I know that you want me to live there, too. Help me, therefore, to get out of my head. Help me get back to the basics. Give me the wisdom to know how to properly use the tools you've given me and the grace to understand all that you want me to understand. Live in my heart, Lord. Enlighten me, heal me, raise me up. I love you! I thank you! I praise you!

Read, Think, Pray: Psalm 19:8-10

"The literal observance of the precepts is something sterile if it does not change the heart and is not translated into concrete attitudes." - Pope Francis

SIMPLIFIED

10/21/2014

Complexity makes me crazy! It seems, though, that I have a tendency to complicate everything. I mean, sure, my heart is filled with simplicity. Sure, my heart knows the truth and holds the answers to all of my questions, but I too often live in my head, and my head turns the simple truth into a jumbled mess.

Yes, complexity is maddening. It leaves me feeling stressed out, overwhelmed, and overworked, and, if I let myself live in this state of complex confusion and survival, it makes it easy for me to believe the lie that simplicity is not obtainable. It makes it easy for me to ignore my heart and live from my head. The problem with this, of course, is that my head never leads me to true happiness. No, true happiness, at least as I have experienced, always comes when I live from my heart.

Rationally speaking, living from my heart seems backwards, though. After all, it makes sense to think that if I hide or ignore what's in my heart, then I'm protecting myself from getting hurt, but I've learned that happiness comes from exposing myself. Yes, I've learned that happiness comes from living with my heart wide open. So, contrary to what seems like popular opinion, I have come to believe that it's not living from my heart that's so damaging, it's refusing to live from it that is. The challenge for me, therefore, is to tell my head "no" and my heart "yes" when it seems like every part of my being (and every person in the world around me) is telling me to ignore what's inside and "stick to the facts."

With all that being said, the following has now become clear: I need to stop making my life harder than it needs to be and remember that simplicity is the way to true peace. Yes, I need to start living from my heart.

Prayer

Complexity stresses me out, Lord, and yet I'm always tempted to make life more complicated. Please, help me! Teach me to seek out simplicity. Give me the courage to move forward in simple ways. Life is about love, Lord, and love is simple. Weed out the complexity in my life, and show me how to live from my heart. I love you! I thank you! I praise you!

Read, Think, Pray: Psalm 119:130

REFLECTION #123

A LIFELONG STUDENT

10/21/2014

221

There is nothing more annoying than a know-it-all. I say this with the utmost humility because I, myself, am a know-it-all. Yes, I am. The Lord convinced me of this years ago when, as the result of my know-it-all attitude, (and the actions that followed) my life fell apart around me. In the mess, (the mess that I myself had made) I eventually found my pride; my attitude of "My way is best," "I am always right," "Everything is about me (or should be anyway.)" Thankfully, though, as I let go of this pride and humbly started my walk towards God, I finally learned, what I am now convinced, is one of life's greatest lessons: to always be a student; a student of Christ, that is.

Yes, I'm convinced that to "always be a student of Christ" is one of life's greatest lessons because just when I think I've figured things out, he reminds me I don't have anything figured out. Just when I think I'm starting to know things, he reminds me I don't know anything. This truth never leaves me feeling discouraged, though. No, it, instead, always leaves me feeling really excited because, after becoming aware of the fact that the knowledge I have is nothing in the grand scheme of things, I'm always left in awe excitedly calling out, "There's more? This is so good, so freeing, so complete! How can there be more?"

So, though my limited mind may not be able to tell you how there's always more, I can tell you this: if God isn't done with me, then I'm not done with Him. If He isn't done teaching, then I'm not done learning. If He isn't done giving, then I'm not done receiving. If He isn't done loving, then I'm not done returning that love. I, you see, am filled with an inner desire to be better, to give more, and to love more completely, so I'll stop showing up to class when He stops having something to teach. (Oh, and I'm guessing this won't be anytime soon.)

Prayer

May I always be your humble student, Lord. Come into my life and teach me. As I learn, remind me often that the goal isn't for me to be perfect but for you to work perfectly through me. Remind me often that the goal isn't for me to know everything but to know the One who does. Guide me in your Truth, Lord. Teach me. I love you! I thank you! I praise you!

Read, Think, Pray: Matthew 23:8

EVER-PRESENT

10/21/2014

One morning at Mass several weeks ago, my mind was in a constant state of distraction. To be honest, I was distracted by just about everything. I was distracted by the clothing on the people in front of me, distracted by the parents playing what looked like a game of hot potato with their toddler, distracted by the new view that came from sitting in a pew on the opposite side of church. (On a side note, have you ever switched seats at Mass? It's like you're in a whole new world!) Anyway, I could list hundreds of things I was distracted by that morning, and these many distractions caught me off guard. I mean, I used to get distracted like this every time I went to Mass. To be honest, I don't think I ever even *tried* to pay attention, but this distracted mental state is far from "normal" for me now. In fact, now I'm usually so engaged in what's happening in front of me that I rarely notice anything that's happening around me. This super-focused engagement was far from being present at that Mass a few weeks ago, though. Yeah, that day I was anything but engaged. Instead my mind was in a constant state of, "Say what now? Could you repeat that? What did you say?" and as much as I wanted to and tried to focus, I just couldn't get centered. I just couldn't stop my mind from wandering. I just couldn't get tuned-in.

Although I tried to center myself and pay attention to what was going on, I spent almost that entire Mass in a constant state of distraction. And, as it went on, I became more and more mad at myself for allowing it to happen. I just couldn't understand why I couldn't get it together. I just couldn't understand why I couldn't stop my mind from racing. I just couldn't understand why I couldn't get focused. I mean, I should have known better, I should have been more disciplined, I should have been more in control, right? Well, thankfully, God didn't let these lies run in my head for very long. Yeah, thankfully, He called out to my heart in the midst of all the distractions...

"I am here," I "heard" Him tell me somewhere in the noise. "I am here, even when you are not."

223

This may not have always been the case, but I find it incredibly comforting to know that God is always present. I find it incredibly comforting to know that He is always fully engaged. I find it incredibly comforting to know that He is always at work. Yes, I find it incredibly comforting to know that "He is always here," especially since I know that "I am often not." And that is why I now recall these words as often as needed. I recall them in the chaos-filled moments of my day when my mind is running from one thing to the next. I recall them when the temptation is heavy, and it seems like God is nowhere to be found. I recall them when my prayer feels dry, and I find myself wondering, "What's the point?" I recall them when life gets away from me, and I want to beat myself up about my many imperfections. Yes, I recall them each and every time I need a reminder. "I am here," I remind myself calling to mind God's words in the midst of the noise of my life. "I am here, even when you are not."

Prayer

It's comforting to know the truth, Lord. It's comforting to know that you can work with me, in me, and through me even in those times when I am not perfectly attentive to what is going on. Thank you for reminding me of your love. Thank you for reminding me of your mercy. Thank you for reminding me of your ever-present nature. May I never again lose hope or be led into despair due to my many imperfections. May I never again be fooled into thinking that you somehow leave me if I am not completely focused on you. Remind me often, Lord, of the truth of your goodness. Remind me often that "You are here, even when I am not." I love you! I thank you! I praise you!

Read, Think, Pray: Psalm 46:2-4

REFLECTION #125

TORN NETS

10/22/2014

I'm constantly asking the Lord to show me how to simplify my life because I'm always tempted to complicate things. I'm always tempted to buy more stuff, to do something else to the house, to spend more time planning and preparing. Today is no different. I can feel the uneasiness stirring in my soul, a sure-tell sign that I'm making life harder than it needs to be. The problem with being this way day in and day out is that it means I'm always in a perpetual state of doing, constantly jumping from one thing to the next. This makes it nearly impossible for me to actually enjoy life. It makes it nearly impossible for me to soak up the moments as I live them. I'm, instead, often left thinking, "What's next?" barely noticing life as it passes me by.

Yes, I'm not immune to the perpetual state of overdrive. In fact, if I don't make a conscience effort for this impulse *not* to take over my life, it does take over. That is why it has become a recent habit of mine to pay close attention to how I'm spending my time. That is why it has become a recent habit of mine to invite God into my life and into my schedule. I pray, *Simplify my schedule, Lord! Simplify my life! Show me how to make better use of the time you've given me! I know you won't ask me to do anything you won't give me the time, talents, and resources to do, so show me what you are asking me to let go of. Show me how to make room for the new things you are sending my way.*

As I prayed today I was reminded that a constant state of "busyness" is not what God wants for me. I was reminded that He is not some unsympathetic slave-driver yelling, "Go! More! Faster!" I was reminded that He, instead, tells us, "Even though there were so many, the net was not torn" (John 21:11). I guess my life gets so busy at times that I feel like my net is tearing, but I know it's not tearing because God is asking too much of me. I know, instead, it's tearing because I am asking too much of myself. Yes, I know, instead, it's tearing because I have taken on projects He hasn't asked me to take on; because I have held on to tasks He has asked me to let go of; because I have refused to delegate, refused to let someone help, refused to give up control. Yes, I know a "torn net" has less to do with my ever-increasing responsibilities and more to do with my pride.

Look, I know I'm here to work, and I know there are crosses for me to carry along the way, but a self-induced, over-complicated schedule with no time to breathe in God's abundance isn't one of them, so I'm returning now to my prayer: *Help me, Lord, to wisely make room for all the new things you are asking me to do. Remind me that You, and You alone, belong at the top of my list; that you, and you alone, are #1. Remind me that people are more important than possessions and work and to-do lists. (Yes, even the most noble ones.) Remind me that being entrusted with much to do doesn't mean my net has to tear. Teach me how to live an active life, Lord, not a busy one.*

There is a difference between living an active life and a busy one. Do you know what that difference is?

Prayer

You are my God, my loving, patient, understanding Father; the Master of my life. I work for you. Help me, therefore, to always consult with you so that I know what it is you're asking of me and what it is you're not. Show me how to simplify my life. Fill me with your Spirit. Give me the wisdom, counsel, and fortitude I need to know what to say "yes" to and what to say "no" to and what to say "no for now" to. Teach me how to live an active life, a life that serves many and is filled with peace, not a busy one in which I'm running around frantically, trying to squeeze everything in. Fill my net with as much as you want to fill it with, Lord, and remind me often that, as long as you are in control, it will never tear.
I love you! I thank you! I praise you!

Read, Think, Pray: John 21:10-11

REFLECTION #126

PAINFULLY OBEDIENT

10/23/2014

I just took action. I just did something I thought God was asking of me. Up until this point I prayed, discerned, and sought wisdom from trusted advisors about what to do. In time, I got my answer: "Yes, do it!" I was as certain as any human could be that taking this step was God's will, so, although it wasn't an easy decision to make or an easy thing to do, I did it. I ripped the Band-Aid off. The thinking, the praying, and the discerning were over with. All that was left to do was take action, so I did it, and did it quickly. (Before I had time to talk myself out of it.)

Shortly after taking action, I felt OK. "That wasn't a big deal," I thought. "Let's move on." Now, a few hours later, the doubt is setting in. "Aaahhh," I find myself nervously thinking. "What did I just do? Was this the right decision? I've been working so hard for the past 5 years to get here, and now, when all that work is finally starting to pay off, I'm walking away. Did I just make a huge mistake?"

Though the anguish is real, I know these overwhelming thoughts filling me with doubt, worry, and fear are not coming from God. Yeah, I know these thoughts are the voice of resistance; the voice of the enemy; the voice of the evil one. I know these thoughts are lies meant to torment me; to confuse me; to send me into a panic and distract me from what it is I'm here to do. Yes, I know the action I took this morning was a necessary part of doing what it is God put me here to do, so, contrary to what Satan would like me to believe, I know this tormenting is *not* a sign I did something wrong. I know, instead, it's a sign I did something right.

Recognizing the voice of the enemy and calling it out for what it really is isn't always enough to end the nagging, though. Yeah, Satan's job is to torment, and he's good at it. That's why I'm still being tormented. That's why he's still here. And that's why I've picked up my pen. Yes, writing has become therapeutic to me. It helps me shed light on the darkness. It helps me find my way through the noise in my head and get back to the truth in my heart. In fact, now that I'm writing, I once again "hear" God's whispering voice. I once again "hear" Him reminding me of my calling. I once again "hear" Him reminding me why what just happened needed to happen. I once again "hear" Him reminding me that this is what dying-to-self feels like; this is what it feels like to let go of my will and embrace His.

"It's not easy at first," He "says." "It's not pain free. It's not without a cross. In fact, it usually comes with one, and that's why so few people actually live the abundant life I offer them. Many can't get past the temporary pain. Many don't trust that something better is coming. Many are unwilling to let go."

"Not me!" I call back. "No! You have made me strong-willed and stubborn and, in situations like this, these traits come in handy, so I will not run away from the pain! No, I will go wherever it is you ask me to go, even if it hurts!"

"Then pick up this cross," God gently responds. "Follow me. The pain is necessary, but it is temporary, and I will not make you go through it alone. Move forward. Be unafraid."

And so, I pick up the cross. I pick up the cross forcing me out of my comfort zone. I deny myself. I move past my desire to figure it all out, to know the plan, to take care of all the details. I move forward. I take one small step into the future which, as is always the case, is completely unknown.

Prayer

You ask me to take such small steps, Lord, and this was such a small step. Still, I know it is in the taking of the small steps that you will complete your big mission in me. Yes, I know the small steps will add up to the big ones. So, I thank you, Lord. I thank you for the wisdom and courage to do what it is you asked me to do. I thank you for the grace and strength to carry the cross that came along with it. May I always be your humble servant, obedient to you in all ways, big and small. Yes, even if this obedience hurts.
I love you! I thank you! I praise you!

Read, Think, Pray: 1 Samuel 15:22

REFLECTION #127

THE SILENT RESPONSE

10/26/2014

I recently found myself (unbeknownst to the person speaking) as the butt of an anti-Catholic joke. Since Catholicism is a fairly common, perhaps even acceptable, area of prejudice, I wasn't surprised by what was said. What did surprise me, though, was my response to it. As always, I have learned much.

You see, in the past hearing something like this would have sent me into defense-mode. I would have felt so personally attacked it would have been hard for me to take the high road and respond with love. In fact, the last time I was faced with such a conflict, I was so hurt by what was said I was brought to tears. I just couldn't understand how someone could misunderstand Catholicism so much, and I couldn't keep my emotions from pouring out of me. My "disapproval" of what was said was obvious, but, because I was so worked up, it likely came across as disgust and judgment instead of coming across for what it really was: love for Christ and his Church. Something has changed in me recently, though, and this little joke-telling experience proved it. Yeah, it proved that it's much easier for me now to take the high road. It proved that it's much easier for me now to meet others where they're at. It proved that it's much easier for me now to let the Spirit guide my response. Most surprisingly, it proved that it's much easier for me now to hold my tongue.

Though much has been necessary for this transition in my heart (and in my tongue) to take place, St. Augustine's words helped tremendously. He put it this way: *"The Truth is like a lion. You don't have to defend it. Let it out of its cage, and it will defend itself."* Yes, the Truth will certainly defend itself. All I really have to do is love. After all, it's love that changes hearts. Arguments, even if won, only change minds.

"It's love that changes hearts. Arguments, even if won, only change minds."

Prayer

Fill me with deep faith, steadfast hope, and endless love, Lord. Help me to face times of persecution in a spirit of victory knowing

> *that there is no need to defend what's true. Remind me often, Lord,*
> *that the Truth is what draws people in and that the essence of this*
> *Truth is your everlasting, merciful love. May this love pour out of*
> *me whether the Spirit prompts me to speak up or to be still, to take*
> *action or to lovingly listen, to respond with words or to respond*
> *with silence. May I always be an instrument of your great*
> *love, Lord, even if this means I never open my mouth.*
> *I love you! I thank you! I praise you!*

Read, Think, Pray: Sirach 20:5-8

"No one can more safely speak than one who knows how to refrain from speech." - Thomas à Kempis, *The Imitation of Christ*

REFLECTION #128

FILLERS

10/30/2014

As I work at "making room" for some of the new by delegating, simplifying, and letting go of some of the old, I'm realizing how easy it is for other things, - things that are seemingly coming from nowhere - to jump in and take their place. I have been having to make a serious effort *not* to let this other stuff fill in. And you know what? It's hard! I mean, where are these "other" things even coming from? Aaahhh! I'm all over the place today! Something is not right. Something is going on.

Help me, Lord, to proceed calmly. Help me to breathe and let go of all of these seemingly urgent "fillers." Show me how to put them in their place so that I can spend the time you give me doing what it is you're asking me to do. I know *what* needs to happen, Lord, and I understand *why* it needs to happen. I just don't know *how* to do it. Please help me! I want to do, do, do. Help me instead to be, be, be.

Prayer

There are so many "urgent" things that come up throughout the day trying to keep me from doing what I know is the most important, Lord. Help me to live attentively so that I might recognize these fillers for what they are and stay disciplined in doing what it is you're asking me to do. Don't let me get swallowed up by the noise, Lord. Don't let me get lost in the details. Instead, keep my mind, heart, and soul always focused on the big idea. I love you! I thank you! I praise you!

Read, Think, Pray: Psalm 90:12

REFLECTION #129

HEARTFELT PRAYER

10/30/2014

"Why do you pray, Julia?...Why do you pray?"

Well, when I first started praying, my why was simple: I was miserable. I was caught up in some serious habitual sin, and, as a result, was empty inside. Nothing in my world made sense, and everything I tried outside of me to fix it only made it worse. So, I started to pray because I was desperate. Yes, as a last resort, I dropped to my knees. I needed help. I was in a huge mess. I prayed in a desperate attempt to get out of it.

Once I was out of the mess, my reason for praying changed. At this point, I wasn't praying to be rescued anymore. No, now my prayer was different; still selfish, but different. Now I was praying to stay out of the mess. Now I was praying because I didn't want to fall back into old habits. Now I was praying because God got me out of trouble, and I was sure if I kept Him around He'd keep me from getting back into it.

After praying this way for a few years, prayer became habitual to me. It officially became part of my routine. Once this happened, it wasn't long before I wanted more. It wasn't long before I desired something deeper. It was here that my reason for praying changed again. It was here that it went from being centered on myself to being centered on others. At this point I prayed because I had found help, and I wanted others to find this help, too.

As my prayer for others continued, I began paying more and more attention to God working in my life and in the lives of those people I was praying for. This is when I started to become more and more amazed by Him, and this is when I started to fall more and more in love. To be honest, it was at this point that God and I were on our honeymoon. In my eyes He could do no wrong. He was perfect, the man of my dreams, the friend I always wanted, the companion I always longed for. He filled every part of me and swept me off my feet.

Since entering into that "honeymoon phase" a few years ago, my reasons for praying have changed again. Now I pray because I like to. Yes, now I pray because I like being with God. I enjoy His company. I enjoy getting to know Him. I enjoy being in His presence. Sure, prayer makes me a better me. Sure, prayer helps me make sense of my life. Sure, prayer helps me stay focused. Sure, prayer redirects me when I need redirected, comforts me when I need comforted, dries my tears when they need dried, hugs me when I need a hug, and makes me laugh when I need a good laugh. But, first and foremost, prayer keeps me connected to God. And, as I see it, there is no other reason I'm here.

"Prayer keeps me connected to God, and, as I see it, there is no other reason I'm here."

So, *"why do I pray?"* Well, it may not have started out this way, but I pray because I'm in love, and the One I love is on the other end of the line.

Why do *you* pray?

Prayer

Draw me to yourself, Lord. Come, sweep me off my feet. Show me what it means to pray. Show me how to spend more heartfelt time with you. I love you! I thank you! I praise you!

Read, Think, Pray: Psalm 73:28

REFLECTION #130

FRESH WOUNDS

11/3/2014

It was in some of St. Francis de Sales writings that I first heard the phrase *"fresh wounds heal quickly."* As is often the case, time has proven these words to be true in my life. Yes, I have found that the quicker I let something go, the easier it is to let it go, and the longer I let something fester, the harder it is to do anything about it. I guess that's why I've learned over the years *not* to let my emotions and thoughts hit the repeat button when I'm in a state of crisis. Yeah, I guess that's why I've learned *not* to let things stew. I guess that's why I've learned to apologize, forgive, and move on.

I mean, we all mess up. Yes, we all make mistakes. We should just learn from them, apologize, and move on.

I mean, other people will hurt us. Yes, it will happen because we all make mistakes. We should just learn from it, forgive, (even if they don't apologize, even if we're right) and move on.

Yes, experience has taught me that we shouldn't waste our lives beating ourselves up. It has also taught me that we shouldn't waste our lives beating others up either. We should just apologize, forgive, and move on remembering that *"fresh wounds heal quickly."*

233

Read, Think, Pray: Proverbs 19:11

REFLECTION #131

THE FIXER

11/4/2014

I just realized I'm a fixer. Yeah, I just realized I want to "fix" things. More specifically, I want to "fix" people. Now, I know this desire to "fix" isn't necessarily "bad." In fact, I'm sure God has given me this desire for good reasons, but it seems I have taken it too far because the more I try to "fix," the worse things seem to get. Still, it's hard for me to sit back and let God do the work. It's hard for me to wait on His perfect timing. It's hard for me *not* to take control. And, yes, therein lies my real problem. I, you see, don't just want situations (and people) fixed, I want to control the fixing. This can only mean one thing: the time for more growth has come!

Yes, as I see it, the root of this self-controlled desire to fix must be pride. I mean, a humble person wouldn't want to control the process, would they? A humble person wouldn't think they had all the answers, would they? A humble person wouldn't think, "Do what I did, and you'll get what I got," would they? No, a humble person wouldn't do any of this, so I must take this time to remind myself of the truth.

The truth is, I am nothing and can do nothing without God. The truth is, He and I are on the same team. The truth is, He sees things I can't and knows things I don't. The truth is, He loves these "broken" people way more than I ever could. The truth is, as much as I want people to be "fixed," I am not, and never will be, The Fixer.

Prayer

Shepherd me, O God, beyond my want to "fix." Help me to better embrace your will for my life and the lives of others. Remind me often that I am only an instrument in your fixing and that you are The Fixer. Show me how to help you by giving up control. Show me how to help you by following your lead. I love you! I thank you! I praise you!

Read, Think, Pray: Isaiah 45:9-12

REFLECTION #132

DISGUISED OPPORTUNITIES

11/6/2014

Obstacles are all around me. They keep coming up, day after day, rearing their unwelcomed heads. They are never pleasant, their timing is always terrible, and with them always comes a sense of discomfort and pain. Oh, how I hate the obstacles when they first show up, but, oh, how I love them in the end. Why? Because, by showing me the way through them, God proves to me that they are nothing more than opportunities in disguise; opportunities for growth, opportunities for transformation, opportunities to become more like Him.

Yes, it hurts to work through the obstacles. In fact, it hurts so much it's as if I can physically feel the pain. But you know what? It hurts more to be complacent. It hurts more to stay where I am. It hurts more to resist the change. So, yes, even though it hurts, I won't let the obstacles hold me back. I won't let them stop me from getting closer to my goal: my goal to love more completely; my goal to become the woman-of-virtue I know I was created to be; my goal to become a saint.

Julia Monnin

Prayer

Thank you, Lord, for the discomfort that keeps me moving forward. Thank you for the opportunities to put into practice the very things I pray for: to see others at their best, to understand rather than to be understood, to love as you love. I offer you my sufferings, Lord. I place all of these obstacles into your hands. I trust you to work out the details. I trust you to untie all the knots.
I love you! I thank you! I praise you!

Read, Think, Pray: Romans 8:37-39

REFLECTION #133

PIERCED HEARTS

11/6/2014

We all have crosses. Sure, some may be heavier than others, but we all have them. We have crosses that are unique to us like physical or emotional illnesses, ailments, and diseases. We have crosses caused by our sin and the damaging effects of it like broken relationships. We have crosses associated with our vocations like the crosses that come with marriage, parenting, and the religious life. This is probably not a surprise to anyone. In fact, I think most of us are painfully aware that crosses are a part of every authentic Christian life. What is coming as a surprise to me, though, is which of my crosses are becoming the heaviest.

I guess I always expected the unique crosses in my life and the crosses caused by the damaging effects of my sin to always carry the most weight, but I'm realizing this isn't actually the case. In fact, I'm realizing it's the crosses associated with what I'm now discovering is my vocation - my vocation within my vocation; my call within my call - that are becoming the heaviest. Yes, these are the crosses that are dropping me to my knees the most. So, I have to wonder, why?

236

Why is it that the thing we are created for, the thing we are here to do, the thing that brings us the most joy and deepest sense of purpose in life is the very thing that causes us the most hurt, pain, and sorrow? Why is it that the thing that makes "our soul proclaim the greatness of the Lord" (Luke 1:46-47) is the very thing that "pierces our heart" (Luke 2:35)? Why is it? Why?

Could it be that pain hurts most in those areas in which we love most? Could it be that it takes pain to truly understand love? Could it be that love, by definition, comes with pain? I'm guessing, yes. In fact, I'm guessing this is one of the reasons so many of us close ourselves off from love to begin with. Still, as much as it hurts to carry the cross that comes with love, I think it hurts more not to. So, continue to carry it, I will.

> "As much as it hurts to carry the cross that comes with love, it hurts more not to."

Prayer

*Open my heart to love, Lord. Remind me that it is through the cross that I find love. Remind me that it is through the cross that I find you. Help me to love more completely. Yes, even if doing so pierces my heart.
I love you! I thank you! I praise you!*

Read, Think, Pray: Luke 1:46-48, Luke 2:34-35

RENEWED

11/7/2014

I am not perfect. To be honest, I'm far from it. In fact, I'm reminded every day of all the things I have yet to work on; of all the ways I'm still coming up short. Even so, I'm not discouraged. No, I'm encouraged; motivated to keep working, to keep striving, to keep fighting. I may enter prayer broken, painfully weighed down by the weight of my cross, but I leave it renewed, recharged, and refocused on what really matters: love. Yes, I leave prayer with a heart filled with love; love for God, love for Christ, love for His Church.

I am secure in who I am and in who I am called to be. I know I am loved. In fact, I know I am not only loved, I am *adored* by my Creator. And, if I ever doubt this, I need only to look at a crucifix. Yes, it's clear. God loves me. Out of His deep love for me Christ died; he suffered, he bled, he wept, he carried his cross and nailed himself to it. All for me. All for us.

Sure, I'm undeserving. Sure, I'm unworthy. Sure, I'm imperfect, but God loves me anyway. And not just *anyway* as if He puts up with me. No, God doesn't just love me *anyway*, He loves me *every way*. And, oh, does it feel good to be loved!

Prayer

Thank you, Lord, for this time with you. Time with you brings me back to reality. Time with you reminds me what this is all about. Time with you reminds me why this is so important. May I move forward with this renewed sense of hope and peace becoming more and more of the person you created me to be. May I move forward living more attentively, rejoicing more joyfully, and loving more whole-heartedly. Perfect my love, Lord. Make it more like yours. Make me more like you. I love you! I thank you! I praise you!

Read, Think, Pray: Isaiah 40:28-31

REFLECTION #135

WHITE LIES

11/12/2014

A few days ago I was playing a game with my 3-year-old nephew. He, like most kids his age, likes to win. He, like most kids his age, is also super-honest. Yep, he'll tell you who he pushed, and when he did it, and won't deny his fault even if it means he's going to get into trouble. That's why it surprised me when I caught him trying to get away with something during our game. Yeah, that's why it surprised me when I saw him give in to the temptation to cheat after he accidently saw that his next honest move would likely cost him the game.

I watched the whole thing happen. I watched him blamelessly fall into the temptation. I watched him struggle internally about whether to give in to it or not. I watched him go against his gut and choose wrong. I then watched his face fill with shame after I asked him what happened. Oh, he knew he had messed up. Yeah, he knew he had made the wrong choice. That's why, when he ended up winning, he wasn't excited about it like he usually is. Yeah, that's why his victory didn't feel like a victory to him. It, you see, was missing one thing; the one and only thing that really matters. It was missing the peace and joy that come from a clear conscious.

We can try to convince ourselves that it's sometimes OK to be dishonest. The problem with "little white lies", though, is they're still lies. Young children know this. At what point do we start telling ourselves otherwise?

The problem with "little white lies" is, they're still lies."

Prayer

Help me to overcome the temptation to lie, Lord. Give me the courage to choose truth always, everywhere, and in everything. Yes, even in those things that seem small and meaningless. May my honesty in small matters prove to you my honesty in big ones, and may I always choose this honesty even when I think no one else is looking. I love you! I thank you! I praise you!

Read, Think, Pray: Luke 16:10

TAKEN AWAY

11/13/2014

I was recently asked the question, *"What are some words of God that have made an impact on your life?"* My immediate response to this question was, "How do I choose? There are so many!" But, as I took it to prayer and thought about it some more, I eventually recalled the words that, hands down, have made the biggest impact on my life thus far. These are the words that truly set me free. Yes, I am convinced that without these simple words, I never would have had the ability to move forward, and, without that, nothing else in my life would have mattered. So, yeah, there are some words of God that have, without a doubt, made an impact on my life. Here's what they are.

Several months ago, I was at Mass on a Wednesday afternoon. It was just an ordinary day. I wasn't feeling super high or super low, I just was. I wasn't expecting anything extra-special from the Lord that day because it didn't seem like I needed it. In fact, all seemed right in my world, and I was sure that it was "just another day." God, however, had different plans. Yeah, that day was anything but ordinary for Him. That day, you see, was the day He chose to answer my many years of prayer. Yes, that was the day He chose to set me free, once and for all.

While at Mass the priest took the consecrated Host in his hands and held it for all to see. As he did I heard him say, "This is the Lamb of God who takes away the sins of the world." To which I responded, "Have mercy on us." I then heard him repeat, "This is the Lamb of God who takes away the sins of the world." And again I responded, "Have mercy on us." I then heard him say the words a third time. This time, however, I heard them differently. Yeah, this time it was as if he was staring directly at me, talking louder and much slower. I heard him say again, (but this time more matter-of-factly) "*This* is the <u>Lamb of God</u> who <u>TAKES AWAY</u> the sins of the world." Suddenly it hit me. My sins were *taken away*! Christ's death on the cross *took away* my sin! They no longer existed! They no longer had any bearing on me! They were gone! I was free! In less than a second, I realized for the first time in my life

240

what I should have realized a long time ago: my sins were wiped away on the cross. I fell to my knees as tears of joy, gratitude, and awe streamed down my face. "Grant us peace," I finally responded through my sobbing.

So, "*what are some words of God that have made an impact on my life?*" Well, they are the most important words every repentant sinner needs to hear: "<u>This</u> is the <u>Lamb of God</u> who <u>TAKES AWAY</u> the sins of the world."...Need I say more?

Prayer

How could I ever doubt your love for me, Lord? You <u>are</u> the <u>Lamb of God</u> who <u>takes away</u> the sins of the world! My sin, all of it, died with you. Yes, through your death, I was set free. Help me not to look back. Help me to live in this freedom forever knowing that you are my God and that my sin is lost in the ocean of your mercy. I love you, my Lord, and I believe in your promises. I believe in the power of the cross. I love you! I thank you! I praise you!

Read, Think, Pray: John 1:29

LOSING MOMENTUM

11/15/2014

When we start out on a race it seems that the initial excitement, adrenalin, and passion we have is enough to carry us through the first part of the journey. When we are close to the finish line, - when the finish line is in sight - it seems that we are filled with a rush to continue, so we find the strength we need to push through. What happens in the middle though? What happens if we never continue long enough to see the finish line? Or, worse yet, what happens if the race seems too difficult, and we never even start to begin with? In my experience, what happens is emptiness. Emptiness that stems from an inner longing and desire for more. Emptiness that stems from settling for "good enough" when you know you were made for more than "good enough." In my experience, what happens is disappointment, indifference, jealousy, and anger. In my experience, what happens is complete loss. Complete loss that leads to despair.

It has become painfully clear to me over the course of these last several months that those of us who are serious about fulfilling our missions here on earth have to learn how to persevere. It has also become clear to me that there is really only one thing we need in order to do this: love.

Love, you see, has a way of taking "rational" logic to "irrational" places. It has a way of shattering the doubts of the mind and centering in on the hopes of the heart. It has a way of leading us, willingly even, to places we don't really want to go. It is, therefore, the only thing we really need to keep us moving forward because it is what gives us a reason to hope. Yes, it is what gives us a reason to proceed.

"Love has a way of leading us, willingly even, to places we don't really want to go."

So, if we want to fulfill our earthly missions, then we have to persevere in love. We have to learn how to let God work through us. We have to learn how to push through the resistance. We have to learn how to let our hearts take the lead. Persevering in love doesn't mean we have to become superheroes who never feel the pain of the fight. No, it doesn't mean we can't lose some momentum along the way. All it really means is that we can't quit. I'll say it again. All it really means is that we can't quit.

Prayer
Thank you, Lord, for the many examples of men and women who are persevering in love. Thank you for the challenges, resistance,

and obstacles in my own life that are helping me learn how to trust less in myself and more in you. Bless us all as we continue our work for you. Fill us with resilience and courage. Fill us with hope and peace. May we proceed in a spirit of victory knowing that, with you on our side, we cannot lose.
I love you! I thank you! I praise you!

Read, Think, Pray: Hebrews 10:32-36

"I myself hold that the measure for being able to bear a large or small cross is love. " – St. Teresa of Avila, *The Way of Perfection*

REFLECTION #138

FOREVER TRYING

11/16/2014

As Christians, we should live in truth. Sometimes, though, when we're standing up for what is true, the world can make us think that we're unkind and, perhaps even, ignorant. When this happens, - when we're made to feel like fools - the truth seems to get a little confusing, but, in reality, the truth is never confusing. Yeah, in reality, the truth is always simple, and the only thing we need to concern ourselves with when sharing it with others, is that we're doing it in love.

I pray daily that I "speak the truth in love and in the power of the Holy Spirit," but I've learned that what happens from that point isn't up to me. Yeah, I've learned that sometimes it's *not* God's will for people to understand. And you know what? That's OK. Why? Because it only proves that someone much wiser than me is in charge.

Yes, God is in charge, and all He really asks us to do is try; to put forth some sort of effort in sharing the Good News. All God really asks us to do is plant and water seeds trusting that He will take care of the growth; trusting that those people He puts in our path are in His loving hands.

Well, I can't speak for anyone else, but "trying" is something I can do. Yes, "trying" is something I am capable of. So, "trying" is exactly what I'll do. Yes, I'll keep trying, even if it seems like it's all in vain.

Prayer

Help me, Lord, to approach all situations with steadfast trust and patience. Fill me with your wisdom, and help me to speak the truth in love and in the power of the Holy Spirit. I love you! I thank you! I praise you!

Read, Think, Pray: Ephesians 4:25-30

"Never doubt your impact, even if you don't know what it is." - Dr. Brian Deal

REFLECTION #139

EYE CONTACT

11/17/2014

I want all I say and do to do one thing: point others to Christ. With that in mind, my daily prayer has become, *Lord, I pray that when others see me, they see you. When others hear me, (or read my words) they hear you. When others even think of me, they think of you. Similarly, O' Lord, I pray that you reveal yourself to me in others. May I look for and see the good in everyone I meet.* Still, though this sounds really good on paper, the question for me, until very recently, remained the same. How? How do I go about doing this? How do I make sure this prayer becomes more than just words on a page?

Although there are, no doubt, countless ways one can go about being God's presence to others and seeing God's presence in others, I recently got a more concrete answer to this question of, "How?". Yes, God, in His very loving, but straight-forward, God-like way, recently showed me that *how* I go about being and seeing His presence in the world around me is as simple as looking up; as simple as looking *at* people instead of *through* them. He convinced me of this one day in the checkout line at the grocery store.

"Look up," I could "hear" Him call out as I avoided the cashier across the counter and instead busied myself on my phone in the hopes that she would get the point that I was in a hurry and therefore not slow down her work by making small talk with me. "Look *at* me," He "said" again as I continued to stare at my phone. "My child, I am present in this young woman standing across from you, and it is here in the ordinary moments of your day that you can see me in others and that you can allow others to see me in you. You are overlooking me when you overlook these people in your life. You are ignoring me when you ignore them. Even worse, you are missing an opportunity to let them see me through you when you don't take the time to look up; when you don't take the time to make eye-contact with them and listen to them whole-heartedly. This is one of the many opportunities I give you throughout your day to point others to me and instead you are pointing them to the world. This is one of the many opportunities I give you throughout your day to let others know they matter to me and instead your half-hearted attention is telling them they matter to no one." "Look up," He "told" me again. "Look *at* the people I send into your life. Get in the habit of looking compassionately into the eyes of every person you meet. 'Why?' you ask. Because this is *exactly* how I look at you."

Get in the habit of looking compassionately into the eyes of every person you meet. Why? Because this is exactly how Christ looks at you.

As the message sank in, I quickly realized I couldn't ignore this call-to-action. I quickly realized I couldn't argue with God's reasoning. Yes, He was right, and I knew it. He always looks me in the eye. He always listens to me whole-heartedly and gives me His undivided attention. He always comes from a place of understanding. He always embraces me with patience, kindness, love, and mercy. Likewise, I never catch Him at a bad time. He's never too busy for me, and I'm never too much for Him. He never looks past me. He never hurriedly responds to me on His way out the door. No, He is always fully engaged with me all day, every day, and His message to me at the grocery store made this all very clear. If I want to be His presence to others and want to see Him in the people I meet, then I am going to have to be fully engaged, too. Yes, I am going to have to learn how to look *at* people the way Christ looks *at* me.

Prayer

I want to be your presence to those around me, Lord. I want to point others to you. Help me, therefore, to slow down and live attentively so that I might look <u>at</u> others instead of through them, past them, or around them. May I give all the people you send into my life the same kind, loving, and purposeful attention that you give to me. May I look compassionately into the eyes of every person I meet. I love you! I thank you! I praise you!

Read, Think, Pray: Psalm 33:13-15

REFLECTION #140

ONE BODY

11/18/2014

We all know that suffering is a part of life. (Life on earth, anyway.) Yeah, we all know that there is no resurrection without the cross. In the midst of our suffering, though, we need reminded of this because suffering is painful, and, well, the pain sometimes clouds our better judgment. I am in one of those moments right now. Yes, I am in one of those moments where my suffering is clouding my better judgment. I need reminded of the truth. So, here goes...

The truth is, God gave me life to live in communion with Him and with others. He put me here to carry out His work living as one small part in His one large body. With that being said, as difficult as it may be to come together with others at times, I must never try to do things on my own. No, I must never try to separate my one part from the One Body. It will never work. I will never survive. Worse yet, my leaving would ultimately lead to the destruction of others.

Yes, the truth is, we are all in this together, and nothing - no, not even living together as the One Body in Christ that we are - is impossible for God.

Prayer

Help me, Lord, to live as one with all. Help me to know my role, to play my part, and to do everything in my power to complete my mission. Not, of course, for my gain but for your glory. Not, of course, so that I can have life, but so that I can willingly lose my life for others. We are many parts, Lord, but we are all One Body (1 Corinthians 12:12). May the actions of my life start to prove my belief in these words. I love you! I thank you! I praise you!

Read, Think, Pray: 1 Corinthians 12:12-26

REFLECTION #141

UNHEALED MEMORIES

11/18/2014

During a conversation with a friend a few years ago, I (much to my surprise) found myself getting all worked up as we innocently talked about some events of the past. I was surprised by my reaction because, although these events were in fact hurtful ones at the time, I thought I was over them. Yeah, I thought I had forgiven the people responsible for my pain. But, since even the memory of their actions brought back all the painful emotions, I quickly realized this was not the case. Yeah, I quickly realized I had not yet truly moved on. My unhealed memories shed light on a dark area that I, unknowingly, was trying to keep hidden. To be honest, I was shocked I was still so hurt by something that

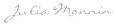
happened years before. After all, I had *said* I had forgiven them, and I had *thought* I really meant it. My reaction that day, though, told me otherwise.

Now that I'm thinking about my reaction to this conversation again, I have to ask: How do we really know for sure we've forgiven someone? How do we really know for sure we've moved on? How do we really know for sure our hearts match our tongues?

How do we really know for sure our hearts match our tongues?"

It seems to me that, aside from looking at any unhealed memories we may have, another way we can know for sure we've truly forgiven someone is by paying close attention to what's going on inside when we're around them. I mean, it's easy to smile on the outside and "play nice" with those who have hurt us, but what we're really thinking about when they're around may give us greater insight. For example, when someone who's hurt us enters the picture, do we find ourselves keeping tabs on them? Do we look at them and immediately recall all they've said or done in the past that has hurt us? Do we walk around in defense-mode waiting for them to strike again? Well, if *I* have not truly forgiven someone, then this is what happens to me. Yes, it's sad but true. And that's why I make myself answer questions like these from time to time. You see, the honest answers help me gain a better understanding of what's really going on in my heart, and, as I see it, this is a good thing.

Yes, as I see it, knowing what's really going on inside is a good thing because I want to be free from my past. I want to know that I've let things go. I want to know that my heart matches my tongue. I don't want to keep tabs on people or remember all the ways they've hurt me, I want to give them a clean slate regardless of how many times I have to give them one; regardless of whether or not they "deserve" it. I don't want to walk around with hate in my heart because a few people in my life have made some mistakes that have injured me, I want to choose love even when it's hard. I don't want to hold a grudge against each and every person that has ever done me wrong, I want to forgive even when it hurts. Why? Because this is what Christ does, and I am convinced that his way is *the* Way to live.

Prayer

Help me, Lord, to forgive like you forgive, for the world tells me to "forgive but never forget," but I want to forgive and forget. Yes, I want even my memories to be free from the grudges. I want to look at people and see them as you see them, not look at them and recall all the ways they've hurt me. Show me, therefore, what I need to do to let go and move on. Teach me how to forgive without limits. I love you! I thank you! I praise you!

Read, Think, Pray: Proverbs 17:9, Ephesians 4:31-32

REFLECTION #142

SHORT LINES

11/19/2014

Sin creates darkness. Lies create darkness. Secrets create darkness. Basically any thoughts we have tormenting us about our past, our future, and everything in between create darkness. The good news, though, is that the way out of the darkness is pretty simple: you just have to turn on the light.

The way out of the darkness is pretty simple: you just have to turn on the light.

How do we do this? How do we turn on the lights in our darkened world? Simple: we talk about it. We say things out loud. Yes, even those things we don't want to say; even those things we want to keep hidden. It really is that simple. I wonder, then, why more of us aren't speaking up.

249

Regardless, I'm not here to judge. In fact, I actually prefer a short line at the confessional, so if others have found a way to stay out of the darkness without taking it straight to the Man himself, then I have no business telling them otherwise. I, for one, *need* Confession. It's *not* an option for me. It's where I'm reconciled with God. It's where I'm renewed and restored. It's where I'm set free. I, therefore, will continue to go. Yes, even if I'm the only person in the world standing in line.

Prayer

Give me the grace and courage, Lord, to turn on the lights in my life. Help me to persevere in my efforts to rid myself of the darkness forever. You, Lord, are the light of the world. May I walk always as a child of the light. I love you! I thank you! I praise you!

Read, Think, Pray: 1 Thessalonians 5:1-6

"Right is right even if no one is doing it; wrong is wrong even if everyone is doing it." - St. Augustine

REFLECTION #143

GOOD TEACHERS

11/21/2014

"What makes for a good teacher?" Well, in my opinion, good teachers are those who bring out the best in their students by helping them discover, nurture, and grow their inner strengths, gifts, and talents. In my opinion, good teachers guide their students, showing them how to go through the steps of getting from point A, the question, to point B, the answer. In my opinion, good teachers challenge their students to think, to work through problems, and to search for answers using the tools, knowledge, and insight they've gained during their instruction. In my opinion, good teachers help their students understand the process of learning, not just understand how to pass a test. In short, in my

opinion, good teachers teach their students *how* to think, not *what* to think.

I've had good teachers like this in my life, and I'm just now realizing what a gift they really are. Yeah, I'm just now realizing how much wisdom I've gained from them as the result of them lovingly guiding me instead of them forcefully pushing me. Now that I realize this, I want to make sure that I, too, "teach" in this same way. I want to guide not demand, direct not conquer, listen not condemn. I want to point out the Way, not force anyone to take it. In short, I want to teach people *how* to think, not *what* to think. How can I be so confident this approach will work? Simple: as I see it, the Truth needs little explanation.

Prayer

Help me, Lord, to become one of those good teachers whose patience, kindness, and humility guides people to the answer, not forces them to accept it. May I teach like you teach, as a gentle, loving friend. I love you! I thank you! I praise you!

Read, Think, Pray: Luke 6:40

REFLECTION #144

A CALL FOR HELP

11/22/2014

To priests everywhere striving to finish your race and finish it well:

Thank You! Know that we, your flock, are forever grateful for your service to Christ's Body, the Church, for it is through you that we, the members of this Body, receive the best gifts we could ever ask for. Yes, it is through you that we become children of God reborn in the waters of Baptism. It is through you that we receive the Holy Spirit in the Sacrament of Confirmation. It is through you that two of us became one as we are united with our spouses in Holy Matrimony. It is through you that we are nourished by the Word of God. It is through you that we are healed and given new life in the Sacrament of Reconciliation. It is through you that we are shown what it means to die-to-self, to serve others, and to love like Christ. And, as if all of that wasn't enough, it is also through you that we receive the Lord in His very Body and Blood in Holy Communion. So, yes, we are grateful. We are forever grateful. Thank you! Thank you for saying "Yes" when you heard the Lord call.

Now, as if you haven't already done enough for us, our dear Shepherds, I cry out to you for more. Yes, I cry out to you for more. Many of our lives are still empty: feed us. Many of us are still lost: find us. Many of us have still forgotten our Savior: remind us who He is. I know that we, your flock, make life hard on you at times and that none of us will ever fully understand what it is you are sacrificing for us, but we need you. Yes, we need you. We need you now more than ever. We need you even if we never admit it. In fact, we need you *especially* if we never admit it. Our lives are noisy; super, super noisy. So, please, on behalf of those of us who often feel swallowed up by the noise of our lives, help us to hear the whisper.

Your Once Lost Sheep,
Julia

Prayer

Thank you, Lord, for the gift of the priesthood. Thank you for the gift of the Church. Pour out your blessings on the Church throughout the world. Bless our Pope and all priests, religious, and clergy everywhere. May the light of your Church shine brightly, and may it be the beacon of hope, peace, and mercy you have created it to be.
I love you! I thank you! I praise you!

Read, Think, Pray: Hebrews 5:1-4

REFLECTION #145

STRONG MARRIAGES

11/24/2014

Several months ago a woman commented on my marriage. She said, "I want a marriage like you have." Her comment made me think. I mean, my marriage didn't get this way overnight, so, though I understood what she was saying, I wondered what "advice" I could actually give her to help her reach her goal. After all, my husband and I are far from having a perfect relationship, and I am no expert on marriage! After reflecting on her statement some and thinking about how our marriage has grown over the years, though, I eventually realized what it took to have, as she put it, "a marriage like ours." Simply put, it took (and takes) work. Lots and lots of work.

Yes, my husband and I have had to work really hard to make our marriage a strong one, and we have to continue to work really hard to keep it that way. The foundation of all this work for us is communication. To be honest, nothing is off the table for us topic-wise. Nothing is taboo. Nothing is hidden. Nothing is off-limits. It certainly didn't start out this way, though. In fact, in the beginning we talked very little about anything that was actually important and instead just went through our days "playing house." We quickly learned, though, that this approach would get us nowhere, so we made some changes. Now we talk about just about everything, especially the important things. Especially the things we don't have time to talk about. Especially the things that are hard to talk about. Especially the things that, on the surface, just seem easier to keep "hidden." So, yeah, for us, step one of the work was learning how to talk and listen to one another. It all started with learning how to have open and honest conversations.

In addition to communication, we also work at our relationship by committing ourselves to continuous growth and learning. After all, we both know that (as our current parish priest continuously reminds us) "if our faith isn't growing, it's dying," so we do everything we can to make sure it's always growing. We read good books, go to Mass and Reconciliation, attend retreats, and pray daily, just to name a few. But, as important as all of this is, (and it's all super-important) I think the most important way we work at our marriage is by forgiving one another. I mean, we could argue all day about what every good marriage really needs, but if it's true that no marriage is perfect, (and I think we would all probably agree that this is true) then the only way any of them will last is if those in them choose (as often as necessary) to give them a fresh start.

So, my "advice" for getting a good, strong marriage grounded in truth, love, and mercy is simple: work on it! Strong marriages aren't given, they're made.

Prayer

Thank you, Lord, for the gift of marriage. Thank you for coming into ours so many years ago and for showing us what it means to love and forgive like you. Keep us in your loving care and help our marriage grow as we grow in our relationship with you. Bless all married couples, Lord, and all those preparing for marriage. Under your loving guidance, may all of these fragile, human relationships become strong, holy ones. I love you! I thank you! I praise you!

Read, Think, Pray: 1 Peter 4:8

REFLECTION #146

THE WRITTEN WORD

11/24/2014

I've been journaling now for over a year, and, although I didn't realize this when I first picked up a pen, (yes, I literally write with pen and paper) I've come to realize that part of the reason I write is because I find it therapeutic. I mean, I know God doesn't need me to tell Him every little thing that's on my mind. I know He knows me better than I know myself and, therefore, has no need for me to try to explain my life to Him, but *I* have a need to explain it. Yes, *I* have a need to process what's going on. *I* have a need to work through my problems. *I* have a need to think out loud. Writing is one of the ways I fulfill this need.

Another reason I write is because I need an outlet to process my emotions. Look, I know emotions, in and of themselves, aren't "good" or "bad." I know anger isn't always sinful, guilt isn't always unhealthy, and sadness isn't always despair, but I also know that how I react to and act upon my emotions matters, so I need a way to work through them healthily. Writing is one of these ways. Yes, writing helps me spot, so that I can then clean up, the many messes in my heart. And, I like this, because although I think it's true, "there's no use crying over spilled milk," I also think it's true, there's no use ignoring the huge mess it left on the floor either.

As if that wasn't enough, writing also helps me avoid delaying the inevitable. It keeps me accountable to myself and to God. After all, when I've written some heartfelt reflection about what I was feeling in the moment something took place, it's kind of hard to gloss over it later and categorize it as "no big deal." This is good for me because I'm often too quick to move on and say, "Next!" Writing keeps me from doing this by forcing me to live in the present and heal through life's hurts thoroughly. I've learned to like this. In fact, I think it's one of the reasons I've found so much peace. The truth is, life just isn't as scary when I'm not the one hiding.

So, what's my point? Well, I guess my point is, I like to write! (Yeah, I know...Who knew, right?)

Prayer

Be my light and my strength as I go through my days, Lord. Show me how to work through all the ups and the downs with you at my side. Show me how to find the meaning and purpose of my life. Show me how to process my emotions in healthy and constructive ways. Keep me accountable to what it is you're calling me to do, Lord, and teach me how to live (and write) like I've got nothing to hide.
I love you! I thank you! I praise you!

Read, Think, Pray: Psalm 144:1

REFLECTION #147

A PIECE OF THE PUZZLE

11/26/2014

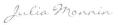

Imagine, if you will, that each one of us is a single piece in God's giant puzzle of creation. Now imagine God pouring us, the pieces making up His giant puzzle, out in front of Him. There we all lay, in front of our Creator, a jumbled, incoherent mess. As with all puzzles, when we are in this state scattered all around, one - or even many - of us could get "lost" without anyone noticing; without anyone caring; without anyone even being bothered by it. As is also with all puzzles, though, as it gets closer to completion, every "lost" piece is eventually noticed. Yes, even if only one out of a billion pieces went missing, the whole puzzle would still be incomplete; less than perfect; unfinished. This, as I see it, is what is meant by "mission" or "purpose" or, what Paulo Coelho calls in his book, *The Alchemist,* our "Personal Legend." Yes, as I see it, if we, the pieces in God's puzzle of creation, don't get put in place by doing what it is we are here to do, then the whole puzzle mourns our loss. It's kind of a big deal.

I bring this up again today because, although I thought I had a good understanding of this whole "mission" thing, I recently read Coelho's book and it, like so many others, has opened my eyes and deepened my level of understanding. It has reminded me that I am here to do something that no one else can do. It has reminded me that if I don't play my part, then my part isn't going to get played. It has reminded me that if my piece goes missing, then the whole puzzle will be incomplete. And, well, as you can imagine, this has refocused my attention on what really matters.

I can easily place myself in Coelho's story. I know what my "thief" is. I know what my "crystal shop" is. I know what my "treasure" is. I'm even learning, as he points out, that there is nothing greater than discovering your mission and working to fulfill it. As I reflect back on this year I've had, though, I can't help but recall the many times I've been filled with anything but "feel-good" feelings, and I also can't help but wonder where all these "not-so-feel-good" feelings have been coming from. Before reading this book I just couldn't quite figure it all out. I just couldn't quite put my finger on it, but I get it now. Yeah, now it is painfully clear. Some of the resistance I've been feeling *has* been the result of the world trying to hold me back from doing what it is I'm here to do like I thought for sure it was, but some of it, sadly, has been coming from me. Yeah, some of it has been because *I* have been holding *myself* back from doing what it is I am here to do. Yes, it's true. In many ways, *I* have been the one creating the resistance because *I* have been the one avoiding my mission.

In my defense, I didn't realize I was doing it. In fact, I would have told you that I *was* doing everything in my power to do what it is I'm here to do, but Coehlo's book has shed some light on the truth for me. And the truth is, I have been fighting against what it is I'm here to do because I have been afraid of the unknown. Yes, I have been hanging out in my "crystal shop" because I got comfortable and lost track of why I started working in it to begin with. I can no longer ignore the uneasiness in my heart telling me it's time to move on, though, so the time has come for me to take action. I mean, sure, I'm still frightened. Sure, I still have lots of questions. Sure, I'm still filled with uncertainty, but I can no longer resist the longings in my heart. I can no longer deny where I feel the Lord is leading me, so it is with great confidence in Him that I stare into the face of my fear and say, "Goodbye crystal shop! So long! The time has come for me to move on."

Prayer

I'm beginning to understand why I'm here, Lord. I'm beginning to discover my unique mission. Thank you for opening my eyes. Thank you for enlightening me. Thank you for filling me with even greater understanding. Now, give me the courage to take the next step. Give me the courage to do what it is you have created me to do. Don't let my fear get in the way of you doing something great with my life. Don't let me stand in your way. I love you! I thank you! I praise you!

Read, Think, Pray: Deuteronomy 8:2

THE HOLIDAYS

STUFFED AND CONSUMED

11/27/2014

It's time for me to get serious. Why? Because the season of consumerism and binge eating (aka, *The Holidays*) is upon me, and when this time of the year rolls around I'm always tempted to do two things: (1) buy more stuff, and (2) eat more food. I mean, I want the holiday season to be a time of grateful celebration, praise, and worship, but it instead often becomes a time of burdensome noise, chaos, and stress. Since I know this, though, - yeah, since I know I'm going to be tempted to make this season more about parties, presents, and food than about peace, love, and joy - I'm heading in to these upcoming weeks with a different approach. That's right, this year, I'm doing the unthinkable: I'm inviting God into my holiday schedule.

I've learned over the years that consumerism and binge eating do nothing but leave me feeling empty, so I've finally decided to take a stand against them. To be honest, this has been a long time coming for me. For years, I have wanted "The Holidays" to leave me with more than just a room full of stuff and a body full of sweets. I'm just now taking action to make sure they do. Yes, this year I want these weeks to leave me feeling inspired, enlightened, and filled up, not drained, burnt out, and wanting more. This year I want them to leave me feeling hopeful,

259

empowered, and joyful, not depressed, beaten up, and disheartened. In short, this year I want them to leave me, and all others, feeling loved, and if I'm serious about this happening, then I know I'm going to have to make some changes in my life. Yeah, I know I'm going to have to make the intentional effort to invite God in.

And, so, it is with this newfound intentionality that I now turn to prayer. I pray that God fills me with the grace and strength I need to be more concerned with giving than with spending. I pray that He fills me with the grace and strength I need to be more concerned with savoring the treat than with stuffing my face. Most importantly, I pray that He fills me with the grace and strength I need to be more concerned with Him than with the things of this world. After all, Christmas should be about Christ, shouldn't it?

Christmas should be about Christ, shouldn't it?"

Prayer

Thank you, Lord Jesus, for this joyful time to prepare for and to celebrate your birth. May your presence be known to us all, and may this season be centered and focused on what really matters: You. I love you! I thank you! I praise you!

Read, Think, Pray: Colossians 2:6-8

LOAVES AND FISHES

12/3/2014

Have you ever wondered why, in the miracle of the multiplication of the loaves and fishes, (John 6:1-15) Jesus asks his disciples to bring him what they have? I mean, he could have made food from nothing. Yeah, he could have just had God drop it from heaven like He had done before. (Does manna in the desert (Exodus 16) ring a bell?) So why didn't he? Why didn't he just take care of this little problem all on his own? Why did he *choose* to involve us this time around? Why did *we* actually have to bring him the loaves and the fish before he fed the crowd? Why did he ask *us* to participate?

Yeah, I can't help by wonder why. I can't help but wonder *why* Jesus asked us to play such an integral part in his plan when he could have, much faster and with much greater ease, done it on his own. I can't help but wonder *why* he gave us more and more chances to help when it seems that all we did was question our contributions and doubt his power. I guess this just tells us a little more about Christ, doesn't it? Yeah, I guess this just proves that he really *does* want to be in a relationship with us, huh?

I mean, why else would he have purposely and intentionally asked us to play a part in his miracle that day? And, for that matter, why else would he *still* be purposely and intentionally asking us to help him today? After all, that is what's going on here, isn't it? Isn't he just asking us to help, day in and day out, by giving him what we already have? He isn't asking us if we understand everything. He isn't asking us to do all the work. He isn't asking us to perform the actual miracle. No, he knows what we know and what we don't. He knows what we're capable of and what we aren't. He knows what we can do and what we can't, and all he really asks us to do is bring him what we already have, no matter how small it may seem, trusting that he can do great things with it. And, well, if our part really is that simple, why would we refuse?

Prayer

Time and time again you remind me of your goodness and power, Lord, yet time and time again I find myself doubting your abilities to work in my life. Why is it so easy for me to believe that you fed thousands with a few pieces of bread and a couple of fish, but so hard for me to believe that you could do the same thing in my life? Increase my faith and trust in you! Help me to believe in your mercy and power! May I be quick to give you what I already have, no matter how small it seems. May I be quick to assist you in whatever way I can, even if it doesn't seem like enough; especially if it doesn't seem like enough. I love you, my God, and I want to trust you more. Come, take my few loaves and fish, and work a miracle in my life. I love you! I thank you! I praise you!

Read, Think, Pray: John 6:1-15

REFLECTION #150

UNMOVABLE

12/3/2014

I hate the feeling of being on a treadmill (literally and figuratively). I hate feeling like I'm taking steps forward but somehow getting nowhere. It's never enough for me to *think* I'm making progress, I want to *see* it. Yeah, I want some sort of "proof" that it's happening. I'm learning, though, that most of the change we make happens so slowly it can seem like we're standing still. I'm also learning that what we think needs changed isn't always what God thinks needs changed. Oh, and, on top of that, I'm learning that God's "why" is often much different than our own.

"God's 'why' is often much different than our own."

Yes, for years now I have been obediently following God's command to reach out to a person in my life who is in need of some spiritual healing. For years now I have been reaching out to this person (in response to the Spirit's promptings) in an attempt to help. I thought for sure I knew *why* God was sending me there. Yeah, I thought for sure God was going to heal, or at the very least comfort, this person through me, but after years of having the same conversation with them it's becoming clear that little progress is being made. In fact, it's becoming clear that "healing" may never actually happen on my watch, so, as you can probably imagine, I've been frustrated. And, in my frustration, I dropped to my knees.

"Why can't I help them?" I asked God angrily. "Why can't I make a difference?...And why would you send me there in the first place if you knew I couldn't move them?"

As I asked God this last question, I was reminded of a story I heard months ago; a story about a man pushing a rock.* As soon as God brought this story to mind I "heard" His response.

"I didn't ask you to move them," He "said." "I just asked you to go. Look at yourself. Look at what you've learned through this. Look at how this situation has shaped you. Moving them, my child, was never the goal. The goal was for you to be trained in virtue, and, this, as you can see, has happened. Just look at how you've learned to listen. Look at how you've learned to be patient. Look at how you've learned to be gentle. Look at how you've learned to be compassionate. This was the reason I sent you to them. I didn't ask you to move them, I just asked you to go."

What more could I say? Seriously, how could I argue with God's reasoning? He has, once again, put me in my place by reminding me that my understanding isn't His understanding, my way isn't His way, my why isn't His why. Now it's clear to me what I need to do. Yes, now it's clear that I need to keep going wherever it is He asks me to go, even if it seems like I'm getting nowhere.

Prayer

Thank you, Lord, for hearing my cry and for lovingly responding to my needs. Help me to be less concerned about how I'm progressing on the outside and more concerned about how I'm growing on the inside. May I never again doubt the road you have me on. May I never again assume that I understand your why. I love you! I thank you! I praise you!

Read, Think, Pray: Isaiah 49:4, Isaiah 55:8-9

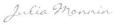

*Pushing Against the Rock

There once was a man who was asleep one night in his cabin when suddenly his room filled with light and the Savior appeared to him.

The Lord told him He had work for him to do, and showed him a large rock explaining that he was to push against the rock with all his might. This the man did, and for many days he toiled from sunup to sundown; his shoulder set squarely against the cold massive surface of the rock, pushing with all his might. Each night the man returned to his cabin sore and worn out, feeling his whole day had been spent in vain.

Seeing that the man showed signs of discouragement, Satan decided to enter the picture - placing thoughts in the man's mind, such as "Why kill yourself over this? You're never going to move it! Boy, you've been at it a long time, and you haven't even scratched the surface! etc." Thus, giving the man the impression the task was impossible, and the man was an unworthy servant because he wasn't moving the massive stone.

These thoughts discouraged and disheartened the man, and he started to ease up in his efforts. "Why kill myself?" he thought. "I'll just put in my time putting forth just the minimum of effort and that will be good enough." And this he did, or at least planned on doing, until, one day, he decided to take his troubles to the Lord.

"Lord," he said. "I have labored hard and long in Your service, putting forth all my strength to do that which You have asked of me. Yet after all this time, I have not even budged that rock even half a millimeter. What is wrong? Why am I failing?"

To this the Lord responded compassionately, "My friend, when long ago I asked you to serve Me and you accepted, I told you to push against the rock with all your strength and that you have done. But never once did I mention to you that I expected you to move it. At least not by yourself. Your task was to push. And now you come to Me, your strength spent, thinking that you have failed, ready to quit. But is this really so? Look at yourself. Your arms are strong and muscled; your back brown. Your hands are calloused from constant pressure and your legs have become massive and hard. Through opposition you have grown much, and your ability now far surpasses that which you used to have. Yet still, you haven't succeeded in moving the rock; and you come to Me now with a heavy heart and your strength spent. I, my friend will move the rock. Your calling was to be obedient and push, and to exercise your faith and trust in My wisdom, and this you have done."

- Author Unknown

REFLECTION #151

RESIST AND RECHARGE

12/3/2014

OK, so we're weeks in to the hustle and bustle of "The Holiday Season," and the temptations I've been having to make this season about the things of the world instead of about Christ have been real. They've been so real, in fact, that I feel like I've been at war. On the inside I'm filled with immense love and joy as I await Christmas during these days of

Advent, but on the outside all I hear is the world screaming, *"Forget about Christ! This time of the year is about the decorations, the perfectly prepared holiday meals, the endless parties, and, of course, the stuff; all of the new stuff!"* Yes, my soul whispers, *"Sit. Be. Celebrate life by reflecting on God's love and on the birth of His son. Be with those you love and enjoy your time together."* But my flesh screams, *"Go shopping! Get the tree up! Cook and clean! Skip your prayer time, you have stuff to do! Go! Do! Buy, Buy, Buy!"* Aaahhh! I knew this was coming. Yes, I am at war.

Though the struggle is real, I am not defeated or in any way discouraged by what has been going on internally these past few weeks. In fact, I'm certain that, in time, God will free me from my worldliness, but I have just realized something about being in a spiritual war that I don't think I've ever really realized before: the importance of recharging. Yes, after weeks of resisting this heavy temptation, I now realize how drained I am, and this exhaustion has forced me to take the time to sit down and regroup. It was during this regrouping that I realized that if I don't do this, - if I don't take the time to sit down and recharge my batteries - then the tempter is going to wear me down until my good, pure, and even holy intentions are lost, and I'm too tired and worn out to resist his attacks. As you can imagine, this is the last thing I want to happen.

So, I need to recharge. Yes, I know I need to recharge. But I wonder, how, exactly, do I do this? I mean, I know how to resist. I resist the temptation by facing it head-on. I resist it by bringing it to the light. I resist it by meeting it face-to-face, by calling it out, by giving it a name. I resist it by diving into it, - by getting to understand what the temptation is, how it's been working in my life, and who it's been working through - then I place all of it in God's hands and trust that He will somehow make the impossible task of being free from it, possible. I know I won't conquer this on my own. I know the only real way I can resist it is by giving it to Christ and by letting him show me how to defeat it, so that's what I've been doing. That's how I've been resisting, but the question remains: How do I recharge? How do I make sure the resisting doesn't wear me down to the point that I'm just so tired I give up?

I guess I recharge by going to Mass, by spending time in silence, prayer, and Adoration, by taking naps, by watching silly movies, and by playing games with the children in my life. Yeah, I guess I recharge by doing whatever it is I do (that is healthy and constructive, of course) that fills me with joy and brings me peace. Oh, and I guess one of the most important ways I recharge is by spending time with my Heavenly Mother. After all, it was her "yes" that made all of this possible in the first place.

And, so, that is what I'll do. Yes, I'll recharge. I'll resist the temptation when it shows up and recharge between the fighting. I'll make sure I'm set up to win. I'll make sure I have the strength I need to come out victorious. And, with this strategy, I'm sure it won't be long until I'm saying, "Goodbye 'Holidays!' Hello 'Christmas.'"

Prayer

You came into this world "so that [we] might have life and have it more abundantly," Lord, (John 10:10) but (as you know) I'm having a hard time embracing this abundant life. Please, help me resist the temptation to over-do it this Christmas. Show me how to rest and recharge in your presence. Don't let me lose sight of what this season is really about. Don't let me lose sight of you. Come into my life, Lord, and save me. I need you. The world needs you. I love you! I thank you! I praise you!

Read, Think, Pray: Deuteronomy 20:1, Hebrews 4:10-11

REFLECTION #152

HIDE AND GO SEEK

12/4/2014

If God came to us in all His splendor and in all His glory, who would approach Him? Probably none of us. In fact, probably even the most courageous of us would run away in fear. Who, though, is afraid of approaching a baby? Who, though, is afraid of approaching something as simple as bread and wine?

Sure, it's true that God comes to us "under a veil" so-to-speak, but why? Why doesn't He just let us see all of Him? I think it's because He longs for us to approach Him. I think it's because He longs for us to come towards Him. I think it's because He longs for us to get close.

It, of course, would be easy to believe that God is somehow "hiding" from us, but I don't think we should mistake the innocence of a child for weakness or the simplicity of bread and wine for powerlessness. In fact, I think life kind of *is* like one big game of hide-and-go-seek. I just don't think God is the one hiding.

"I think life kind of is like one big game of hide-and-go-seek. I just don't think God is the one hiding."

Prayer

The world tells us to be afraid of you, Lord. The world tells us that you are out to condemn us, that our sins are unforgivable, and that we are unworthy of your love and mercy, but you tell us differently. Remove from us any fear we have about approaching you. Soften our hearts, and give us the courage to walk towards you. Soften our hearts, and give us the courage to turn back to you. Soften our hearts, and give us the courage to receive your mercy. Call us out of hiding, Lord, and draw us into your loving presence. I love you! I thank you! I praise you!

Read, Think, Pray: 2 Corinthians 3:7-18

"My child, do you fear the God of mercy? My holiness does not prevent Me from being merciful. Behold, for you I have established a throne of mercy on earth - the tabernacle - and from this throne I desire to enter into your heart. I am not surrounded by a retinue or guards. You can come to me at any moment, at any time; I want to speak to you and desire to grant you grace." - The words of our Lord, Jesus Christ, to St. Faustina as recorded in her Diary, *Divine Mercy in My Soul*, 1485.

267

LOVING FREELY

12/4/2014

"The problems aren't here for us to solve, they're here to solve us." - I heard Matthew Kelly say this years ago, and it has stuck with me ever since. Not surprisingly, I was reminded of these words again when, after trying for weeks to solve a problem in my own life, I finally realized I was looking for the solution in all the wrong places. As soon as I realized this, I started asking God some better questions. Here was Question 1: "If the problems aren't here for us to solve and they are, instead, here to solve us, then what are you trying to solve *in me* through this problem, Lord?"

To back track a little, here's my problem: I'm frustrated with the "noise" associated with all the holiday parties. I just can't understand why everyone can't take it down a notch and focus more on each other and less on the turkey. This little problem eventually led me to Question 2: "Why does this bother me so much?"

It could bother me because I'm offended that Christ seems to be taking a back seat in the celebrating, but it could also bother me because I hate cooking and cleaning. It could bother me because I'm legitimately concerned about the well-being of the women in my life who seem stressed out, overwhelmed, and consumed, but it could also bother me because I have to take time out of my schedule to help clean the party venue. Yeah, Question 2 really got me thinking. As I prayed about it, God reminded me that all He ever asks us to do is love. And, well, this, at first, gave me nothing but more questions. Questions like, Question 3: "What is love?" And, Question 4: "What does it mean to love?" And, Question 5: "How do I show this love to others?"

James Martin's book, *The Jesuit Guide to Almost Everything,* answered some of these questions for me. This book helped me realize that what this problem was really trying to solve in me was *how* I showed my love to others. It helped me realize that I need to "love freely." That is, I need to show others I love them by allowing them to love me as they can, not as I want them to.

You see, I prefer others show me their love by being present with me, by conversing with me attentively, and by spending quality time with me, but others might prefer to show me their love by cooking me a nice meal. If this is the case, if our "love languages" (as Gary Chapman, author of *The Five Love Languages*, would say) don't match, then I can show them I love them by loving freely; by accepting the fact, for example, that they want to cook and by helping them in the kitchen. After all, love doesn't mean getting everyone to conform to my way of thinking. No, of course, it doesn't! Love means accepting people where they're at, and this means if something is important to someone I love, then it should be important to me. (Yes, even if this means I'll spend extra time in the kitchen when I'd rather spend extra time in meaningful conversation.)

Prayer

Help me to love freely, Lord. Help me to love more like you: completely, unconditionally, and without regulations. May I show my love to others by accepting the love they want to give me in whatever ways they want to give it, and may I always try to love them in a way that best speaks their language. I love you! I thank you! I praise you!

Read, Think, Pray: Romans 12:9-13

REFLECTION #154

HOLES

12/6/2014

There is nothing in this world like the love of a child. Nothing. I was reminded of this as I sat in prayer thanking God for all the graces He has given my husband and I throughout our marriage, especially for the grace He's given us as we carry the cross of infertility. Yes, the desire for children is real, and we, too, long to have a house full of kids, but even with this longing, I still find myself truly happy and perfectly fulfilled. I

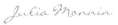

know this can be a little hard to believe. In fact, it's even a little hard for me to believe at times. And this is why, after thanking God that I am, by some miracle, still carrying this cross with a smile on my face, I followed up with a simple question: Am I kidding myself? I mean, come on. Is my happiness real, or is it just a facade?

I asked myself this question for one reason: I wanted to know the answer. I wanted to know for sure that I wasn't just putting on a brave face. After all, sad, angry, hateful, hurtful, and jealous-filled feelings would all be completely understandable and even natural, so my lack of them just seems a little "odd" at times. Yeah, even to me. I mean, don't get me wrong, I've *had* all these feelings before. Yes, I've mourned the absence of children in my life on several occasions, but every time these natural (and they really are natural) feelings come up, I work through them by talking about them and by taking them to Christ. Then I somehow find the strength to pick up my cross again with a smile on my face and without a grudge in my heart. Isn't that strange? I mean, even I am somewhat surprised that I'm not living a life of despair, hence my question. Yeah, hence the reason I asked myself if my happiness was real. I wanted to know what was really going on inside. I wanted to be sure I wasn't lying to myself, and, after some honest conversation, I found out I wasn't. I found out that my answer to the question of, "Am I really happy?" is a resounding "Yes!"

Yes, my happiness is real. Yes, it is genuine. Yes, it is authentic. I mean, sure I would love to have children of my own, but I, in no way, feel lost or abandoned without them. Besides, it's not like God isn't answering my prayers. He's answered every last one of them, and He's even blessed my husband and I with a daughter. Yes, He's even given us the joy of being used in His creative miracle, and, even if this child was only with us a few short weeks, the joy of having her is still very much present. Oh, and as if that wasn't enough, God has also given me the joy of "the barren wife who bears seven" (1 Samuel 2:5). Yes, I know this joy, too. In fact, I know that I, "the barren wife," have borne way more than seven, and I am reminded of this each and every time I am around any of my, what is now 24*, nieces and nephews. So, yeah, I know the love of a child, and the children in my life remind me that I am *not* childless. With that being said, of course, I'm happy! I mean, why, exactly, would there be any reason for me to be otherwise?

270

THE WORLD IS NOISY - GOD WHISPERS

Yes, God has given me plenty of reasons to be happy. To be honest, now that I think about it, I'm kind of surprised I was even questioning my happiness to begin with. I know I'm happy, and to me, it's clear *how* I'm carrying this cross with a smile on my face. Yeah, to me, it's clear *how* this is all possible. It's possible because of God. After all, since the hole in my heart that only He can fill is overflowing, it makes perfect sense that all the other, seemingly empty ones, would be filled up, too.

> *When the hole in your heart that only God can fill is overflowing, then all the other, seemingly empty holes, fill up, too.*

Prayer

I love you, my Lord! You are the answer to every one of my prayers. Yes, you. The answer is always you. You, my God, fill every part of me. I need nothing but your love because with it I am perfectly fulfilled. I am truly at peace. I am genuinely happy. Thank you, Lord. Thank you for filling me with your joy and for proving to me that it's the only joy that can ever really be complete. I love you! I thank you! I praise you!

Read, Think, Pray: Wisdom 7:7-11

* As of the date this book went to print, this number has increased to 28.

REFLECTION #155

HEADS AND HEARTS

12/13/2014

The truth is inside. I believe this. I understand this. I try to live this. Yes, I know the truth is inside. Do you ever wonder, though, *where* inside it is?

271

Well, I can tell you where I *don't* think it is. I don't think it's in our heads! In fact, I'm pretty sure our heads are *not* a good place to take up residence. I mean, our heads are good, helpful, and holy even. (And we need them to help us sort through things and weed through the garbage. After all, we're not animals. Our minds are a gift, and we're meant to use them.) But I don't think we should live in them. Yeah, I think that would be a bad idea. You know where I do think we should live, though? That's right, our hearts.

Yeah, I think we should live in, from, and through our hearts. After all, God tells us to become like children, (Matthew 18:3) and children, especially young children not yet "educated" in the ways of the world, live in, from, and through their hearts, don't they? It seems to me that they do, anyway. I mean, they let us in on what's going on inside them whether it's good, bad, or ugly. They don't filter themselves. They don't give much thought to what other people are thinking. They don't spend hours wondering what they should say or what they shouldn't. No, they just live and love and feel, and, since they're doing this without trying to hide any of it from us, we can see right through them. We can see right in to their most "truest" selves. I think that's what God wants with us, too. Yeah, I think when it comes to our relationship with Him, He wants us to live, like children, with our hearts on display.

Prayer

Help me to live in, from, and through my heart, Lord. Don't let the noise in my head confuse me into paralysis and disbelief. Come, teach me how to live like your child. Teach me how to live my life in an open and honest way, sure of your Fatherly love and guidance. Show me how to get out of my head and into my heart.
I love you! I thank you! I praise you!

Read, Think, Pray: Deuteronomy 30:11-14, Proverbs 4:23

"... The heart is our hidden center, beyond the grasp of our reason and of others; only the Spirit of God can fathom the human heart and know it fully. The heart is the place of decision, deeper than our psychic drives. It is the place of truth, where we choose life or death. It is the place of encounter..." - Catechism of the Catholic Church, Paragraph 2563

THE SLOW AND PAINFUL PROCESS

12/16/2014

I feel like I've been all over the place recently. I'm such a structured creature of habit that if I get out of my routine a little, I'm tempted to freak out and go crazy. (And, unfortunately, that's *not* an exaggeration.) I know, though, that life is rarely predictable, so I'm learning that I can't have a "take-no-prisoners" or a "stick-to-the-plan at all costs" approach. Yes, I'm learning that I need to be more flexible and that my wants need to come after other people's needs, so I know what needs to happen. Yeah, I know what I need to do. The problem, of course, is that knowing and doing are two different things. I repeat, knowing and doing are two different things.

Sure, it's become obvious *what* I need to change. It's even become obvious *how* I need to change it. (Prayer, Sacraments, fasting, and lots and lots of practice.) But where I'm struggling, (and where I always seem to struggle) is with the "waiting" part. Yeah, I'm struggling with the *process* of change. You see, I just want to get to where I'm going, so nothing ever happens fast enough. Everything, instead, is always way too slow. And therein lies my problem. I, you see, need to be patient. I need to trust that I'm exactly where I'm supposed to be.

The process of change is always slow and painful. In fact, the reason it's so painful for me is because it's so slow, but it's always worth it, so I'll keep at it. Yes, I'll keep moving forward holding on to the hope that, in the end, I will indeed be free from my many, many vices. (Yes, even if it takes a lifetime.)

Prayer

Give me what I need to make it through this slow and painful process of change, Lord. Set me free from my sin and teach me how to trust more completely in you. You are my God, and I love you. Come, prove to me that there's no reason for me to rush

273

*or push or force anything into happening. Come, prove to
me that I am exactly where I'm supposed to be.
I love you! I thank you! I praise you!*

Read, Think, Pray: Proverbs 19:2

REFLECTION #157

THE SICK DAY

12/22/2014

Though I've been blessed (at least for now) with good health and don't find myself sick often, today I'm not feeling my best. Being physically sick has reminded me how weak I really am. It has reminded me that life is more than what I "do." In fact, it has reminded me that I can "do" nothing without God. Before I was reminded of this, though, I spent my morning in a state of distress knowing that my illness meant I wouldn't be able to work like I normally do. At some point, I even found myself wondering things like, "Who am I if I can't work?" And, "What am I worth to anyone if I can't perform my duties?" I guess, in a way, I felt like a big waste of space since I was unable to get anything "done."

As I sat asking myself questions like these the temptation to believe the lie that my self-worth is somehow dependent on what I can accomplish crept in. Thankfully, God came to my rescue by reminding me of a story I just read yesterday. (Coincidence? I think not!) This story* was about a bishop, who, after being put in prison, found himself devastated since being in jail meant he wouldn't be able to complete the projects he had started for God. After many stressful days he was eventually comforted in his affliction when he heard a voice tell him, *"Everything you have done and desire to continue doing...are God's works, but they are not God. Choose God and not the works of God."*

As I recalled this story and reread the words that this bishop heard in his cell, God reminded me that His works, though good and righteous, are not Him. He reminded me that there's more to life than doing good and avoiding evil. He reminded me that there's more to *me* than what I *do*.

Most importantly, He reminded me that my self-worth has nothing to do with what I'm able to accomplish. And this, sadly, is something I need reminded of often. So, yeah, though it certainly didn't start out this way, I'm now incredibly grateful for the sick day.

> *There's more to us than what we "do." Our self worth has nothing to do with what we're able to accomplish.*

Prayer

Help me, God, to choose you and not only your works. Free me from the lies enslaving me to a life of "doing." Show me the truth about your love and help me to believe it. Remind me often that I am not loved for what I do but for who I am: your beloved child. I love you! I thank you! I praise you!

Read, Think, Pray: Galatians 4:1-7

* This story is about the late Vietnamese cardinal, Nguyen Van Thuan. I read this story on 12/21/2014. It was in the mediation that day in the Catholic Devotional Magazine, *The Word Among Us*. (www.wau.org)

REFLECTION #158

WANTS VS. NEEDS

12/30/2014

This season of gifting has got me thinking about the difference between the gifts we "need" and the gifts we "want." This thinking has made me realize that the gifts we "want" are often more exciting to receive than the gifts we "need." After all, our "wants" fill us with pleasure, and this makes us think that these gifts are somehow more "fun." The gifts we "need" are often a different story. Yeah, even though we make good, practical use of them, it somehow feels "boring" to receive them. All of this has made me wonder, is it better to give people the "fun" gifts they "want" or the "boring" gifts they "need?"

All this wondering has made me realize that this doesn't have to be an "either/or" situation. Yeah, all this wondering has made me realize that God has a way of giving us, His beloved children, the "fun" things we "want" and the "boring" things we "need" all at the same time. With that being said, I think this is how I should try to give to others, too. Yeah, I think I should try to give people what they "want" while, at the same time, trying to give them what they "need." How am I going to do this, you ask? Well, I'm going to trust in the creativity of the Holy Spirit and start by meeting people where they're at.

Prayer

Teach me, Lord, how to give like you. Send your Spirit upon me, and show me how to meet people where they're at so that, through me, you can give them what they "want" and what they "need" all at the same time. I love you! I thank you! I praise you!

Read, Think, Pray: Matthew 7:9-11

REFLECTION #159

EAGER ANTICIPATION

12/30/2014

Some of my best Christmas memories are "waiting" for Christmas morning. For me anticipating what was to come was always as exciting, if not more so, than the actual day. There was (and still is) a joy in the air the weeks before Christmas; a joy that's a little different than the day itself. As an adult, I often get this same feeling before a long-awaited vacation. Just thinking about "getting away" somehow puts me in a better mood. The reality of this joyful waiting got me thinking. I now wonder, is waiting really the hardest part?

At first, I would have said "Yes!" I mean, come on. I'm sure you've noticed I'm usually one who does *not* like to wait. In fact, I'm sure you've noticed I'm usually a no-nonsense, "let's get to where we're going so that we can get to the next place we're going," kind of a person. After some reflective thought, though, I've come to realize (much to my surprise) that my real answer is "No." No, the waiting isn't really the hardest part. That shocking discovery left me with another question: What, then, is? What is the hardest part?

The hardest part for me is getting to the destination and being let down. It's realizing my joyful expectations don't match the less than joyful reality. It's waking up Christmas morning only to discover I didn't get the gift I wanted. It's arriving on my dream vacation only to discover I'm staying in a run-down hotel with less than dreamy accommodations. Yeah, the hardest part for me is the disappointment. It's the colossal let-down I feel after realizing my expectations weren't met.

Still, though this is true, I'm convinced that, unlike some of the situations (and perhaps people) of this world, God won't let me down or disappoint me. Yeah, I'm convinced God will live up to the hype. I'm convinced God will not only meet my expectations, He'll exceed them. With that being said, I'm going to be a more joyful waiter from now on. Yeah, I'm going to let myself get excited about the life that is to come. I'm going to let myself get excited about Christ and his promises. After all, I'm certain heaven will be nothing like the gift-less Christmas or the not-so-dreamy trip of a lifetime. Yes, I'm certain it will vastly exceed even my wildest expectations.

"I'm convinced God will live up to the hype."

Read, Think, Pray: Romans 8:18-25

REFLECTION #160

HEAVEN ON EARTH

12/30/2014

I was recently asked the question, *"Why do you go to Mass?"*
Surprisingly, I had to think about my answer. You see, Mass, (yes, daily
Mass even) has just become something I do. At this point, it's a habit. I
don't have to plan it. I don't have to think about when I'm going. I don't
have to wonder if I'll make it. No, there's no question about whether or
not I'll be there. I'm going, every weekend, and as often as possible
during the week, no questions asked. Still, the question remains: Why?
Why is Mass so important to me that it has become engrained into my
inner-most being?

Perhaps my answer will surprise you because it's not, "I go to Mass
because I find it entertaining." Or, "I go to Mass because of the
fellowship." Or, "I go to Mass because I have nothing else to do." No,
none of these are my reasons for going. Mass, you see, isn't
"entertaining" to me, and, as much as I love being around others, I
actually find private devotion "easier" than devotion with the
community. My why, therefore, is different; much different. (Oh, and
just to be clear, "because I have to go" hasn't been my reason for years.)

So, why do I go to Mass? What gets me out of bed on days I'd rather sleep in? What gets me going at noon in the middle of a busy work week when there's no "obligation" for me to attend? Why do I plan my whole schedule, day in and day out, around this one event? Simple: Christ. I go because I yearn for God. I go because I long to be near Christ. I go because I'm hungry to receive him in the Word and in the Eucharist. I go because I'm a big sinner, and I'm convinced I was created to be a saint. I go because I'm nothing, and Christ fills my nothingness. I go because I want to be united with my Savior, and I know of no other place where I can unite myself with him in such an intimate way.

"I go to Mass because I'm a big sinner, and I'm convinced I was created to be a saint."

Yes, I've fallen in love with the Mass, but it's not because of the perfectly sung hymns or the life-changing homilies or the friendly smiles and handshakes of my fellow brothers and sisters. No, I've fallen in love with the Mass because I've fallen in love with Christ, and, to me, the two are inseparable. The question for me, therefore, isn't, *"Why do I go to Mass?"* it's, *"Why wouldn't I go?"* You see, to me, *nothing* in my life is more important.

Prayer

Mass is one of your greatest gifts, Lord, but until we understand it, it can feel like a chore. Help us, therefore, to grow in our understanding. Help us to come to appreciate your gift. May we never again take for granted the very real, personal, and tangible way we meet you at Mass. May we never again take for granted how close you come to us in these moments we are in, and receive, your True Presence. Come, open our minds and hearts. Show us the beauty of what you've given us. Show us why it's been said that Mass is heaven on earth. I love you! I thank you! I praise you!

Read, Think, Pray: John 6:48-67, Luke 22:14-20

A SHORT MEMORY

12/31/2014

At this point in time, lots of us have heard about Jesus. At this point in time, lots of us have even been baptized and, in so doing, have become God's adopted children. Yes, at this point in time, lots of us have been Sacramentalized, it just seems that few of us remember why.

I'm saddened by the realization of how quickly we, God's children, forget about Christ. I'm saddened by the realization of how quickly we, God's children, forget the Good News. Why are we so quick to forget?

Maybe our lives have just gotten a little noisy. Yeah, maybe we just need a little reminder. Well, it's worth a shot anyway, so here goes...

A gentle reminder to all of God's children who have forgotten the Good News:

Jesus Christ came into this world to show us, His chosen ones,
how to live. He died so that we wouldn't have to. He is the Way,
the Truth, and the Life (John 14:6), and with him, in him, and through
him, everything - yes, everything - makes sense. Let us not be so quick
to forget! Let us not be so quick to forget that we are children of
the King! Let us not be so quick to forget that we are free! Let
us not be so quick to forget that we are loved!

*This message has been humbly brought to you
by the most forgetful one of all: Julia*

Prayer

*I haven't forgot about you, Lord, I just got a little distracted.
Come back into my life, and help me re-center my mind and
heart on you. Enlighten me. Strengthen me. Encourage me.*

Fill me with your great love. Heal my short memory,
Lord. May I never forget the Good News again.
I love you! I thank you! I praise you!

Read, Think, Pray: John 3:16-18

REFLECTION #162

THE RESOLUTION

12/31/2014

I like to take advantage of the opportunities a new calendar year brings with it. Yeah, to me, the New Year is a great time to refocus and restart. It's a great time to look back on what I've learned and think about all I'm grateful for and to look ahead at what's to come and set new goals for the future. With that being said, this year I have one resolution: to get in the habit of noticing.

This past year I've felt God calling me to live a more contemplative life. I've felt Him calling me to spend more time in the silence; to spend more time thinking about Him, about life, and about love. As a result of this calling, I've been training myself to live life in a more reflective state of awareness. I've been training myself to pay closer attention to what's happening around me so that I can spend time thinking about what it all means. Well, I think this training is starting to pay off. Yeah, I think it's starting to bear fruit. In fact, I think it's because of this training that I now "hear" God speak so often. And, well, in case I ever forget, (I have, after all, been known to have a short memory) here are a few examples of what He's been saying to me recently:

Example 1: A few weeks ago I was out driving my car. Although I was out during the day it was a little cloudy, so I turned on my headlights as I headed down the road. As soon as I turned my lights on, I *noticed* the two cars heading in my direction turn their lights on as well. After *noticing*, I "heard" God say, "See, Julia, light is contagious. Once

281

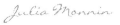

someone sees yours, it reminds them to turn theirs on, too. Don't make what I'm asking of you harder than it needs to be. Just turn on your light. Others will follow your lead."

Example 2: For several months now I have felt "the call" to share my writing with others. In recent weeks, this "call" has become "louder," and the door has been opened to begin. As the time got closer for me to walk through this open door and begin sharing, fear and nervousness began to consume me. Suddenly, I found myself questioning everything. "What will people think?" I wondered. "Who do I think I am to do this? Maybe I should just wait. Maybe now isn't the time. Maybe I didn't 'hear' God correctly. Maybe I shouldn't do this at all. Maybe this isn't my 'calling.'" Etc., etc., etc. God put my fears to rest after I *noticed* Him "speaking" to me through some lyrics of a song. Through this song I "heard" Him tell me that the time had come for me to share. I "heard" Him tell me to remove my mask, to "never go back" because "the past is in the past." I "heard" Him remind me of my story. I "heard" Him remind me of where I have come from and what has all happened. I "heard" Him remind me that the "perfect girl was gone" and that was OK because no one is perfect, and no one is helped when we pretend that we are. I "heard" Him tell me, "it's time to see what you can do," encouraging me to "let others in" and to "keep it in" no longer. I "heard" Him tell me that the time is now, that I need to begin, that I need to come forward and "stand in the light of day." Yes, I "heard" Him tell me, over and over and over again, to "let it go" all because I *noticed* Him "speaking" to me through some lyrics of a song. (On a side note, I never would have guessed a song from a Disney movie I watched with my nieces and nephews a few months ago would become my personal anthem inspiring me to take the next step. Never!)

So, anyway, yes, I've been *noticing* things these past few years. I've been paying closer attention to what's been happening around me and in me and through me and have, as a result, been "hearing" God's voice more and more. What I hope to improve with my *noticing* skills in the new year, though, is *how much* it's happening. Yeah, I want this *noticing* to go from being something I have to think about doing to something I just naturally do. I want it to become engrained into my inner-most being. Yes, I want it to become a habit. And that's why, this year, my resolution is simple. This year, I resolve to get in the habit of noticing.

Prayer

*Help me, Lord, to "tune-in" to you on a more regular
basis. Help me to listen to you more attentively so that I can
"hear" your voice in the ordinary events of my day. You have all the
answers to all of my questions, Lord. You know me better than I know
myself. Help me to take advantage of this knowledge by focusing
my mind and heart on you at all times. Speak to me always,
my God, and help me get in the habit of noticing.
I love you! I thank you! I praise you!*

Read, Think, Pray: 1 Samuel 3:1-10

THE WAIT

THE CHAIR

1/7/2015

For the past few years, one chair in my home has become what I would call my "prayer chair." It's in this chair that I begin each of my days with Scripture, spiritual reading, and, of course, my journal all within reach. Though it certainly didn't start out this way, I have come to love my time in this chair. To be honest, I can't function (not virtuously anyway) without it. Yes, I'll admit it. I'll own up to who I really am. My name is Julia. I am a wife, a daughter, a sister, and an aunt; a worker, a student, and an over-achiever; a sinner, a wanna-be saint, and, most importantly, a child of God. And you know what? This child needs her Daddy and needs Him often!

The daily need I have for my Father is met in this chair. Yes, this chair is where He and I get together, day in and day out, and where everything in my life comes to make sense. Sure, every day in this chair is a little different. Sure, there are some days my prayer leaves me feeling more uplifted and inspired than others, but regardless of how I "feel," I never doubt my Father's presence when I'm here. No, never.

Sometimes when I'm in this chair God has a lot to say to me. Sometimes when I'm in this chair I have a lot to say to Him. Sometimes when I'm in this chair neither of us say a word. It's during these times that our time together is really just a recognition of each other; I notice Him, He notices me. (Or, what is more accurate since He always notices me, is that I notice Him noticing me.) Although my mind always tells me that prayer has to have words in order to be "engaging," my heart always tells me that our relationship is most sincere when neither of us are talking. After all, in some relationships a "look" can say it all, and there are just some days a "look" is all either of us need.

So, yes, though this place in my home could never replace the real and true way I encounter the Lord at Mass and Adoration in the Eucharist, it is in this chair that I've really come to know my Father. It is in this chair that our relationship has blossomed. It is in this chair that I have learned who He is, who I am, and what this all means. With that being said, it's no wonder I have come to love my time in this chair! I mean, this is where it has all happened for me. This is where it has all come together. This is where it has all started to make sense. And why? Because this is where I have come to know how very much I am loved. What else could any child need?

Prayer

I never knew what life was until I met you, Lord. I never knew how great life could be until I let you come into mine. I need you in my life! I want you in my life! Please, don't let me walk away from you. Please, don't let me stop taking the time to meet up with you. May I never forget why I'm here, Lord. May I never forget what you've shown me and taught me and told me. Most importantly, may I never forget how very much I am loved. I love you! I thank you! I praise you!

Read, Think, Pray: Psalm 5:3-4

REFLECTION #164

CALLED TO GREATNESS

1/13/2015

I've had a feeling for awhile now that God has made me for something "different;" that the life He's planned for me isn't an "ordinary" one. Yeah, I've had a feeling for awhile now that God has made me to be a saint. Oh, and not just any saint, a great one. And you know what? I'm terrified by even the thought!

I mean, I can think of no one *less* worthy of "greatness" than I, yet, as much as I try to ignore it, I can't seem to shake "the call." (Oh, and you wanna know a secret? This "call" is so strong, so intense, and so real that I just realized it's even one of the reasons I would like to have kids. Ssshhh, don't tell anyone!) Seriously, I know that sounds awful, but it's true. You see, I'm so frightened by this "call to greatness" that I'm already coming up with ways I can get out of it. Children, sadly, have become one of those ways. I mean, if my call was to be a mother, then that would give me a great reason to have a "normal" life. And if I had one of those "normal" lives, then when God told me to "become a great saint" I could easily tell Him, "You've got the wrong person! I, my Lord, am a mother with lots and lots of kids. There's no way I can be a great saint in the world and be a great mother to my children. No, there's no way! You'll just have to make me one of those 'normal' saints. You know, one of those saints whose greatness is revealed through the changing of dirty diapers and the wiping of runny noses. Yeah, you'll just have to make me one of those saints. Any greatness other than that just isn't for me."

Oh, I hate that this is how I've been thinking. Yeah, I hate that I'm so afraid to fail I'm already coming up with reasons why I shouldn't even try. But I'd be lying if I said these thoughts hadn't crossed my mind. Yeah, I'd be lying if I told you I'm not afraid. The good news, though, is that God hasn't let these fear-filled thoughts fester in me for too long. Yeah, the good news is that God has put these fear-filled thoughts to rest by reminding me of the truth.

Sometimes we're so afraid to fail we come up with reasons why we shouldn't even try.

"You're right," He "told" me confirming my suspicions about being called to greatness. "You *are* called to something 'different.' I *have* made you for something 'more.' 'Normalcy,' as you define it, is *not* for you. But, trust me, my child. You'll be more than happy with the life I'm calling you to; the life I made you for."

"But what about my husband?" I asked Him still looking for reasons to dodge my calling. "What about him? Will he be more than happy, too?"

"Yes, of course!" God replied extinguishing the last of my excuses. "He's as much a part of this as you are."

And, so, I'm ashamed to admit it, but I've obviously been having a hard time accepting my calling. Yeah, I've obviously been having a hard time accepting the fact that I'm being called to greatness. I guess there's just a part of me that thinks it would somehow be easier to ignore the call and go back to living a "normal" life, but every time I try to tell God that He's got the wrong person, - that I'm a nobody from nowhere who is incapable of living anything but an ordinary life - He "tells" me, "You, My child, may be nothing to this world, but you are *everything* to me! Don't be afraid of the life I'm calling you to, for I have been preparing you for it from the very first moment of your existence. You are my light! You were *made* to shine. You are my apostle of love! You were *made* to love. Trust me, my child. Trust me. I have never, and will never, steer you wrong."

And, so, I'm running out of excuses. Yeah, I'm running out of reasons to tell God why I can't do this. I guess there's really only one thing left for me to say.

"So, you made me to be a great saint, huh, Lord? Well, you better get to work! I've got a long way to go!"

Prayer

I love you, Lord, and I would like nothing more than to want what it is that you want for me. Yes, I would like nothing more than to want what it is that you desire. So, bend my heart to your will. Make your will my own. Help me to accept the fact that I've been made for greatness. Help me to accept the fact that I've been made for more. Don't let my fear stand in the way of your plans for me. Don't let my fear stop you from doing your work in me and through me. Give me the courage to proceed, Lord. Give me the courage to let my light shine. I love you! I thank you! I praise you!

Read, Think, Pray: 1 Peter 2:9, Matthew 5:14-16

REFLECTION #165

RELIGIOUS SPIRITUALITY

1/13/2015

There's an idea in our culture that there's a difference between being "spiritual" and being "religious." From what I understand of it, the idea is that "religious" people practice some sort of organized religion and that "spiritual" people find God (or what they might refer to as some "higher power") outside of church. Regardless of how these two terms are actually defined, it seems to me that the world is (for the most part) OK with people being "spiritual," but that it's *not* OK with people being "religious." Why is that? Why are there so many negative associations with the word "religious?" I mean, when I answered the question of someone I just met a few weeks ago after he asked me what I was writing about, he immediately turned his nose up in disgust and gasped in horror, "That doesn't mean you're religious, does it?" So, yeah, I definitely think there's a negative connotation to the word "religious." I'm just kind of curious why.

I can understand parts of the "spiritual" side of the argument. In fact, I would agree that God is everywhere and in everything and that we can, and should, seek Him in the world around us. I would even agree that God is "bigger" than religion. Yes, I would agree that we can find God, have a relationship with Him, and even "be saved" outside of "church." (After all, that is what the Catholic Church actually teaches.) I also know that organized religion is far from being perfect. Yes, I know that over the course of its history it's been associated with, and even responsible

289

for, many unthinkable scandals. Still, I just can't wrap my head around the idea that a "spiritual" life is somehow a substitute for a "religious" one. I guess, to me, the two seem inseparable. Yeah, I guess, to me, the "spiritual" side is missing something without the "religious" side. And, perhaps, in time, God will unveil to all of us what that "something" is.

Prayer

Guide us to the truth about religion, Lord. Give us the courage to ask, seek, and knock. Teach us how to live openly so that we might hear and understand your voice. Set us free from the lies of the world. Set us free from any falsehoods keeping us from uniting ourselves with you in the ways you have intended us to. May we walk in peace as your beloved children standing firm in our faith as chosen members of your Church. I love you! I thank you! I praise you!

Read, Think, Pray: Matthew 16:13-19

REFLECTION #166

THE MESSAGE OF REASSURANCE

1/14/2015

It's been fairly easy for me to understand that we all have a mission to fulfill. What's not been so easy for me to understand is *what* my mission is. That's why I've been living my life with an open heart these past few years, eagerly waiting on God to let me in on it. Over the course of this time, I've given God one small "yes" after another, and with each of these "yeses" my mission has become more and more clear. Still, there have been (and still are) times when I want to complicate things; times when I want to doubt; times when I want to stay in my comfort zone and keep everything as it is. I have learned, however, (time and time again) that never getting out of my comfort zone means never becoming all I was created to become, so I wake up each and every day ready to get uncomfortable. Today was no different. But, as I started diving into my work, I quickly realized the discomfort I was feeling was "heavier" than normal. It was so "heavy," in fact, that I was afraid it would actually keep me from proceeding this time. Well, thankfully, God didn't let it. Yeah, thankfully, God came to my rescue by sending me a little message of reassurance.

This message came to me after Mass. After hearing a homily that really spoke to me, - one during which I specifically thought, "This is so perfect. I would change nothing about it. It needs no elaboration; no simplifying. It's wonderful." – I went up to the priest to ask him for a copy of it. (Which was not, by the way, my first time doing this. He probably knows what to expect when he sees me coming. HA!) Anyway, after kindly agreeing to give me his copy, I asked if he would mind if I shared it with others. "No," he told me. "Just put it in your own words."

As I left church and drove back home, his words kept repeating themselves in my mind. "Just put it in your own words...Just put it in your own words...Just put it in your own words." It didn't take long for me to realize why.

"Just put it in your own words," I thought. "Hmmm, that's kind of what I do. Yeah, that's kind of what I've been doing all along, and that's kind of why I've been doubting this whole 'writing thing' to begin with because it's not like I'm saying anything that hasn't already been said a million times before by millions of other (much more intelligent and much more holy) people. Oh, I think God is sending me a message here. Yeah, I think these seven words spoken through that priest are words He wants me to pay close attention to."..."Just put it in your own words," I can "hear" Him reassuring me. "That's all I've ever asked you to do."

And, so, it is with sincere gratitude that I say, "Thank you, Lord, for this message of reassurance; this message of 'just put it in your own words.' This short, little sentence has reminded me what it is you are asking me to do. So, from now on, I *will* 'just put it in my own words' and trust that you will take care of the rest."

Prayer

You are so good, my God, and I love you! Thank you

for sending messengers into my life to lift me up, to remind me of you, and to reassure me of my mission. May I always be open to hearing your voice and receiving your guidance in and through the people around me. May the reassurance I hear from them be enough for me to keep up the good fight and to do what it is you have put me here to do.
I love you! I thank you! I praise you!

Read, Think, Pray: Proverbs 2:1-6

REFLECTION #167

A LOVE STORY

1/15/2015

Once upon a time as a young tween-age girl, I received a phone call from a boy in the grade ahead of me. At the time, I didn't think much of it. It, you see, was one call of many. I remember thinking, though, that this particular boy on the other end of the line had some guts. I mean, sure, I knew who he was, (when you're from a small town like me you know who everyone is) but I had never really met him before. He was just some quiet boy I knew nothing about. And that's why it wasn't hard for me to turn him down that day when he asked me "out." (Whatever "out" means at that age.)

As the years went on I thought very little about this phone call or about the boy on the other end of the line. For years he remained the quiet boy I knew nothing about. In high school, though, an innocent friendship began to blossom between the two of us as we were "coincidentally" paired up for a few things that sort of forced us to get to know one another. Still, I never could get past the fact that he was so quiet, so, even though he always wanted more from our relationship, I continued to turn him down each and every time he found the courage to ask me out. Although always disappointed by my response, he never took my "no" as a final answer. He just kindly accepted defeat, continued being a friend, and quietly held on to the hope that I would someday change my mind.

At some point in this game of boy-chase-girl, the quiet boy finally decided that if he was going to get me to change my mind, then he was going to have to get some outside help. I guess he realized he wasn't going to break through my heart of stone without some reinforcements, so he got himself a middle-man; a trusted friend whose mission was to warm me up to the idea of giving him a chance. This friend of his talked him up constantly for months on end, and, much to my surprise, it actually worked. Yes, slowly, over time my heart began to soften, and I started to see the quiet boy as more than just the quiet boy. Although at this point my head was still trying to tell me he wasn't "right" for me, my heart (and this guy's buddy) finally convinced me to give him a chance. So, after years of patiently waiting in the background of my life, the quiet boy finally got his "Yes."

Now, I may not remember all the details of our first date like he does, but there is one moment in the early months of our dating that I will never forget. After a meal, we sat in the car getting ready to leave when he took a deep breath and nervously reached over to hold my hand for the first time. At the moment his hand touched mind a wave of electricity filled my entire being, and I immediately found myself (for what was probably the first time ever) speechless. "How could this quiet boy, who said so little, speak so loudly to my heart?" I wondered. "How could he say so much without saying a word?" Well, after years of ups and downs and countless "rough patches" that all seemed to stem from my doubt that this quiet boy really did love someone as flawed as me, we finally became husband and wife. Now I, too, realize what he seemed to have realized way back in elementary school: we really are the perfect match.

I wish I could tell you that my husband was the only man in my life that I refused to give a chance to, but I can't. No, I spent years refusing to give God a chance, too. Yeah, just like the relationship with my husband, my adult relationship with God started with me closing my heart off to Him. It started with me being sure that He wasn't the one; sure that He was too quiet, too distant, and too mysterious to be my "type." But just like the quiet boy did so many years ago, God, too, sent someone into my life to soften my heart so that I could get to know the real Him. And (just like the quiet boy's buddy) that someone did her job. Yes, that someone revealed to me the truth about the man my soul was really made for: her son, Jesus Christ.

I guess this just goes to show that sometimes we need an intercessor to get the job done. Yeah, I guess this just goes to show that sometimes we need someone in the middle, someone who understands both sides, to bring two people together. I guess this just goes to show that without a little intercession, some of us have a really hard time saying, "Yes."

> *"Sometimes we need an intercessor to get the job done."*

Prayer

You have turned my once cold and hardened heart into mush, Lord, and I thank you for it. I thank you for patiently waiting on me, just like my husband, until I could see the light. I thank you for loving me, just like my husband, even when I didn't love you in return; even when I just kept telling you, "No." I love you, Lord, and I thank you for coming into my life. Please, send your Mother into each of our lives. Use her to soften our hearts, break down our walls, and help us to get to know you for who you really are. May your silence speak loudly to our hearts, and may we all come to tell you what you have always longed to hear: "Yes!" I love you! I thank you! I praise you!

Read, Think, Pray: Ezekiel 11:19-20

REFLECTION #168

THREE LITTLE WORDS

1/20/2015

A few years ago, (early on in my spiritual journey) I was at a meeting in church praying with the group I was with when we got to a part in the prayer where we told God, "I love you." Though I didn't expect it to be, it was awkward for me to say those three little words out loud to God. After thinking about it some, I eventually realized why.

The words "I love you" are powerful. They're meant to be heartfelt and meaningful. They're meant to be told to someone you know, someone you care about, someone you're in a relationship with. And, well, at that time in my life, (though I was taking steps in the right direction) I was far from knowing God. Sure, I knew *about* Him, but I didn't *know* Him, and there's a big difference between the two. With that being said, it's not really surprising it felt so strange for me to tell God I loved Him that evening. After all, how could I love someone I didn't really know?

There is a difference between knowing about God and knowing Him.

Though I don't like to live in the past, I do like to remind myself of stories like these from time to time because they prove to me how far I've come. Yes, they prove to me how much my heart has changed in just a few short years. Oh, and you know what else? They also prove to me that once you get to know God for who He *really* is, it doesn't take long to fall in love.

So, you see, my whole life God has been telling me, "You are precious in my eyes and honored, and I love you" (Isaiah 43:4), and I just realized I'm finally at the point where I can respond with ease, "I love you, too." It's such an awesome place to be!

Prayer

*Yes, Lord, I love you! I love you! I love you! I love you!
Now, may the rest of my life do one thing: prove it.
I love you! I thank you! I praise you!*

Read, Think, Pray: John 21:15-17

THE CRUCIFIX

1/20/2015

I've heard many people ask why. "Why do you keep Jesus on the cross?" "He is risen," they say. "Let us rejoice!" To this I say, yes, of course. Christ *has* conquered death. He *is* risen. He *is* no longer on the cross, but I think we are seeing two different things when we look at a crucifix. You must be seeing death, but that's not what I see. I see love.

When I look at a crucifix I don't see fear and defeat; I see triumph and redemption. When I look at a crucifix I don't see mockery and violence; I see honor and sacrifice. When I look at a crucifix I don't see death; I see love. I see Christ, the love of my life, giving up everything for me. I see his arms stretched out wide saying loud and clear, "How much do I love you? I love you this much!" I see his heart pierced, vulnerable, and wide open begging me to love him in return. I see the loving face of my Savior consoling me by crying out, "Do not weep for me. I would do it all over again if I had to. In fact, there is *nothing* I wouldn't do for you. *You* are *my* everything. I love you."

So, you may look at a crucifix and see hatred and brutality, but I see something completely different. I see God who became man to prove His love for us by doing the one thing that, as God, He could never do; die. And that doesn't leave me feeling sad, it leaves me feeling loved; completely and totally loved.

Prayer

It is unfathomable to me how much you love me, Lord; how much you love us all. What more could you do to prove this? There is nothing else. - It is finished. - May the crucifix remind me of your love each and every time I look at it. Through it, my God, may I learn to love more like you. Through it, my God, may I be set free. I love you! I thank you! I praise you!

Read, Think, Pray: John 15:13

DADDY'S LITTLE HELPER

1/20/2015

God is my Father; my friend; my everything. My heart burns with love for Him, so my heart aches when I notice others distancing themselves from Him. That's why, as I sat in prayer thinking about all the people in the world choosing to walk away from Him, I cried out in a panic, "What are they doing, Lord? Where are they going? Don't they know the answers aren't out there? Don't they know they're going the wrong way?" I had no idea what God had in store for me next.

"Fear not," I "heard" Him call out in the stillness of my heart. "They will return. Yes, I will break their hearts of stone and give them hearts made only for love. That, my child, is where you come in. Yes, that is what you are here for. Go, tell them about me. Share with them what's in your heart."

"Oh, Lord," I replied, "I really *do* want people to know you, and I really *do* want them to love you, but why me? Why do *I* have to be the one to tell them? Why don't you just make yourself known? Why don't you just remind them who you are all by yourself? After all, you are more than capable of doing this without my help."

"My child, listen to what it is you just asked me," I could "hear" Him respond gently redirecting me. "Why don't I just make myself known? Why don't I just remind them who I am all by myself? That *IS* what I'm doing! *What do you think I'm doing through you?*"..."These people aren't waiting on me to reveal these truths to them," He continued, "they're waiting on you. They're waiting on the message I will send to them *through* you. Do not be afraid of your mission! I made you for this and will only ask you to do things that you are more than capable of doing. You will not fail, my child. In fact, you *cannot* fail because I am with you always." "Besides," He concluded, "when have you ever *not* finished something that you've started?"

With that, any and all fear I had subsided. With that, any and all doubt I had disappeared. I then found myself pleading, "Let me help you, Lord! Please, let me help you! I can help! I want to help! In fact, there is *nothing* I want to do more!" And you know what? I'm pretty sure that's a prayer He'll have no problem answering.

Prayer

I want to help you share the Good News, Lord. I want to let
you use me as your instrument to break down stony hearts. So,
please, Lord, use me. Make me my Daddy's little helper.
I love you! I thank you! I praise you!

Read, Think, Pray: Isaiah 6:8

REFLECTION #171

THE EMPTY CLASSROOM

1/20/2015

Dear Jesus: HaHaHa! You are so very funny! Your humor, my Lord, is not lost on me. Thank you for the laugh! - Yours Truly, Julia

Yes, isn't it "funny" that on the day I'm preparing to e-mail a group of my readers my reflection titled *An Audience of One,* I show up to church to lead a new book study only to discover that no one else is coming? And, this, after I *begged* God to let me help Him. Ha! It's a good thing I'm doing this for Him and not just to hear myself talk, huh? I mean, if my intentions were self-centered I'm sure I would feel defeated right now because, by the world's definition, this looks like a complete failure. Oh, but I'm not worried. No, and I'm not mad that the work I did to prepare for this seems to all be in vain.

I, you see, read to learn, and I write so that I can better understand what it is I'm learning. (And, of course, so that I don't forget!) I did these things long before anyone knew I was doing them, and I will continue doing them even if no one ever reads a word I write or shows up to a talk I give. I, of course, am happy to share what it is I'm learning. Yes, I'm happy to let people "listen in" on my prayer and study, but sharing my discoveries with others is *not* the reason I'm "searching." And, well, my response to this empty classroom tonight just proved that to me.

Prayer

May tonight's "failure," Lord, be a reminder to me that none of this is about me. May it be a reminder to me that you are the Master of all of this and that you are the One who will make it all come together. Even if on the outside it looks like a total loss, Lord, don't let me doubt what it is I'm doing for you. Instead, allow the work you're inspiring in me to bear great fruit. Yes, even if, like with this empty classroom, it looks like there's nothing to bear it in. I love you! I thank you! I praise you!

Read, Think, Pray: Galatians 6:9

REFLECTION #172

DYING TO SELF

1/22/2015

In frustrated prayer I asked God, "How many times, Lord, must I say the same thing? How many times must I go over this incredibly simple task with this same person?"

"As many times as it takes, my child," I "heard" Him gently respond. "As many times as it takes."..."Oh, and don't forget to do it with great love and patience."

Aaahhh! I have so much more work to do on myself! I have so much more to learn! I have so much more to overcome! I need to stop being so impatient, rude, and unkind. I need to learn how to serve instead of walking around expecting to be served. Ugh! I'm so stinking sick of this pushy, demanding person living inside me! I am so ready for her to take a hike!

299

I think it's important to note here that, in spite of my obvious flaws and my even more obvious awareness of them, I, in no way, feel discouraged or condemned by God's redirection. I feel humbled, sure, but one of the fruits of prayer is greater humility, right? Yes, I'm convinced this is all about humility. I'm convinced this is all about

becoming so completely humble that I'm dead-to-self; that "I live, no longer I, but Christ lives in me" (Galatians 2:20).

"I'm convinced this is all about becoming so completely humble that I'm dead-to-self."

I have been asking myself the same questions over and over again. "What is going on? Why can't I figure this out? Why can't I just be nice and patient and loving without having to try so hard?"

"Humility," God reminds me. "The answer is always humility. Strive to grow in the virtue of humility."

And, so, before I go any further, here is another quick note to self:

Dear Julia - Get over yourself! Admit your mistakes, be reconciled, and try again. This is really <u>not</u> as hard as you're making it out to be!

Prayer

I, my Lord, am a prideful person. Just when I think, "I'm getting really good at being humble," you remind me that I'm really not. Keep reminding me, Lord. Fill my heart with deep love for you and for those around me, and remind me often that I am a pushy, know-it-all without you. Soften my heart. Make it more like yours. May I be quick to put myself aside and even more quick to admit when I don't. You are my God, and I love you. May my actions start to prove that I mean it.
I love you! I thank you! I praise you!

Read, Think, Pray: Mark 10:42-45, 1 Peter 4:9-11

"There are two types of people in the world – those who are humble and those who are about to be." - Anonymous

REPENT AND BELIEVE

1/22/2015

In Mark's Gospel, Jesus begins his public ministry with the words "repent and believe," (Mark 1:15) and I just realized that everything we need to know about how to live our lives while we're here on earth is in these words. Now that I've come to realize this, - yeah, now that I've come to understand that the words "repent and believe" say all that really needs to be said about what I need to "do" while I'm here - I've got a question to ask myself: Which of these two parts gave me (or is still giving me) the most trouble?

Believe it or not, I think the "repent" part of this has been the easier part for me. And that, of course, is saying much because repenting, especially in the beginning, was no easy task. In fact, it took me years to come to terms with it, years to understand it, and years to work up the courage to do it. But actually doing it, - actually turning my heart back to God with true contrition for my sins and resolving not to sin again - was (and still is) "easy. " Yes, especially when compared to the next part.

Yeah, without a doubt, the next part, the "believing" part, has always been the harder part for me. I've always had a hard time *believing* I'm forgiven. I've always had a hard time *believing* I'm loved. I've always had a hard time *believing* I'm worthy. It's a fear-induced slavery I wouldn't wish upon my worst enemy. One that I was victim to for years.

So, yeah, in my opinion "repent and believe" kind of says it all. In fact, if my life is proof of anything, it's proof that our freedom lies within these words...I'm beginning to understand why Jesus led with them.

Prayer

Help me to believe in your promises, Lord. Help me to believe in your truth. May I remind myself often that you are a God of love, that you are a God of mercy, that you are a God of patience and understanding, that you are a God

301

> *of light. May I never again become enslaved to the*
> *darkness, especially the darkness of disbelief.*
> *I love you! I thank you! I praise you!*

Read, Think, Pray: Mark 1:14-15

REFLECTION #174

THE SHEPHERD'S VOICE

1/22/2015

"I like him," I thought as the shy man I had gotten to know a little approached the ambo to proclaim God's Word.

"Yeah, me too," I "heard" God humorously tell me back. (I mean, of course He likes him! Duh!)

"Wow, this is beautiful, " I thought as I took in all the sights, sounds, and smells of an empty church one evening.

"If you think this is nice," I "heard" God reply, "just wait until you see heaven!"

Though God's voice isn't always this clear and direct, I have come to know the truth. And the truth is, His sheep really *do* hear His voice (John 10:27). I'm just glad I finally started listening!

Prayer

> *You are my rock, my refuge, and my strength, my Lord.*
> *You are my Good Shepherd. Thank you for calling out to*
> *me and for helping me come to know what your voice*
> *"sounds" like. Lead me, Lord, and I will follow you.*
> *I love you! I thank you! I praise you!*

Read, Think, Pray: John 10:14, 27

DADDY'S LITTLE GIRL

1/29/2015

As my husband and I stood at a prayer service listening to the speaker who had the floor, I noticed a young girl standing to my left. This girl (who I would guess was around 5 years old) stood, unmoved, staring in my direction. Her eyes were tightly locked on mine throughout the entire presentation, and, as the speaker continued, I kept being drawn to her gaze. I looked down at her often and smiled because it was obvious that she was, for some reason unbeknownst to me, drawn to me. I didn't wonder much about what that reason was. No, her look didn't let me wonder. It was a consuming look of awe, a peaceful look of love, and she gave it as if in a trance, undisturbed by anything that was going on around her. "A beautiful little girl," I thought at one point as I again smiled in her direction. Then the service came to an end, and we went our separate ways. As the days passed and life continued, I gave little more thought to our encounter.

In the week that followed I sat in conversation with my spiritual director when suddenly, kind of out of nowhere, the image of this little girl staring up at me came to mind. As it did, I shared the story with him and asked, "What do you think she saw? Do you think she saw something in me that the average person doesn't see?"

"Sure," he replied, "that's a possibility, but perhaps God used her to give you a message. Perhaps God, for a brief moment, switched roles with you. Perhaps this is how He sees things. Perhaps this is what He sees when you look at Him."

"Is it?" I wondered after he made this suggestion. "Oh, I hope so! I hope God knows how much I love Him just by the way I look at Him. I hope He feels my love as easily as I could feel the love of that little girl just by looking into my eyes." After conversing about it a little more, I left his office and headed back home. As the hours passed and life continued, I gave little more thought to his suggestion.

As planned, later that evening I went to Mass. At one point during Mass I caught myself staring. I had never noticed I did it before, but in that moment it became obvious that I was doing it. It also became obvious that I had been doing it for quite some time. Yes, it became obvious that, from the moment I entered the pew, my eyes had been staring; staring at Christ. I had been looking at him intensely, lovingly filled with wonder, gazing at him on the crucifix and in the Eucharist. A thought (a thought in the "tone" that I have come to recognize as God's voice) then entered my mind.

"Yes," I "heard" God reassure me. "The man you spoke with today was right. That girl *was* giving you a message. As he suggested it might be, that *is* exactly how you look at me. As he suggested it might be, that *is* exactly how I see you. You, my child, will always be my little girl; my beautiful, little girl. And, yes, even your gaze fills me with great joy."

And, well, with that being said, I think the following is worth repeating: sometimes a "look" says it all.

Prayer

I look to you now, Lord, and thank you for calling me into your family. I thank you for choosing me to be your child. I will keep my eyes locked on yours trusting in your Fatherly care, trusting in your Fatherly protection, trusting in your Fatherly love. May this gaze of wonder remind me often that I have always been, and will always be, your little girl. I love you! I thank you! I praise you!

Read, Think, Pray: Zephaniah 3:17

"God loves each of us as if there were only one of us." - St. Augustine

REFLECTION #176

A STEADFAST GAZE

1/29/2015

My husband and I went to see the third movie in *The Hobbit* series, *The Battle of the Five Armies*, a few weeks ago. Though I know these movies have a Christian message, I can assure you this was his movie pick. I, you see, usually prefer movies that get me laughing not ones that get me thinking. Even so, I went because my husband enjoys these movies, and I enjoy him. (And, of course, love him enough to let him pick the movie every once in awhile.)

Not having seen any of the other movies in this series, (or any of those in the Tolkien series for that matter) I didn't really know who was who or what was actually going on. I was able to keep myself entertained, though, by trying to look for the Christian themes that I knew were throughout by guessing who each character in the story was supposed to be depicting. I guess this strategy worked because there was one part of the movie that spoke to me that evening and has stuck with me to this day.

In the opening scene there was a village under the attack of a huge, evil dragon. As fire rained down, everyone in the village panicked. All were sure that everything would be lost and destroyed, for it seemed certain that good would be conquered by evil. As the terrorizing continued, however, the hero made his way to a tower to give himself a shot at killing the dragon. After failing a few times to do so, the hero's young son somehow made his way to him in the tower with an arrow in hand; an arrow that was sure to defeat the dragon once and for all. The son handed his father the arrow trusting that his dad would be victorious. (I mean, what young son doesn't believe his dad can do anything?)

Anyway, the father took the large, heavy arrow, put it in his bow, and placed the end of it on his son's shoulder for leverage and support. The son then stood in front of his father facing him. You could tell by looking at the son that the evil and destruction didn't scare him anymore because his eyes were locked on the eyes of the man he knew was going to destroy it: his father. As the father took aim, though, the son couldn't help but turn around. As he did he immediately caught sight of the dragon, and the evil, pain, and suffering he saw filled him with fear. The father noticed his fear and got his attention reminding him not to look back. "Look at me," he told his son. The son listened to his father's instructions and locked his fearful eyes back on the eyes of his father. As his gaze changed direction, the fear subsided, and he was, once again, filled with faith, hope, and trust. In that moment, the father was finally able to do what needed to be done. He released the arrow, which struck and killed the dragon, and, in spite of what seemed like sure defeat, good prevailed.

Sadly, I, too often, relate to this young son. Yes, sadly, I, too often, find myself having immediate faith and trust in my Savior only to give in to the temptation to turn around and look at the destruction behind me. Thankfully, though, Jesus doesn't let me stare into the darkness for too long. Yes, thankfully, he always gets my attention and reminds me to turn back around. "Look at me," he says. "Look into my eyes. Don't turn around. Don't let the darkness frighten you. Remember, 'in the world you will have trouble, but I have conquered the world' (John 16:33). Yes, I am the arrow that has conquered death. Keep, therefore, your eyes firmly locked on mine and know that there is nothing to be afraid of."

So, as it turns out, my husband's movie picks aren't always bad after all. In fact, I should probably let him pick out what we're watching more often. (But, if you ever read this, dear, don't hold your breath!)

Prayer
This world is only scary when I look away from you, Lord. This world is only scary when I take my eyes off you. So, I beg you, please, keep my gaze firmly locked on yours! Don't let me look back! Don't let me stare into the darkness! May my steadfast gaze in your direction always remind me that there is nothing to be afraid of. No matter how "ugly" things seem to get. I love you! I thank you! I praise you!

Read, Think, Pray: Proverbs 4:25, Hebrews 12:1-3

REFLECTION #177

PREMATURE

1/29/2015

I've been doing a lot of thinking lately about this idea of things happening too soon; of things happening before we're ready. As I meditated on the words of Jesus in the parable of the sower, (Mark 4:1-20) I was drawn this time to the soil with the rocky ground. (You know, the one where the seed sprouts up quickly but is then scorched by the sun.) Well, I think the Lord was sending me a gentle reminder through this story because I was, once again, being tempted to push things into happening. Yes, "bigger, faster, more" always seems to be the temptation for me. God reminded me, though, that faster isn't always better. He reminded me that lasting, abundant fruit springs forth from seeds with deep, deep roots. And how does one grow such deep roots? Well, slowly and steadily, of course! So, yes, I must stop "pushing" God. I must not be too eager to make things happen because if it hasn't happened yet, then there must be a good reason for it. Perhaps I'm not as ready as I think I am. Perhaps others aren't quite where they need to be. Perhaps we all need even deeper roots.

This all got me thinking about my niece, Megan. Megan was the long-awaited child; the first child of my older sister and her husband, the one for whom was prayed (1 Samuel 1:27). But Megan's life, though fruitful, was shortly lived. Megan was born premature, too small to survive outside the womb. Her first tiny breath quickly became her last, and, in an instant, the hopes, dreams, and joys of all who knew her vanished. As perfect as she was, - and trust me, she was perfect; a clear image of her mother with ten fingers and ten toes and eyes, though never open, you could tell were a deep, dark brown just like her mom's and aunts' - she just wasn't ready to come into this world. Her birth was just too soon, too premature, and I told her this as I held her beautiful, but lifeless, body in my arms for the first and last time. "You just didn't wait long enough, Megan. You needed more time. You weren't quite ready." In time, though, our mourning turned into joy, and we were all reminded that her mission, though short, was very much accomplished. I mean, sure, this world was not for her, but that didn't mean her life was in vain, and today I was reminded that her short, little life is still producing great fruit.

Yes, as I found myself tempted to "jump the gun," tempted to "put the cart before the horse," tempted to "push to make things happen faster," Megan came to mind. Her life brought me new insight and enlightened me with greater understanding.

"You're not ready," she "told" me in prayer repeating the same words I once told her. "You need a little more time. Wait for God's perfect timing. He'll fulfill His mission in you even if by the world's standards it's shortly lived. Trust in Him. Sink your roots. It's not happening yet because the world is not quite ready for you, and you are not quite ready for it. Trust, Aunt Julia, and be patient. When it's time, it will happen."

When it's time, it will happen."

And, so, I say, "Thank you, Lord, for the message you have given to me through my dear, sweet niece, Megan. I know you're right. Yes, I know you're right. I will get back to work, waiting on your perfect timing. I will get back to work, trusting that, when it's time, it will happen."

Prayer

*I know your timing is perfect, Lord, so I will patiently
go back to work waiting on this time to get here. I will not
push. I will not force. I will not release any of this too soon.
I trust you, my Lord, and I will wait until you say it's time.
(Oh, but just so you know, I'm bursting at the seams!)
I love you! I thank you! I praise you!*

Read, Think, Pray: 2 Peter 3:8-9

THE DISCOVERY

DEEPLY SPEAKING

1/29/2015

After taking a closer look inside my journal these past several months, I have discovered that my reflections have two "tones." Some of them are what I like to call "cutesy." These seem (at least to me) to be more entertaining than they are heart-warming or thought-provoking. They are just simple explanations about what's going on inside my head; my simple, little "cutesy" head. The others are different; way different. They are (again, at least to me) more "real." They take me, - yes, even now, months after writing them - to another place emotionally and spiritually. It's easy for me to tell which of my reflections are of the first of these two "tones" and which of them are of the second. I wonder if others will be able to tell, too.

Regardless, now that the Lord has convinced me that I am meant to share my writing with others, I want what I write to be the window of my soul. I want what I write to express the deepest longings of my heart. Why? Because I love making myself completely vulnerable to others. No, wait, of course, that's not why! No, the real reason I want to open my heart up to others is because I want others to open theirs up to Christ.

I read a quote recently by Carl Rogers that says, *"What is most personal and unique in each one of us is probably the very element which would, if it were shared or expressed, speak most deeply to others."* Well, this most "personal and unique" part of me is the very part I want to share in my writing. I pray that it does, in fact, speak most deeply to those who read it.

Prayer

My writing is simple, Lord, but it has always been from my heart. And, now that I know your plan includes me sharing this writing with others, I pray that it reaches whomever it is meant to reach whenever it is meant to reach them. Speak through me, Lord, and touch the soul of the community, "not permitting any word of [yours] to go unfulfilled" (1 Samuel 3:19). I love you! I thank you! I praise you!*

Read, Think, Pray: 1 Samuel 3:19

* *"When one has the courage to enter where life is experienced as most unique and most private, one touches the soul of the community."* - Henri J.M. Nouwen, *The Wounded Healer*

REFLECTION #179

SPIRITUAL MOTHERHOOD

1/29/2015

I don't know if I'll ever have any children of my own in this life, but I do know I'll be a mother. In fact, I would argue that I already am. Yeah, I would argue that I already am a mother; a spiritual mother, that is. And here's why...

My niece took me by surprise the other day when I asked her, "What do you think one of the hardest things for an adult to do is?" And she answered, "Put up with kids." (The answer I was looking for was forgive!

I was trying to get her to understand how hard it is to love and forgive, especially when you're an adult.) Well, not surprisingly, her answer caught me off guard, and, to be honest, broke my heart. I hated that she felt like she, and all the other children like her, were a burden to the adults in her life. After all, I am one of the adults on this list! So, after processing her answer, I quickly told her how much she was loved, (and made sure she knew it) but I never forgot her words. They were the very words that finally made me realize how much of a "mother" I already am.

Yes, there are already children in this life entrusted to me; lots and lots of them. These children look up to me and watch everything I do. And that is why I need to do a better job at making sure they know how much they are loved. Yes, that is why I need to do a better job at making sure they know how much of a gift they really are. After all, I don't want my vices to be the traits I pass on to the generation that is coming after me. No, I want my virtues to be. So, in order that they are, I am going to start living with the following truth at the forefront of my mind:

My thoughts, words, and actions - all of them - aren't just affecting me. I am a mother, a spiritual mother, and my children - all of them- are counting on me to get it together!

Prayer

I may never be a mother in the most literal sense of the word, Lord, but you remind me often that I am already a mother to all of your beloved children. I am not, therefore, disheartened because of my "empty" home. I, instead, am filled with great love for all your children, young and old. May I be a kind, gentle, loving "mother" to everyone I meet.
I love you! I thank you! I praise you!

Read, Think, Pray: Matthew 12:46-50

SNOW DAYS

1/30/2015

"When was the last time you built a snow fort?" I asked my husband the other day as we enjoyed a beautiful winter day playing in the snow with a niece and a few of our nephews.

"Probably when I was like 8," he answered after giving it some thought.

"Yeah, me, too," I told him. "I was probably about the same age as some of these kids are now."

Then, after reminiscing a little, we both shook our heads in disbelief saying, almost simultaneously, "Time really does fly by, doesn't it?"

Oh, yes, time seems to fly by. I've been thinking a lot about this, though, and I don't think the real problem is that time goes by too fast. No, I think the real problem is that, as it does, we become so consumed with work that we forget how to play. That's my real problem anyway. Yeah, and that's why I just realized how thankful I am for snow days.

Yes, this has been an eye-opener for me because before this fun-filled, snow fort building, snow day, I would have told you that the only way to get that carefree, "there's nothing to do and nowhere to go," vacation day feeling was to go on an actual vacation, but I was wrong. I now know that this relaxing, playful feeling I look forward to all year long is obtainable in my own backyard. I just pray that, from now on, I'm wise enough to stop working every once in awhile, and go get it!

Prayer

I thank you for giving us time to work and time to play, Lord.
Please, give me the grace I need to do both. Show me how
to better enjoy all life has to offer; downtimes included.
May I take frequent "vacations" throughout the year,

> *even if I never leave my house to go on one.*
> *I love you! I thank you! I praise you!*

Read, Think, Pray: Genesis 2:2-3

REFLECTION #181

SUPERHEROES

1/30/2015

My siblings are super-parents. Well, I think so anyway. Yeah, I think they, and all parents out there like them, are the superheroes of our time. Sure, they're not perfect, - after all, no superhero is - but they, without even thinking about it, put their lives on the line for their children each and every day. I admire this about them. In fact, I admire this about all parents. Parents like these are selfless in every sense of the word. They are Super-Moms and Super-Dads, and I thank God for all of them. For they have been gifted with many "special powers."

As I think about the many superheroes in my life, one of my brothers-in-law comes to mind. This man doesn't just give his kids a fish (or even just teach them to fish). No, he jumps in the water while they're fishing to show them how it all works. One way he does this is on the ski slopes. Although it's more difficult for this Super-Dad to bring his youngest daughter along because she's quite young and needs much help making it down the hill, he doesn't question her being there. Nope, he just takes her down with him by placing her little skis carefully inside his so that they can both go down together. After talking about this "training strategy" with my husband one evening, he said something I will never forget:

"What he's doing is genius, you know," he told me. "I mean, who would be afraid when their dad is right there?"

"Yeah," I thought as I pondered his words. "Who would be afraid when their Dad is right there?"

You see what I mean? My siblings are superheroes! And one of their many "special powers" is making my "invisible" heavenly Father, visible!

Prayer

I love you, my Lord, and I thank you for the many superheroes in my life. May the care they have for their children be a constant reminder of your care for me, and may I live fearlessly remembering that I am riding up and down the hills of my life completely and totally surrounded by you. I love you! I thank you! I praise you!

Read, Think, Pray: Isaiah 41:10

REFLECTION #182

WHAT'S IN THE NAME?

1/30/2015

In 2010 my husband, Tony, and I entered into a Covenant of Love* with Mary, the Blessed Mother. In so doing we placed ourselves - our full, complete, broken selves - into her hands; a place (after much prayer, study, and discernment) we were confident was safe and secure. Along the journey of living out our covenantal lives with the Blessed Mother, we were asked to come up with a name for the place in our home where we would invite her to take up residence; the place where we, as humans on earth, would be able to connect in some way with her and her Son who are in heaven. In Schoenstatt* terms, this place in a home is called a "Home Shrine" and when you "dedicate" it, (yes, we Catholics like our ceremonies) you give it a name; a name that is meant to describe the home, and therefore the hearts of those living in it, that you are asking Christ, through Mary's intercession, to help you form. Why a dedication? Simple: It's one way we show God we're serious about moving forward. It

315

helps us experience Him in real, tangible ways, and the witnesses present keep us accountable to our good intentions. Why a name? Simple: We name what we love. Why Mary? Simple: We need help! That's why Christ gave her to us in the first place (John 19:25-27).

Anyway, at the time of this official ceremony, my husband and I weren't very far along on our spiritual journeys, so, although our hearts were beginning to open up to God, we didn't so much "care" what the name of this place in our home dedicated to Christ and his mother would be. I suppose that's why when the priest who was with us during our covenant ceremony suggested that the name of our home shrine be *Mary's Welcome Home* we said, "Sure, why not?" (Besides, who could argue in a situation like that?)

As we went through the process of dedication, (and through the years of formation and ongoing conversion that followed) this name - this name chosen for us - began to make more and more sense. You see, at first it always meant two things to us: (1) Mary (and, therefore, Christ) was always welcome in our home and others who entered would be welcomed in it, too. And (2) We were always "welcome back" to her (and, therefore, to Christ) anytime we had wandered off. Although this level of understanding has served us well and has helped us along the way, I recently gained a deeper, more profound understanding of this name.

One ordinary morning in prayer, I found myself thinking about the name of our home shrine. As I did, I thought about the meaning of the name. (Specifically, the two meanings listed above.) At one point in my prayer, Mary joined my train-of-thought. It was then that I had this enlightenment:

"Yes, my child," I could "hear" her say in the stillness of my heart. "Yes, the meaning you have placed with this name is true, but there's more. You see, *you*, yourself, are my welcome home. I have taken up residence in *you*. *Your marriage* is my welcome home. You invited me in long ago, and I immediately entered and made myself comfortable. *You* are my home. *Tony* is my home. *Your marriage* is my home. And, yes, I feel most welcome."

Clearly I had no idea what was in the name! And, well, this got me thinking. I now wonder if, in some situations, we're *not* the ones choosing our names like we think we are. Yeah, I now wonder if, in some situations, our names - yes, even our own - have been chosen for us by God from the very beginning.

I wonder...I really wonder...

Prayer

What's in the name, Lord? What's in the name?
Come into our lives and speak to our hearts. Help us to
understand what it is you want us to know about what
you have named us and what you have made us for.
I love you! I thank you! I praise you!

P.S. - Here are some descriptions I found for my name (and my husband's name as well). These descriptions describe us so well! Could they be examples of situations in which God, through our parents, chose these names for us? Oh, I think so!

What does your name mean?

"Julia" - *From the Latin meaning "youthful." She is bright, lively, and hardworking; she will persist long after others have given up. She thirsts for knowledge.*

"Anthony" - *From the Latin meaning "priceless." He is strong and manly, independent and happy with his own company. A loyal friend if you can get close.*

Read, Think, Pray: Isaiah 49:1

*The Apostolic Movement of Schoenstatt is a Roman Catholic Marian Movement founded in Germany in 1914 by Father Joseph Kentenich. "Schoenstatt is a movement of moral and religious renewal in the Catholic Church, working to help renew the Church and society in the spirit of the Gospel. It seeks to reconnect faith with daily life, especially through a deep love of Mary, the Mother of God. As an international movement it is present on all continents and has members from all vocations and walks of life." (from schoenstattofohio.org)

PLANTING SEEDS

2/5/2015

I just realized, due to my increased level of stress, that I am in need, once again, of one of those friendly little reminders. So, here goes...

Dear Julia:

Take a deep breath, and calm down. You are putting *waaaay* too much pressure on yourself. You are depending *waaaay* too much on you. Please, take a deep breath. Remember who you are. Remember who your Father is. Remember who is really in control.

My dear friend, remember, God knows what you are capable of and what you are not. Remember, He knows what you can do and what you can't. Remember, He knows what you are able to do now and what you will only be able to do later after much time and practice. Yes, please remember, God is not some impatient, slave-driver demanding you to work until exhaustion. No, that is not God! So, breathe. Relax. It doesn't have to be this hard.

Good. Now that your focus is back on the Truth take hold, once again, of that freedom gained for you on the cross. Go, live in this freedom; live under the ease of Christ's yoke (Matthew 11:28-30).

Prayer

It's easy for me to push myself too hard, Lord. Way too easy. Please teach me how to live my life focusing on planting one tiny seed at a time. May I always remember that the seed grows because of you, not me. I love you! I thank you! I praise you!

Read, Think, Pray: Mark 4:26-28

"Judge each day not by the harvest you reap but by the seeds you plant."
- Robert Louis Stevenson

318

CHRISTIAN THINKING

2/6/2015

"Learn to think and live like a Christian. - For what has occurred was not a death but a crown, not an end but the beginning of a greater life." Should we begin thinking and living like this *"we will not only remain unharmed by these events, but will reap the greatest benefits."*

As I read these words of St. John Chrysostom, it was as if I could hear him asking me, "What is it that you don't understand, Julia? Have you forgotten the Good News? Have you forgotten about the Resurrection? Have you forgotten about the difference Christ makes?"

Yes, apparently I *had* forgotten these truths, but Chrysostom's words rekindled the fire inside me. His words reminded me of the Truth. Now I cry out in excitement, "Yes, of course! Of course, there is nothing to be afraid of! Of course, there is nothing to worry about! Of course, there is nothing to fear! The Lord is with us and will never forsake us! Yes, of course!"

The time has come. It is time for me start thinking and living like a Christian. Why? Because I am one!

Prayer

The evil and darkness of this world tempt me to fall into despair, Lord, but I want to live and think like the Christian I am knowing that this is not the end. Come, make your presence known in my life. Give me the courage to follow you. May I move forward fearing nothing, not even death, remembering that worldly death isn't death at all but the crown of eternal life. I love you! I thank you! I praise you!

Read, Think, Pray: 2 Timothy 4:7-8

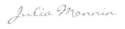

REFLECTION #185

THE VOICE OF REASON

2/6/2015

The other day I witnessed a nephew of mine angrily tell his mom to "Go Away!" after she had arrived to pick him up and take him home. This wasn't the first time I've seen something like this happen. In fact, over the course of my life, I've seen it happen lots of times with lots of different children. This time, however, I realized something I had never realized before. Yeah, this time, I realized how much I, just a few short years ago, spent much of my time doing this *exact* same thing.

Think about it. The real reason my nephew was so upset by his mom's presence was because he was having fun, and he knew her being there meant it was time to leave the party and go home. Sound familiar? Oh, I can't tell you how many times my Father, through the voice of my conscience, showed up while I was out at a party to gently encourage me to go home when all I did was angrily shout, "Go Away!" Yes, many, many times my Dad (again, through the voice of my conscience) tried to keep me out of trouble and many, many times I told Him to, "Get lost!" (Or just ignored Him all together.) You see, what I mean? I really wasn't much different than my 3-year-old nephew. In fact, I was much, much worse.

Still, I'm not going take this as an opportunity to look back and beat myself up about my countless mistakes. No, I'm, instead, going to take this as an opportunity to move forward in gratitude. Yes, I'm grateful. I'm grateful the Lord called me (and continues to call me) into action and gave me (and continues to give me) the grace to start over. My life is different than it once was; much different. And this realization of how far I had fallen those not so many years ago, is just more proof of how far I've come.

Prayer

Continue your work in me, Lord! May I listen

320

fervently and follow obediently never, even for a second, questioning your voice of reason guiding me home.
I love you! I thank you! I praise you!

Read, Think, Pray: Isaiah 30:9-11

REFLECTION #186

LITTLE SIGNS OF LOVE

2/9/2015

Some of my nieces and nephews are getting to that age where their social status is more important than their family status. Sure, it's obvious they love us, their family, but theirs is an embrace and love that is more silent and hidden, especially when their friends are around. Look, I remember what it's like to be that age, so I understand where they're coming from. Yeah, I get it: family doesn't exactly equal coolness. Since I understand this, I try my best to respect their privacy and keep my distance from them when we're out in the world even though I want to hug and kiss them as soon as I see them. (Yeah, I'm that crazy aunt that "pinches cheeks" no matter how old they get. My "cheek pinches" just come in the form of hugs.)

Anyway, it's because of the fact that I try my best to respect their privacy and free will that I resisted the urge to run over to a nephew and give him a big hug recently when my husband and I happened to walk by him as we were leaving another nephew's basketball game. Oh, I really wanted to hug him, but it was clear that he was in the middle of a game with a group of friends, and I didn't want to intrude, so I didn't do it. I, instead, just waved and told him goodbye as we walked away. He kindly waved back, but as I kept walking my heart ached a little. Don't get me wrong. I wasn't hurt by the fact that he wanted to play with his friends, it was just upsetting to admit that I didn't seem to be important enough to get anything more than a quick wave from him. I guess I was just saddened thinking about how quickly kids grow up and how "un-cool" we adults get in the process. Yeah, I guess I was just a little brokenhearted by it all. As I was wallowing in my sadness, though, I suddenly felt a little hand tap me on the arm. I looked down to see my nephew standing next to me. He had walked away from his game to catch up to me to give me a hug, and, as you can imagine, my heart melted as I took him in my arms and graciously accepted his little sign of love. His simple gesture healed my broken heart, and, in an instant, my sadness turned into joy.

I didn't think much more about this little event until a few days later. As I sat in prayer, the memory of this encounter with my nephew replayed itself in my mind. As it did, I "heard" God call out, "Yes, my child, that is what you are to me." "Look," He continued, "I don't expect, nor want, you to take yourself out of the world, I just don't want you to ignore me. I just don't want you to forget about me when you're out fulfilling your duties. Remember me. Think of me. Glance in my direction every now and then. 'Why,' you ask? Because my heart longs for you just like your heart longed for your nephew that day. I love you and adore you and long to be near you just like you did with him. Yes, my heart breaks for you just like yours broke for him, but know this: you have the power to mend it. Yes, you! *You* have the power to console *me*! Just love me. Just embrace me. Just notice me."

You have the power to console Jesus. Yes, you. You have the power to console him.

A part of me is ashamed to have needed this reminder. I mean, who am I *not* to notice Him? Here He is, God, who, out of love, became man to unite Himself with us; who, out of love, allowed Himself to be tortured to save us; who, out of love, rose from the dead to prove Himself to us, and I, a nobody, look past Him; I, unworthy of anything, forget about His sacrifice; I, so weak and lowly, ignore Him. I mean, He should be the one ignoring me! Oh, but now that I understand the joy and consolation that I, a mere human, can bring to my Savior, I will strive to never again stop looking in His direction. I will strive to never again avoid Him when I'm out in public. I will strive to never again be "too cool" to give Him a hug.

Prayer

*Yes, my Lord, I often ignore you when I'm out in
the world. I often forget about you and about what
you did for me. I often forget about who I am and about
why I'm here to begin with. I do love you, though. Yes, you
know that I love you. Help me move forward proving this
to you. Help me reach out to you often - yes, even
when I'm out in public - with little signs of love.
I love you! I thank you! I praise you!*

Read, Think, Pray: Hosea 11:1-4, 8-9

REFLECTION #187

THE SURGERY

2/12/2015

My heart is overflowing with love, joy, and gratitude as I sit at home, safe and sound, recovering from surgery. Yes, I have plenty to be grateful for. Returning home is just one of these things.

Although this surgery was a minor one, I have to admit, I was a little nervous about it. This, you see, was my first time "going under the knife," so I didn't really know what to expect, and I felt a little uneasy about it as a result. To be honest, even though I felt like it was God's will that I have this done, there was a part of me - a very selfish, prideful part - that didn't want to go through with it. I now realize, though, how important this was, not just for me physically but for me spiritually, too.

Yes, as usual, this experience has taught me much. At the top of this list is this: Life isn't about getting what we want, it's about giving all we have. Oh, and sometimes, - just sometimes - giving all we have means going where we don't want to go. Yes, sometimes, - just sometimes - giving all we have means "becoming weak for the weak" (1 Corinthians 9:22).

Prayer

*I give you my "yes," Lord. Today and always, I give you my "yes."
Let it be done to me according to your will. (Yes, even if
this means I will become weak in the process.)
I love you! I thank you! I praise you!*

Read, Think, Pray: Luke 9:23-24

"If you would have all, you must give all." - St. Catherine of Bologna

---

REFLECTION #188

NOT JULIA, JESUS

2/16/2015

I sit, now, in Christ's Presence overcome with thoughts and feelings. Here he is, Jesus, the love of my soul, directly across from me. I wonder, what would I do without him? Where would I go? What would I be? I would be lost, I tell you. Oh, yes, I would be lost. I would be lost. I would be empty. I would be incomplete.

In some ways, I feel guilty for knowing the Lord the way that I do. In some ways, I feel like I have an unfair advantage when it comes to running my race. Yes, in some ways, I feel like I have a "secret" weapon; a "secret" weapon that I would love nothing more than to *not* keep secret. I now see this as part of my mission. Yes, I now see that I'm here to "let the cat out of the bag," so to speak. There is Good News to share, and I am here to share it. There is an answer to all of this, and that answer is Christ.

For the rest of my life, I have but one goal: to become like him whom my heart is so in love with. He is everything my heart longs for. I want nothing but to love like he loves. I want nothing but to make him known so that others might love him, too. We, as I see it, are a hungry, tired, worn-out people in need of one thing: love. It will be my mission to give others this one thing. The rest is nothing.

How can I love more like you, Lord? How can I be more like you? I will start by taking my gaze off myself and placing it on you. Yes, I will start by focusing more on you. Not my will, Lord, yours. Not my timing, yours. Not my plans, yours. Not me, you. Not Julia, Jesus.

Prayer

If it is you who lives in me, Lord, I cannot fail. If it is you who others see, then I will be doing what I have set out to do. If it is you who is revealed through my life and my work, then my life has had great meaning, my work has served its purpose. Infiltrate my entire being, Lord. Make your presence in me unmistakably clear.
I love you! I thank you! I praise you!

Read, Think, Pray: Song of Songs 8:6-7

REFLECTION #189

HOME

2/17/2015

I can count on one finger how many times I've had surgery, but the lessons I've learned so far through this one ordinary event are countless. One such lesson was humility. I've been striving for years to be more humble, but it only takes one day of being physically incapable of taking care of yourself to understand what true humility is. Likewise, I've been striving for years to "let go;" to give up control by letting go of my dreams for myself so that I can embrace God's dreams for me. Well, just a few days of recovery helped me finally understand the expression, "Life is not about what you do, it's about how you love." You see, before this surgery I was certain that "doing" was the most important thing, but when you can't "do" because you're physically incapable of "doing" anything, you realize quickly that the only thing that matters is how you

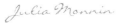

love. This, as you can imagine, is a great lesson for an over-achieving, "do-er" like myself. In fact, it's a life-changing lesson.

As if that wasn't enough, this experience has also given me a more genuine understanding of my heavenly Father's deep, deep love for me; of His deep, deep love for us all. This, as you can probably imagine, is what will stick with me forever. Yes, this, as you can probably imagine, is what I will never forget. Allow me to explain.

My mom and dad met me at my home a few hours after my surgery. As I laid on the couch in pain it was easy to see the sorrow on their faces. (I guess no parent likes to see their child suffering, no matter how old that child is.) Anyway, as they got up to leave after their visit Mom walked over to me, bent down, and gave me a big hug and lots of little kisses. I have to point out here that these were *not* just any kisses. No, they were little, repetitive pecks all over my face similar to what a parent would give to a young child. As you know, though, I am no longer one of these young children, so, as an adult on the receiving end of such affection, I can assure you I was quite "surprised" by it. Perhaps, "surprised" isn't the right word. Yes, perhaps it would be more accurate to say that the 10-year-old in me wanted to roll my eyes, push her away, and "wipe" her many kisses "off," but something stopped me from doing this. Yes, though my instinct was to reject what she was doing, I couldn't help but be drawn to what she was saying. "I'm so glad you're home," she repeated over and over again between her many pecks on the cheek. "I'm just so glad you're home."

The kisses eventually came to an end and Mom stood up to leave. Though she and Dad left right away, the memory of her heartfelt embrace replayed itself over and over again in my mind. Suddenly, I realized why. God was speaking to me through her. Yes, her words to me were actually His.

"I just want you home," He "said" reminding me of the why. "Do your best. Run your race. Fulfill your mission. Then, when it's finished, these will be my words to you. 'I'm so glad you're home, ' I'll tell you between big hugs and lots of little kisses. 'I'm just so glad you're home. '"

Prayer

This was such an ordinary experience, my God.
This was such an ordinary embrace between a mother
and a child, but your message was extraordinary. Thank you!
Thank you for giving me a lifetime of understanding in this one tiny,
unsuspecting package of physical weakness and pain. You are
so good, my Lord, and I love you! Help me to run my race
and to run it well. Help me to make it home.
I love you! I thank you! I praise you!

Read, Think, Pray: 1 Timothy 2:3-4

REFLECTION #190

SET FREE

2/17/2015

Someone once asked me, *"What would you say is the greatest gift you have received from your conversion?"* I didn't have to think much about my answer. No, my answer was, and still is, clear: freedom. The greatest gift I have received from my conversion is freedom; detachment from the things of this world.

Although I've always been a citizen of "the land of the free," I was a slave for most of my life. I was a slave to my closet, a slave to my appearance, and a slave to the number on the scale. I was a slave to my reputation, a slave to attention, and a slave to the letters on each of my report cards and transcripts. I was a slave to my work, a slave to money, a slave to power, a slave to pleasure, and a

327

slave to perfectionism. Yes, I was a slave. I was a slave to others' opinions and a slave to clothes, shoes, coats, and purses. I was a slave to order, neatness, and organization, and a slave to the details always concerning myself more with the ceremonial "washing of the hands" than with the actual feeding of the hungry (Matthew 15:1-9). The priorities of a slave like me were simple: Me, Myself, & I. Yes, everything was about me. Everything was about what I wanted. Everything was about getting my way. I, you see, was a slave to myself; a slave to this lesser, prideful self living inside.

It took me years to realize I was so enslaved. In fact, I would have never guessed that "freedom" was what I was seeking. But time, growth, and the change that has come with it, have proven to me that this was *exactly* what I was longing for. Yes, all along, I wanted to be free. I wanted the chains to be shattered. I wanted the ropes untied. I wanted the grip loosened. Still, the saddest part of all of this wasn't the slavery. No, the saddest part of all of this was that I had the key to unlock the door of my cell the whole time and just never realized it. The saddest part of all of this was that the door, in all actuality, was never even closed to begin with. Yeah, the saddest part of all of this was that I chose to stay in my cell for years when all I had to do was stand up and walk out.

So, yes, without a doubt, the greatest gift I have received from my conversion is freedom. Christ, after all, didn't come to condemn us, he came to save us (John 3:17). He didn't come to sentence us, he came to ransom us. He didn't come to kill us, he came to give us life. He came to shatter the walls around our hearts. He came to free us from the lies of the world. He came to show us the Way out. And that, you see, is *exactly* what my conversion has led me to; it has led me on the path that has set me free.

Prayer

I love you, my Lord, and I thank you for your gift of freedom.
I thank you for showing me, little by little, all that I was enslaved
to and for helping me, little by little, to let it go. You have proven to
me that peace in this world is possible and that this peace comes from
you. Continue your work in me, Lord. Continue to show me the

path that leads to you; the path that leads to true freedom.
I love you! I thank you! I praise you!

Read, Think, Pray: Isaiah 61:1-3

REFLECTION #191

WANDERINGS

2/18/2015

I know very little about St. Cuthmann of Steyning. In fact, until very recently, I had never even heard of him. I can see, though, why God waited to introduce him to me until now. Yeah, I can see why this little introduction of him didn't happen until this exact moment in my life. Here's why...

The legend of St. Cuthmann tells us that at one point in his life he was out wandering the countryside pulling his paralyzed mother around in a cart. Yes, it tells us he was physically out roaming around - *wandering* - begging for alms. Legend has it that while he was out wandering the rope he was using to pull the cart (and his mother who was in it) broke, so he made a new one with what he could find. He was certain the rope would break again, so he prayerfully decided that, when it did, he would take this as his sign from God to stop his wanderings and build a church. Well, time proved that he was right. Yes, the rope did eventually break, and when it did he stopped and prayed, *"Father Almighty, you have brought my wanderings to an end; now enable me to begin this work. For who am I, Lord, that I should build a house to name? If I rely on myself, it will be of no avail, but it is you who will assist me. You have given me the desire to be a builder; make up for my lack of skill, and bring the work of building this holy house to its completion."*

As soon as I read this man's prayer something inside me clicked. All the years of searching, waiting, and wondering suddenly made sense. His words were so similar to my own. His prayer was so much like mine.

And now that I had read them, - yes, now that I had seen them for myself - I, too, realized what he had realized: my wanderings have come to an end.

I never would have told you that I've been "wandering." No, I never would have used that word to describe the journey I've been on these past few years, but that is *exactly* what has been going on, and I think this journal proves it. Yeah, I think the 190 entries before this one prove that I was searching for the "what" of my life. I just didn't realize how intensely I was searching until I read this prayer of a man who lived thousands of years before me.

With this man's words, my "mission" has become clear. It's kind of hard for me to believe it has taken me so long to figure this out, but it's obvious now. Yes, now it's very obvious. *I am a writer!* My entire life, - the good, the bad, and the ugly - has been preparing me for this; all of it has been preparing me to write, to speak, to share my story. Yes, of course! Duh! *I am a writer!*

I have no idea where the road is taking me, but I do know this: my wanderings have come to an end. It's time for me to begin my work.

Prayer

It's time for me to begin my work, Lord. If I rely on myself it will be of no avail, but I fear nothing because it is you who will assist me. You have given me the desire to write, you will make up for my lack of skill. Yes, you will bring this work of my hands to its completion. So, go ahead, Lord. Begin the work you have planned just for me. I love you! I thank you! I praise you!

Read, Think, Pray: Luke 5:27-28

"The two greatest days of your life are the day you were born and the day you know why." - Mark Twain

And this is my prayer: that your love may increase ever more and more in knowledge and every kind of perception, to discern what is of value, so that you may be pure and blameless for the day of Christ, filled with the fruit of righteousness that comes through Jesus Christ for the glory and praise of God.

(Philippians 1:9-11)

ACKNOWLEDGEMENTS*

It's finished. That's right, you heard me. Today I finished my first book: Volume I of my journal, *The World is Noisy - God Whispers*. I've been dreaming about this day for years now. Yes, years. It's been almost three years to the day since I first picked up a pen and began to journal, and it's been about two years (one year into that said journaling) since I've been turning what I originally scribbled down on paper into a reader-friendly book. There have been many times during this process (especially in the last year) when I thought I would never get to this point; many times when I thought I would never find the strength to keep going. But, by God's grace, I'm finally here. Yes, I'm finally to the point where I'm ready to make my "private" journal, public; ready to share what's really been going on inside my heart. I thought this day would never come.

Though the first couple years of this journey came and went relatively easily, this past year has been anything but. In fact, to be honest, last year was an incredibly "heavy" year for me. The "downs" were many, and the "ups" were few and far between. It would be difficult for me to put into words what this process of turning my journal into a book was really like. (Though I would bet the frustration, fear, and pain is evident in what will be Volume II of my journal.) Even so, I somehow made it here. Yes, I somehow made it to the point where I am ready to completely expose myself to the world. Again, I repeat, I thought this day would never come.

There are so many people I would like to thank for helping me make it here. For starters, I would be nowhere (and nothing) without God, so a "thanks" directed towards Him is certainly of the utmost importance. Besides Him, (and, of course, all the angels and saints who have been interceding for me nonstop from the very beginning) there are plenty of people in this world I would like to thank as well. To begin, I would like to thank my 16 brothers and sisters. (To be clear here, I have 2 brothers and 2 sisters, and so does my husband. Add to them their spouses and, yes, I have 16 brothers and sisters.) So, Krista, Brian, Todd, Casey, Tara, Andy, Travis, Tricia, Tina, Dwaine, Chris, Heather, Brian, Kathy, Jill, and Tony, thank you! Thank you for keeping me sane during this process

(Trust me, whether you knew it or not, your love and support and laughs are what kept me moving forward on those days it would have been much easier for me to give up.) I would also like to take a second to thank my nieces and nephews. Yes, all 28 of them. So, Erynn, Bryce, Katelyn, Trevor, Alissa, Will, Andrew, Xavier, Aliyah, Melena, Brittany, Lucas, Tyler, Alex, Jack, Lydia, Ross, Will, Michael, Kaitlyn, Andrew, Hayden, Brody, Audra, Dane, Carlie, Adelynn, and Keegan, thank you! Thank you for inspiring me each and every day and for reminding me what life is really about. Without you, I would have no idea what love is, and, without that, my life and every word I have ever written (and will ever write) would be meaningless. You are all a huge gift to me. Thank you for being you!

In addition to my immediate family, I would also like to thank my extended family and friends. Especially you, Jess and Crystal, my dear friends from whom time and distance can't seem to separate. And you, Grandma Esther and Grandma Shirley, my selfless, God-fearing grandmothers whose solid examples of faith and love (and, of course, countless prayers) have been instrumental in my life. Oh, and, before I go any further, I would also like to thank my high school English teacher (who just happens to be my aunt) for proofreading this book and for, more importantly, teaching me how to write to begin with. Just so you know, Aunt Lynn, I cringed a little every time I used one of those "R.I.P" words and every time I began a sentence with the word "and," "but," or "so." Your lessons have definitely stuck with me! (Although, I must say, I really like this "stylistic liberty" thing that lets me, on some level, make my own rules!) Regardless, without a doubt, your "mission" is to teach, and I was blessed enough to have you, not only as an aunt, but as one of the *Good Teachers* in my life. (Remember that reflection? Well, you are, most certainly, included in this list!)

As I continue, I would, of course, also like to thank my parents. Just like I would be nowhere (and nothing) without God, I would be nowhere (and nothing) without you. I hope this journal, in and of itself, is one long, continuous "thank you" directed towards you because your influence on (and in) my life would be impossible for me to ever thank you for in just a few short sentences. Oh, and thank you, too, Steve and Rita, my father and mother-in-law. You raised such a "good boy;" a boy that I am now blessed to call my husband. The love and support we have both received (and continue to receive) from you has always been (and always will be) beyond measure.

Before I bring this to an end, I have just one more thank you to give. Ok, Ok. Not one, three. First of all I would like to thank my coach, Dr. Brian Deal. Without you, Brian, I would have never realized that "I am a writer." And, as if that wasn't enough, without you, I would have never had the courage to actually share my writing with others. You are a gift to me and always will be. I will forever be grateful to God for bringing you into my life; for using you as His instrument to inspire and enlighten me. (On the flight down to the conference during which we first met, I asked the Lord to speak to me while I was there. (See my reflection titled, *Awestruck*, for proof of that prayer.) You were that "someone" the Lord spoke to me through, and I am still, to this day, *awestruck* because of it!) Secondly, I would like to thank my Spiritual Director, Fr. David Zink. I am convinced, Fr. Zink, that from the very first moment the Lord brought you into my life, He has given you some special grace to understand my soul. Not being understood has been (and still is) one of the biggest crosses I've had to carry on this journey, and your guidance in my life has made the weight of this cross feel as light as a toothpick. So, thank you! Thank you for being such a good and holy priest!

Ok, and last, but certainly not least, I would like to thank my husband, Tony. I know, my love, that our life together looks *nothing* like what we had planned, but I think you'll agree that what we have now is better (way better) than either of us could have ever imagined. Still, to say that this transition from your elementary school crush, to your high school girlfriend, to your college fiancé, to your wife, to your wife who is your office manager, to your wife who is a writer has been "easy" and "carefree" would be a lie. You, and only you, (besides the Lord, of course) saw the frequent moments of torment, wiped away the countless number of tears, and listened to the never-ending "venting sessions" filled with fear and doubt about how I would ever be able to do this. Yes, dear, for most of our relationship, I have been your little cheerleader encouraging you to keep moving forward, but during these last few years you switched roles with me. I'm certain that, without your unconditional love and support, I would have crumbled under the weight of the cross. So, thank you! Thank you for holding my hand through it all and for patiently waiting on your cheery, joyful wife to make her return. I'm happy to say, she's back! Yes, she's back! Oh, and I'm certain that this "wait," just like all the other "waits" in our life, will be worth it!

So, to the Lord for EVERYTHING and to everyone else through whom He gave me that EVERYTHING, thank you! This book is for you!

Prayer

I love you, my Lord, and I thank you for EVERYTHING and for EVERYONE! May my simple life, and these simple words, be a gift of love to all those who loved you (and me) first. I love you! I thank you! I praise you!

There, now it's finished. Oh, my good and gracious, God, it's finally finished! Praise be to you!

Read, Think, Pray: Psalm 30

* This entry, listed here as the acknowledgements, is taken from Volume II of my journal from a reflection dated 3/13/2016.

INDEX OF REFELCTIONS

INDEX OF REFELCTIONS

INDEX OF REFELCTIONS

INDEX OF REFELCTIONS

INDEX OF REFELCTIONS

INDEX OF REFELCTIONS

INDEX OF REFELCTIONS

INDEX OF REFELCTIONS

INDEX OF REFELCTIONS

INDEX OF REFELCTIONS

ABOUT THE AUTHOR

Julia Monnin is a small town girl from west-central Ohio whose "rocky" young adult years were followed by a massive conversion in her mid-20's. After living a life of deadly sin for more years than she would like to admit, she eventually found God's endless love and mercy and her fresh start in the practices of the Roman Catholic faith she grew up in. Since rediscovering her faith and, by God's grace, turning her life around, she now serves God joyfully and gratefully in her vocation as a wife and a Catholic writer, speaker, and spiritual companion.

To learn more about Julia or to schedule her for your next event, visit www.theworldisnoisy.com

27744886R00219

Made in the USA
Lexington, KY
08 January 2019